Yale Studies in Political Science, 19

Published under the direction of the
Department of Political Science

A backcountry classroom in Thailand

INTERNATIONAL AID
TO THAILAND
THE NEW COLONIALISM?

RONALD C. NAIRN

New Haven and London
Yale University Press

ACKNOWLEDGMENTS

Especial thanks are proffered to the Council on International Relations, Yale University, whose generous grant in the summer of 1963 enabled research to be undertaken in France and Thailand. Appreciation is also expressed to the Graduate Program on International Relations and the Southeast Asia Program, with particular thanks to David N. Rowe. Professor Rowe's advice was urbane and wise and he gave unstintingly of that most precious commodity, time. My debt to him however extends beyond professional dimensions. His warm and practical friendship has had its own impact which I acknowledge with gratitude.

It would be impractical to list here all those in the field who gave of their time and information. The following organizations, however, were especially helpful: UNESCO Headquarters, Paris; the regional offices in Bangkok of UNESCO, UNTAB, FAO, UNICEF; and the local offices in Bangkok of WHO and ILO.

Generous assistance was given by many Thai government ministries and departments. The Supreme Command, Ministry of Defense, not only provided data but also helped ease a path through other departments and assisted with travel. Officials at the ministries of Foreign Affairs, Interior, Health, Agriculture, and Education were most helpful even to the extent of assigning personnel to accompany me on various excursions. All Thai Ministries were generous with printed materials. The same can be said of the departments of National Community Development and the National Statistics Office.

The experience and insight of the priests of the Society of Jesus and the Dominican Order and the missionaries and administrators in the Commission on Ecumenican Missions (all in Thailand) were freely given.

A special debt of gratitude is felt toward many hundreds of ordinary Thai country folk who since 1957 have shown unfailing courtesy and kindness to me as a traveler or guest in their villages and homes. Perhaps their views on the changes being intruded upon their world affect this study more than even the writer is aware and deserve special recognition.

All views expressed are my own and I accept full responsibility for shortcomings.

R. C. N.

Prescott, Arizona
June 1966

CONTENTS

Acknowledgments   v

List of Tables   ix

Introduction   1

PART 1. OPERATIONS

1. UNESCO—Its Concept of Strategy and Mission   9
2. Scope of the Operations   20
3. The Dynamics of the Operational Milieu   42
4. Roles, Personnel, and Communication   76

PART 2. THE THAI RESPONSE

5. The Thai Elite and Rural Progress   95
6. The Bureaucracy—Rival or Ally?   110
7. Achievement   126
8. Three Comparable Operations   135

PART 3. THE COMMUNICATION BREAKDOWN

9. Communication in the Field: Some Criteria   155
10. A Perspective at Headquarters Level   176
11. U.N. Aid: The New Colonialism?   187

Appendices   193
    I. United Nations Agencies and Aid Projects in Thailand   195
    II. Foreign Personnel at the Cha Cheong Sao Pilot Project   200
    III. Foreign Personnel at TUFEC   201
    IV. Handicraft Activity Sponsored by TUFEC   202
    V. Achievement of Empathy by Foreign Experts at
        TUFEC—A Thai View   203
    VI. Changes in Villages in the TUFEC Laboratory Area   204

Bibliography   207

Index   225

TABLES

1. Comparison between the UNESCO Budget and New Zealand Expenditures on State Education — 15
2. Education in Thailand, 1908–1950 — 33
3. Educational Activity of Christian Missions in Thailand — 144
4. A Schematic Outline of an Aid Operation — 177
5. Current Aid Methods Based upon TUFEC and the Pilot Project, with Suggested Reemphases — 178

INTRODUCTION

The activity of the United Nations in extending aid to technologically underdeveloped countries offers prospects for wide-ranging studies in international relations. In a general historical sense,
"backward" Asia has, at least since the latter stages of the eighteenth century, faced a massive technological confrontation, posed
by the "advanced" West. Until World War II colonialism was the
main manipulative agency in this confrontation. Its demise in
institutionalized form, however, did not end the technological
confrontation; in fact, its general intensity tended to increase.
The technological confrontation transcended change in the political status of colonial dependencies and remained as a continuum
with an autonomy and dynamic of its own. Nevertheless, with the
disintegration of overt colonialism, new types of working relationships were required, and these could no longer be based upon
omnipotent colonial authority or supported by the administrative
capability of the colonial power *intra muros*. Ideas of equal political status, new military relationships based upon mutuality, and
the advent of multilateral and bilateral aid projects—where ideas,
skills, and material were proffered gratis—are some of the more
significant features of the new postwar relationships between
East and West.

These new relationships brought with them new requirements
for social and cultural contact of a kind that was not part of the
colonial way of life. Social status, social intercourse, and living
habits generally imposed requirements for less exclusiveness and
ethnocentricity; there was a need for Western civil and military
personnel to integrate with local organizations and often to accept
local leadership and administration. Above all, decisions affecting
both East and West were in the main conducted by intercommu-
nication between both parties on a basis of near-equal status. In
general terms, at least, this was the way the new relationships were
supposed to work—in theory this was what was desired by both

parties. Thus superimposed upon the continuing technological confrontation was a social and cultural confrontation that was new and promised to play a significant role in East-West relations.

United Nations field operations in Thailand were representative of the new situation. The United Nations, in the eyes of its founders, did not espouse a particular political or ideological role. It was to be involved only in bringing utilitarian skills common to the technological West to meet an alleged revolution in rising expectations. At first glance, therefore, the charge so often leveled at many bilateral aid operations, that relations between East and West had not really changed, that neocolonialism had succeeded the older form disguised in more respectable clothing, hardly seemed valid relative to the United Nations. Their operations were to comprise untrammeled technological, social, and cultural contacts. They were to be representative of the new relationship and not an old evil under a new name.

I intend to concentrate on two of the major United Nations field programs in Thailand, although other programs and aspects of the operations must also be drawn upon. One program, the Cha Cheong Sao Educational Pilot Project, was concerned with education in a formal sense and with the proliferation of new educational techniques and ideas throughout the kingdom. The other project, known as TUFEC (the Thailand UNESCO Fundamental Educational Center), was nominally concerned with fundamental education but in fact became a full-scale community development enterprise, with all the inferences this type of activity has for a nation whose lifeways are based upon the peasant and small-scale agriculture.

Although the sponsoring agency of both projects was the United Nations Educational, Scientific, and Cultural Organization (UNESCO), other United Nations agencies gave support in their respective fields: the Food and Agricultural Organization (FAO), the World Health Organization (WHO), the International Labor Organization (ILO), the Technical Assistance Administration (TAA; after 1958 the Bureau of Technical Assistance Operations), and the United Nations Children's Fund (UNICEF). The Technical Assistance Board (TAB) performed a coordinating function relative to general administration. Outside organizations also gave support. These included the United States Operations Mission (USOM; now the Agency for International Development but still officially called USOM in Thailand), and the Shell Oil Company.

These projects, the most extensive United Nations activities in Thailand, had an organic life of up to nine years and employed some 63 foreign personnel actually in the field. These personnel were, of course, supported by relevant regional and zone offices, which coincidentally were located in Bangkok. Some specialist personnel from the offices gave their services to the projects on an ad hoc basis, and there was the usual round of visits and reports emanating from Headquarters. For comparative purposes it might be noted that in 1963, when United Nations activity in Thailand was at its maximum intensity,[1] 100 foreign experts were employed. Their activity was highly fragmented, however, being spread over some 41 projects. All but two of these projects had a scheduled life of one year or less, and none absorbed more than two experts. Furthermore, the nature of many of these projects was such that it would be highly speculative to assess their impact in Thailand generally. Such activity fields as reactor physics, documentation center techniques, economic statistics, mineral survey, applied scientific research, rural migration, nuclear instrumentation, and electronics—to mention some—may be highly important at some future time, but in contemporary Thailand their impact is incipient or latent and the nature of many limits contact with the main stream of Thai life. Nevertheless, the two educational projects selected for concentration here had an importance extending well beyond that indicated by their purely quantitative extent relative to other United Nations activity.

The projects studied were aimed at strata of Thai life of intrinsic social, cultural, and economic importance to the great mass of the people in the most immediate sense. Educational policy, planning and development, educational curricula and techniques in the classroom, homemaking, village crafts and industries, village organization and welfare, health, marketing, and agriculture were some of the areas penetrated. Inevitably, activity of this nature brought the projects into contact with Thai officialdom at many levels, to a degree unknown in other United Nations enterprises in

1. "The United Nations Program for 1963," *Siam Rath* (July 13, 1963), p. 2 (in Thai).

Thailand. Because the projects had an organic life lasting nearly a decade, significant written records were accumulated within both United Nations agencies and Thai ministries and departments. Of equal significance from the point of view of available records, large numbers of Thai participated in the projects as students and counterpart workers and from within the Thai government. Again, no other United Nations program in the kingdom made such wide contact.

The overall scope planned for the projects gave them an added dimension. Both projects aimed at proliferation nationally. They were not to be limited efforts confined to advice on inanimate things such as rice storage or the training of half a dozen aero-radio operators. Indeed, the Fundamental Education Project aimed at ultimately providing a training center for all of Southeast Asia.

Perhaps the most important characteristic was that both projects involved the United Nations in major cultural and social contact and communication in its widest sense. When all is said and done, it is the capacity to attain effective relationships in this milieu that determines whether direct transfer of skills and ideas between a technologically advanced donor and a technologically unsophisticated recipient is feasible. This issue has been well summarized by John Montgomery, who, writing of United States efforts in the foreign field, noted: "The abstractions of administrative efficiency and worldwide policy making encounter reality at the point where the essential negotiations and operations take place: that is at the country level."[2]

The main concern of studies on the aid process generally, regardless of whether they are focused on unilateral or international programs, has been with conceptual aspects, usually on a regional or global basis. The problems of donor and recipient at the field level have been largely ignored. The purpose of this study is, therefore, to evaluate what happens at the level where actual transference of skills and ideas is attempted.

I will make no assertion that the patterns developed here are typical of United Nations activity of this kind everywhere. The aid

2. John D. Montgomery, *The Politics of Foreign Aid: American Experience in South East Asia* (New York, Frederick A. Praeger, 1962), p. 152.

process, especially that conducted by the United Nations, is a widespread and complex enterprise. Many different experiences must be evaluated before any but the overconfident would proffer general laws that might cover the extraordinary scope and aspiration of United Nations activity and call for changes in the current methods of extending aid. But a beginning must be made.

PART 1. OPERATIONS

1

UNESCO—ITS CONCEPT OF STRATEGY AND MISSION

The basic philosophy of UNESCO and its concept of function are contained in its Constitution. This document gave UNESCO a unique place among United Nations agencies, containing not only statements of high moral values but also a view of the role that intellectual endeavor should play in preserving peace and in uplifting man's social and cultural existence. Perhaps only the most sanguine would have expected the provisions of UNESCO's Constitution to be readily realized in the postwar world, or to be achieved without a more particularized translation of the Constitution's lofty aims into specific programs and objectives. It was a seeking for compatibility between distant prospects and the immediacy of world problems that concerned the leadership of the organization at its genesis and reflected on the pattern of working relationships that the Organization initiated in its early years.

The basic UNESCO aspiration was best expressed in the Preamble to the Constitution:

> to contribute to peace and security by promoting collaboration among nations through Education, Science and Culture in order to further universal respect for justice, for the rule of law and for the human rights and fundamental freedoms which are reaffirmed for the people of the world without distinction of race, sex, language or religion by the Charter of the United Nations.

A more succinct and particularistic assessment of means whereby these aims might be attained appeared during early sessions of UNESCO's first Program Commission:

> UNESCO will contribute to peace and security by promoting collaboration among the nations in the *preservation* of men's

knowledge of themselves and each other; in the *increase* of that knowledge through learning, science and the arts; and in the *dissemination* of that knowledge through education and through communications generally.[1]

These general statements of intention proliferated rapidly as new members gave voice and as intellectuals in general showed their interest. At the outset, however, it appears that within the organization itself there was uncertainty as to how these still very broad objectives might be translated into viable programs. There was no experience to guide the organization. Educational, social, and cultural transfer between peoples in the past had been, as one commentator stated, "unsystematic, often unconscious of itself, casual, slow moving, individualistic."[2] It was in altering and presumably institutionalizing this historical pattern—to give an *élan vital* to a vast intercommunications spectrum—that UNESCO had to attain success if its general concepts were to become realities.

Julian S. Huxley, UNESCO's first Director General (December 1946 to December 1948), attempted to meet the issue, at least in part, by formulating "a working hypothesis concerning human existence and its aims and objectives and which will dictate, or at least indicate, a definite line of approach to its problems." Dr. Huxley's views were synthesized in the term "scientific world humanism," which recognized that "Peace and security can never be wholly realized through the means assigned to it [i.e. by UNESCO] —education, science and culture. It [UNESCO] must envisage some form of world political unity whether through a single world government or otherwise."[3] Thus in the mind of one important official at least there was a relationship between international political order and the achievement of UNESCO's aims. But the relationship seems to have been that world order might be at-

---

1. Howard E. Wilson, "The Development of UNESCO," *International Conciliation*, No. 431 (New York, Carnegie Endowment for International Peace, 1947), p. 307.

2. Howard E. Wilson, ed., "National Programs of International Cultural Relations," *International Conciliation*, No. 462 (June 1950), p. 304.

3. Julian Huxley, UNESCO: *Its Purpose and Its Philosophy* (Washington, D.C., Public Affairs Press, 1948), pp. 6, 13.

tained, or at least furthered, by an educational, scientific, and cultural program.

Dr. Huxley advocated the promotion of International Centers for Applied Mathematics; a World Bibliography and Library; International Institutes for Home and Community Planning; a National Theatre Institute; chapters on the natural sciences, the social sciences, and the mass media. To meet the immediate problem of repairing war damage he suggested an International Reconstruction Camp, but this particular project was viewed very much as a temporary measure and something of a diversion from longer-term intellectual pursuits.

Practical measures were also included in the concept of "scientific world humanism": references to achieving human betterment through making new sources of energy available to "mankind in general and to certain backward regions in particular"; and the "application of nuclear physics and of microbiology to peaceful ends." The Director General recognized that such issues as widespread illiteracy in the "world's dark areas" might be an impediment to realization of the grand design. Other forms of human wretchedness were ignored. Had he wanted to, Dr. Huxley could well have justified this remoteness on the grounds that there were other United Nations bodies charged with meeting these needs, with far greater resources than UNESCO had.

The emphasis of UNESCO at its beginning was therefore almost entirely toward things of the intellect and, more importantly, toward things that could only be properly understood by the intellectual. Although he did not say so specifically, Dr. Huxley impressed his readers with the belief that creation of "scientific world humanism" was essentially to be the work of an intellectual elite and the results would eventually trickle down to the masses.

These general views of the organization were never officially endorsed by its members. Nevertheless, in its structural shape and certainly in its early attitudes, UNESCO bore the imprint of the first Director General to a marked degree. Evidence of this is apparent in the publications of UNESCO even today. That there are only superficial resemblances between UNESCO's actual operations and its original aspirations is another fact, the significance of which warrants closer examination.

THE PRACTICAL MILIEU

At least two major issues interposed themselves during the early stages of UNESCO philosophizing. These were the urgent demands inherent in postwar reconstruction and the emergence of specifically national as opposed to international demands. Both issues required specific and timely action, and to a large degree events arising in this context determined UNESCO's operational path.

While UNESCO's part in postwar rehabilitation was modest relative to the demand, these activities preempted a considerable proportion of UNESCO's resources—in personnel as well as finances. The emergency needs to which the organization devoted itself included the repair and replacement of scientific, educational, and cultural resources; despatch of skilled personnel to meet specific needs; youth service camps; fellowship grants for retraining of teachers; a program to show devastated countries how they might meet their immediate needs; and small amounts of financial aid for the purchase of scientific and educational equipment.[4] It has been noted that UNESCO at this time became involved in what the United Nations Relief and Rehabilitation Agency (UNRRA) had been specifically set up to handle, with, it might be noted, far greater resources.[5]

These postwar rehabilitation measures engaged the organization from 1946 through 1949. At best they could do little more than attempt to restore recipient countries to their prewar condition. This "bread and butter" activity was a far cry from the detached intellectual goals set for UNESCO at its genesis. Even more significantly, however, these initial operations left their imprint on the structure and capabilities of the organization.

A powerful reinforcement to this grass roots approach came when Dr. Huxley was replaced after a two-year term of office by Dr. Jaime Torres Bodet. Bodet had an abiding concern for the services that UNESCO might perform for the peoples of less economically developed countries and "he set himself without delay to

---

4. UNESCO, General Conference First Session, Report of the *Reconstruction and Rehabilitation Commission* (Paris, 1947), pp. 1–7.

5. Walter C. Laves and Charles A. Thomson, UNESCO: *Purpose, Progress, Prospects* (Bloomington, Indiana University Press, 1957), pp. 27, 71.

further the co-ordination of all UNESCO fundamental education activities with the programs in agriculture and health carried on by the FAO and the WHO."[6] Without overemphasizing the influence of any one man (or indeed the role that a Director General plays in an international organization), the combination of pressing postwar needs and the advent of a new Director General, who saw human welfare in very basic and immediate terms, did reinforce the utilitarian rather than the intellectual emphasis of the organization.

A further and perhaps irresistible factor carrying the utilitarian emphasis forward was the increase in bids for UNESCO's services by member states, especially the economically underdeveloped states. The concept that developed states should help the underdeveloped gave the sanction of "rights" to these requests. That the states seeking aid were technologically and educationally backward determined the nature of the tasks. Under these circumstances it was difficult to maintain the idea of UNESCO as a great scientific and cultural center. Requests were not for sophisticated intellectual products but for aid of the most utilitarian kind.

Despite the considerable variety of UNESCO projects, both as planned and activated during the organization's early years, by the early 1950s concentration had centered around five main areas as follows:

1. Expansion of free and compulsory education at the primary school level.

2. Development of "fundamental education"—a term used to describe not only literacy training but other basic education necessary for overall community development and social and economic progress.

3. Reduction of racial, social, and international tensions.

4. Fostering a more widespread mutual appreciation of Eastern and Western cultural values.

5. Sponsoring and assisting scientific research for the improvement of living conditions.[7]

6. Ibid., pp. 297–98.

7. UNESCO, *Information Manual No. I: What Is UNESCO?* (Paris, UNESCO, 1955), p. 11.

All of these areas are oriented toward alleviating "underdevelopment," except perhaps 3 and 4 which have their own special place in the spectrum of internationalism.

Whether the organization wished it or not, the activities listed above, when carried on in underdeveloped countries, required less an activity of the mind than an activity of the hands. Education, especially in its elementary forms, held a predominant place. Again UNESCO had to proceed in a simple and basic way. To do otherwise would have been to propagate a philosophy of education; and a general philosophy of education required some degree of international consensus as to purpose and method. It is one thing to espouse a literacy program; it is another to institute a particular work program using acquired literary skills. Race, religion, cultural, and political divisions imposed their own educational demands toward which UNESCO could do little in the short term except assist functionally and in accordance with local requirements. This was a substantially different concept from "scientific world humanism," or any other "world" approach. The reality of international differences, on the one hand, and the need to meet immediate problems, on the other, prompted the organization into activity a good deal more prosaic than sought in early aspirations.

UNESCO accumulated statistics concerning functional rather than theoretical aspects of education. It was estimated that more than 700 million of the world's peoples were illiterate and that nearly half of the world's 100 million children did not go to school. Even more significantly, notice was taken that with an annual global population increase of more than one per cent the situation was worsening.[8] UNESCO saw the need to help increase the number of qualified teachers and school buildings, develop curriculum, and make education available for adults. The organization, realizing that the resources available to it could not even begin to affect the problem in the short term, conceived its task "in terms of long range goals, towards which single projects would have little significance but rather towards specific limited objectives which it was felt would generate increasing educational progress."[9]

8. UNESCO, *Compulsory Education in South Asia and the Pacific* (Paris, UNESCO, 1954), pp. 14, 120.
9. UNESCO, *Information Manual No. I*, p. 12.

Just how sparse were UNESCO's resources relative to even the more limited task it had set itself should be illustrated. New Zealand is a good comparison. Virtually all education there is provided by the state, is universal, and offers a range from elementary education to the university. With a population of only two and three-quarter million, New Zealand is probably the smallest country on earth with a complete educational system, and therefore New Zealand's educational budget provides a contrast not only to the resources that UNESCO could employ but also to the immensity of the cost of attacking the problem of world illiteracy.

TABLE 1. COMPARISON BETWEEN THE UNESCO BUDGET AND
NEW ZEALAND EXPENDITURES ON STATE EDUCATION

Year	Total UNESCO Budget: All Purposes	Total UNESCO Budget: Education	Total New Zealand State Education
1947	$ 6,950,000	$ 884,373	$67,421,000
1950	8,000,000	1,624,195	75,890,000
1955	10,314,538	1,995,359	84,617,000

Sources: Department of Statistics, Wellington, New Zealand Official Yearbooks, 1948, 1951, 1956 (Wellington, Government Printer); and UNESCO, UNESCO Information Manual No. 1 (Paris, 1957).

Account must be taken therefore of the obviously wide disparity between the magnitude of the world education problem with which UNESCO became involved and the resources and methods it might mobilize. Much the same disparity probably would be revealed with regard to any other UNESCO aspiration, but the contrast shown by education is most appropriate for this study. UNESCO was led into utilitarian roles but could be utilitarian only to a limited degree. In brief, it found itself making an approach to problems of immense practical magnitude with resources that could do little more than allow it to hover on the fringes.

UNESCO's problem was dichotomous. Was it to construct a synthesis of the world's intellectual resources and to leave the practical aspects of the attack on current ills to others? The Preamble to its Constitution held

> that a peace based exclusively upon the political and economic arrangements of governments would not be a peace which

would secure the unanimous, lasting and sincere support of the peoples of the world, and that the peace must therefore be founded, if it is not to fail, upon the intellectual and moral solidarity of mankind.

Nevertheless the real issues facing UNESCO could not be ignored; they not only embroiled the organization in matters with a strong economic and political content but did so at a most mundane level. And what of the intellectual milieu envisaged by the organization's founders? In reality, was this to be at the level of teaching adult illiterates to read? Was UNESCO to be a temple for the intellectual or a handmaiden for the masses? Circumstances prompted the organization to concentrate on the latter role. At the same time it also did its best to cling to the view of the world espoused in its Constitution. This ambivalence seems to have greatly affected development of a working philosophy for daily guidance of the organization.

A WORKING PHILOSOPHY

UNESCO, in its early years, tried to be all things to all men. It dangled abstractions before intellectuals and it tried to serve refugees and peasants. The gap between concept and reality was so large that UNESCO, virtually before it emerged as a functioning body, found itself drawn this way and that by a diversity of interests, tasks, and objectives. Whether the organization could have resisted this diversification is open to question. Inis Claude has observed that "postwar functional agencies have experienced difficulty in concentrating on important matters, rejecting trivial proposals, and abjuring interesting diversions. They stand in constant peril of being treated as hobby horses to be ridden off in all directions at once." He noted that this "situation appears to prevail particularly in UNESCO which could easily degenerate into a mere international playhouse of intellectuals, scholars, artists and esthetes."[10]

But in its early days UNESCO did have workers in the field who were given practical tasks to perform. In activity related to educa-

10. Inis L. Claude, Jr., *Swords Into Plowshares: The Problems and Progress of International Organization* (New York, Random House, 1959), p. 395.

tion UNESCO assisted with scientific and technical documentation for universities in Mexico, Yugoslavia, the United Arab Republic, India, and Pakistan, and with the establishment of fundamental education centers, or pilot projects, in Liberia, Ceylon, Iraq, Sudan, South Vietnam, Nicaragua, and Paraguay, in addition to the Thailand project to be examined. Teacher training programs were started in Bolivia, Costa Rica, Honduras, Nicaragua, and Ecuador. An educational research institute was established in Brazil. Specific activities within these projects ranged from community development to child psychology studies, from research on school legislation problems to literacy campaigns. As well as these and other educational programs, there were more diverse activities ranging from desert rehabilitation to radio broadcast methods. None of these projects was large; most were quite tiny. All illustrated UNESCO's involvement in quite practical matters. It has been said that a program of practical operations on the part of UNESCO "implies intellectual agreement between men whose views of the world, of culture and even of knowledge are different and even opposed; agreement between minds can be reached spontaneously, not on the basis of common speculation ideas, but on common practical ideas."[11]

In practice, however, even this concept did not seem to mean very much. The picture at the operational level became not one of men "intellectually agreed" but rather one of small groups spread throughout the world, after only a brief preliminary contact with UNESCO and its philosophy. These field workers—or experts, as UNESCO chose to call them—served a few years in a foreign country relative to some very specific skill and then dispersed to their respective homelands. The small cadre of permanent staff, who rarely amounted to more than 2 or 3 per cent of the overseas total, itself had no discernible philosophy. In their reports and memoranda words and phrases like "change" and "social, cultural and economic development" appear, though fairly infrequently. The mass of their reports dealt with administrative matters and day-to-day activity in the field. Thus, when they and the experts in the field, as the ultimate instruments of UNESCO, began to play out their role, they appeared in commonplace form. Personnel over-

11. Jacques Maritain, UNESCO *Proceedings,* Doc. 2c/132, pp. 30–33.

seas were clerks and workmen, bureaucrats and technicians—each with a utilitarian job to do in a strange and alien environment—rather than missionaries of the intellect. Their role was not of the mind so much as of the office and factory.

That servants of the United Nations should make their field debut in this sober way is not entirely unexpected. It is easy to establish roles for the human species which expect more of them than humans have shown themselves capable of achieving; and perhaps this is what UNESCO did in propounding such projects as world centers for applied mathematics or other programs concentrating on the international intellectual elite. But even had the United Nations servants in the field been indoctrinated bearers of new beliefs and ideas, they still would have had the task of propounding them in a specific national environment. It is far from certain that leaders of underdeveloped nations perceived the far-reaching changes that could occur within their societies if in fact the resources, skills, and knowledge of the United Nations donors had been sufficient to achieve the transformation that the more generalized United Nations aspirations implied. It is far from certain that any Southeast Asian government, for example, ever sought a sophisticated educational system for the peasantry which constitutes more than 80 per cent of its population. Neither is it certain that Southeast Asian governments, again, were especially interested in rescinding their long tradition of disassociation from their neighbors and indulging in the form of cooperation essential to regional functional programs. By and large both donor and recipient were experimenting with forms which nobody knew very much about and whose ends were far from clear.

Thus, in ultimately formulating a working philosophy, three major impediments can be discerned. First, at the highest level, the sponsoring agency, UNESCO, was not sure how its very general philosophy was to evolve into a workable program—whether uplift of mankind was to come from a great international intellectual synthesis or through reaching down for the bootstraps of the poor and the untutored. As it happened, the postwar reconstruction pre-empted a clear decision. The organization became involved in all the pedestrian mechanics of aid, though there was a strong carry-over within the higher echelons of UNESCO of the original grand view of the world. But this carry-over probably only bedeviled the functional role from which the organization could not absolve itself, no matter how plebeian that role might be.

The second impediment to the formulation of a working philosophy was that field workers were mainly technicians, and the majority were short-term agents of the United Nations. They had neither the time nor the interest to probe UNESCO's deeper conceptions, even had these been synthesized and generally agreed upon.

The last obstacle was a fundamental one. The field operations, had conflict ever arisen, must have conformed to national—not international—criteria, set in terms of basic national philosophies.

When the specific field operations sponsored by UNESCO in the Kingdom of Thailand are examined, the lack of an overall philosophy and the impact of this lack on operations become more apparent. At this stage, however, it might be said that the UNESCO venture in Thailand was more technical and utilitarian than philosophical. Although I am concerned primarily with practical performance, the basic philosophy of the primary sponsoring agency, which in this case was UNESCO, cannot be entirely divorced from the realities of operations in the field. Aspirations, attitudes of personnel (especially at the headquarters level), selection and guidance of experts, areas of emphasis in planning and in operations, and relations with recipient governments—all must to some degree be influenced by the sponsoring organization's concepts, or its lack of them. This was the general background of the organization that marshaled the resources of its own and other United Nations agencies for specific operations in Thailand.

2

SCOPE OF THE OPERATIONS

THE THAI ENVIRONMENT

Cha Cheong Sao is a country town located some 64 miles by road and rail southeast of Bangkok. The town is on the banks of the Bangpakong River and about 20 miles upstream from the river mouth on the Gulf of Thailand. Although the Bangpakong River is no more than 200 miles long, it does assume quite majestic proportions at Cha Cheong Sao, becoming half a mile wide at flood season from August through October.

The surrounding countryside, especially inland from the town, is fertile paddy, perhaps among the best in the kingdom. Criss-crossing the paddy is a limited canal system, providing water resources for adjacent fields but equally important for transportation. Along the canals are the area's famous windmill water pumps, used almost universally to lift water into the rice fields.[1] Besides rice, pineapples, corn, and coconuts are grown. But rice is the staple, and from the first plowing in July or August to the massive onrush of greenness about October and November, the Cha Cheong Sao plain is a striking spectacle.

In common with most Thai peasants, the local people are avid seekers and consumers of fish. The river, small streams, and canals provide plentiful supplies, and the proximity of the sea makes possible a wide variety of sea food for commercial use, especially the cheap and plentiful *platu,* long a peasant staple. In general,

---

1. When harnessed to the "Rahaad" or "Chinese Dragon Pump" (a simple endless belt with mounted wooden cleats), these wind pumps could develop one h.p. in a twelve-knot wind and irrigate approximately fifteen acres to a depth of one centimeter in twelve hours. FAO representatives in Thailand made detailed plans of these pumps, and stated that they were introduced by FAO to Iraq and Pakistan.

such areas of forest as still exist are not close to concentrations of peasant population. The peasant is therefore denied a place where he can freely gather wild vegetables and fruits, select lumber for building, or hunt for recreation as well as for food.

Surprisingly, the area faces a water problem in the hot season. There is an ever-present risk that if water levels in the river fall too low, sea water will invade the canals and seep into adjoining farmlands. An even more common and always present woe, however, is that most wells in the vicinity of the town become saline during hot weather. This has caused the Teachers Training College in the town to close down during the summer on more than one occasion.

Cha Cheong Sao, with a population in 1960 of 19,809, is the center of administration for the province of Cha Cheong Sao which in 1960 had a population of 322,660, including a Chinese minority of 6 per cent and a Cambodian minority, also of 6 per cent.[2] The population is predominantly Therevada Buddhist, but there are very small religious groups of Christians and Moslems. An administrative seat, the town is also the site of a Teachers Training College, comprising four high schools, two for boys and two for girls. Included in the provincial administrative structure is, of course, the district education officer.

During the early 1950s approximately 65 per cent of the children attended elementary school and 7 per cent attended high school. These figures are close to the national average, which was about 60 per cent for elementary school and 8 per cent for high school.

Perhaps the greatest and most significant landmark in the town is Wad Saotorn, containing a statue of the Buddha which has the status of a national shrine. The Wad (temple) is famous as a center of learning and noted for its size and beauty, attributable to an extensive building program over the last ten years, mainly supported by the local people.

Though data are not available, in general the peasants in the Cha Cheong Sao area are appreciably better off than many of their fellow countrymen so far as having better houses, more elaborate farm equipment, greater variation in diet, and access to more

2. Central Statistics Office, *Thailand Population Census 1960, Changwad Cha Cheong Sao* (Bangkok, Thai Watana Panich Printers, 1961).

Westernized ways of life (through proximity to Bangkok). A "frontier" appearance, so typical of many of the more remote Thai areas, is missing from the Cha Cheong Sao milieu. Overall, therefore, Cha Cheong Sao is a more sophisticated rural area than might have been found elsewhere in Thailand. It was this area that the Thai government chose to be the locale for the Pilot Project (the Cha Cheong Sao Educational Pilot Project) sponsored by UNESCO, with support from other United Nations agencies.

The locale for a second major project receiving United Nations assistance was the town of Ubol. The Ubol project was known as TUFEC (the Thailand UNESCO Fundamental Education Center). Ubol is located near the southeast corner of the Korat Plateau—that is, the Northeast Region of the Kingdom. Ubol is some 400 miles from Bangkok by road and rail and fifty miles due west of the Laotian border. There is also a road connection with the Laotian province of Pakse, one of the two Laotian provinces on the west bank of the Mekong River. Ubol town, with a population in 1960 of 51,118, is the administrative center for the province of the same name. The province has a population of 1,130,712, including tiny minorities of Chinese, Indians, Cambodians, Vietnamese, and Laotians, none of which have reached significant percentages.[3] Data on Laotian nationals require qualification, however. Many Thai nationals in the Northeast Region regard themselves as Laotian even though their political and economic ties are quite firmly riveted to Thailand. The relationship is not dissimilar to that between the Scottish and Welsh in the United Kingdom and the English. It would be difficult to distinguish Laotian from Thai in the area except perhaps through the simple factor of residence, and even here the issue is shadowy. The Mekong River, which for the most part forms the boundary between the Northeast Region and Laos, provides a great highway conducive to movement up and down and across the river. It can provide a link between kindred on either bank. The most observable fact of this ethnic grouping is that the people on the Thai side of the Mekong, while demonstrably Thai subjects, have a somewhat more detached view

3. Central Statistics Office, *Thailand Population Census 1960, Changwad Ubon Ratch-Thani* (Bangkok, Thai Watana Panich Printers, 1961).

of Bangkok and the Thai administrative and governmental processes generally than have, say, the people on the Central Plain.

The Northeast Region is generally regarded as Thailand's impoverished area. The relatively infertile, light, sandy soil is abnormally low in nutriment even for tropical regions. The rainfall is lower all over the region than in the rest of the kingdom, and there is a chronic and sometimes acute water shortage for at least half of each year. Paradoxically, at the height of the monsoon (August through September) the drainage characteristics of the area produce severe flooding, with large areas often lying under as much as twenty feet of water.

Dry and wet rice farming is the most common pursuit, but corn and jute have recently come into prominence as cash crops. The region is also the most important cattle-raising area in the kingdom, involving breeding native cattle and water buffalo for both beef and draft purposes. Each summer great herds of cattle, especially water buffalo, are driven to Bangkok, where those not consumed or used locally are shipped off to other Asian areas, notably Malaya, Vietnam, and Hong Kong.

Of the numerous small towns in the Northeast, Ubol undoubtedly is the most pleasant and distinctive. It has long been important as a religious and educational center, with certain unique qualities. Of the nineteen wads in the town, seventeen were of the reformed Dhammayut School.[4] The tenets of the reformed order relevant to this study include:

1. the responsibility of the wad for providing education for all of the people

2. an intensified and more comprehensive study by the priests of the doctrines of the Buddha, with emphasis on the rationality of the Buddha's philosophy

---

4. This reform was introduced by King Mongkut (Rama IV) during the middle years of the nineteenth century. The reforms were long resisted by the Mahanikaya sect which still comprises approximately 90 per cent of the monkhood in Thailand but over recent years the Mahanikaya have adopted many of the precepts of their rival. See H.R.H. Prince Dhani Nivat, "Some Aspects of the Cultural Background of Thailand," *Vistas of Thailand* (Bangkok, Public Relations Dept. 1963), p. 3.

3. explanation of the doctrine, which should be explainable to all
4. obedience by the priests to the rules of priesthood, without any relaxations

It is remarkable that Ubol should be a center of this order, a tiny fragment of Thai Buddhism but exacting in its practices. It helps emphasize the long-held renown of the town for its learning relative to the rest of the nation and the uncommonly high levels of literacy among the older people in the area.[5] The town also holds a reputation for colorful and widespread community observance of Buddhist and other festivals. Ubol, at the start of the project, was not therefore an ordinary town in Thailand; it was more radical than many and probably more advanced educationally, with a well developed sense of civic responsibility.[6]

Ubol and Cha Cheong Sao provided a home for the United Nations operations for eight years and nine years respectively. Can some assessment be made of the general attitude of these towns and their surrounding districts toward change? Specific and detailed data are almost totally absent, but the advent of most of those material factors popularly associated with change from traditional orientation to modernity can be noted. Relatively cheap road and rail transportation has linked the areas, especially Cha Cheong Sao, to Bangkok, a modern and increasingly Westernized city. For some, Bangkok has been a catalyst to a different conception of life.[7] To all it sets standards far different from the rural environment. Aiding this has been the advent of mass media communications. Daily newspapers from Bangkok appear in both towns within 24 hours of publication. Television reached the

5. There are no statistics to support this widely held opinion. The issue was put to Mr. Aphai Chandavimol, Under Secretary of Education in July 1963, and he said that this opinion was strongly held among teachers and educators who had worked in Ubol and elsewhere.

6. Ubol is also the locale for TURTEP (Thailand UNESCO Rural Teachers' Education Project) which is concerned with teacher training but currently employs only one foreign expert. By and large the activity of TURTEP has been incorporated with my analysis of TUFEC.

7. For the only detailed analysis of one aspect of the modernizing impact of Bangkok, see Robert Textor, *From Peasant to Pedicab Driver* (Ithaca, N.Y., Cornell Monograph No. 9, 1961).

Cha Cheong Sao area in 1957/58 and is extremely popular. The radio has long been a well patronized medium and the transistorized type is now making its way even into the home of the peasant. Movies, both Thai and foreign, have been perhaps the favorite entertainment media and even the newsreel sometimes appears in rural areas.

Data on the impact of mass media communications are non-existent. Possibly it has not been very great. In the villages, as one restricted survey has observed, indications are that the peasant still relies on traditional sources (the headman, the abbot, or the schoolteacher) for information.[8] There are other signs that information is not necessarily accumulated proportionally to the availability of media. It was reported, for example, that TUFEC students, a far better educated stratum than the average rural Thai, revealed "at question time [on United Nations Day, 1957] . . . that many or perhaps most of the students believe that the United Nations is an American organization for combatting communism. This presents a problem for the future."[9]

Thus a note of caution must be introduced when assessing the impact of modern mass media. It is just possible that as far as Thailand is concerned the impact has been less than their relatively widespread use might indicate to the Western observer. The longevity and functional viability of what has been termed the traditional mode is such that the modern media are either resisted or must function along with older forms. The personal liking of the Thai villager for face-to-face relations in a village atmosphere of intimacy and unhurried exchange, for example, does not at this time seem to be threatened by newspapers, radio, movies, or even the fascination of television. These are additions to an existing spectrum of communications rather than replacements. In this area therefore caution is warranted in assigning too catalytic a role to the spread of modern communications media.

Another factor facilitating change would be the growing use of modern drugs as well as the less widely available modern health

8. Robert Kikkert, "A Pilot Village Study in North East Thailand" (unpublished South East Asia Survey Research Report, No. 3, United States Information Service, Bangkok, October 1960), pp. 4, 5.

9. R. Gillet, TUFEC Sixth Quarterly Report (from the files, UNESCO Regional Office, Bangkok, n.d.), p. 3.

services. Moreover, the townspeople, and to a much lesser degree the peasants, have been increasingly exposed to new and variegated products in the market, accessible to the humblest purse. Once fresh fish was carried home strung up on a piece of flax, or fresh meat purchases were wrapped in a banana leaf. Now everything is wrapped in the polyethylene bag. Plastic and cheap metal utensils and containers add greatly to the facilities available in the kitchen, for dining, and for bathing. Well-known brands of soft drinks, toiletries, and tinned foods are allotted a portion of everyone's budget—not only because of lower prices but also because of the admonitions and blandishments of radio and television advertising.

Military conscription plays an important role in introducing new values to an especially important segment of the population. Thailand's military forces have become increasingly mechanized in their material configuration and Americanized in their functional conceptions, whether these be related to the treatment of a sick soldier or the control and management of a logistics system.

On the grander economic scale the peasant has long been aware not only of market prices and their fluctuations but has reacted to them. Indeed he seems more conscious of this feature than probably any other external happening. When asked, he will accurately and perceptively discuss problems of falling prices for jute because of overproduction (both in Thailand *and* Pakistan), or the risks involved in capturing an early market with a crop of pineapples. Except in the remotest parts of Thailand it is rare to find a peasant who is not conscious of these things. Neither is this new. While detailed and comprehensive data are unavailable for earlier times, it must be remembered that Thailand's extraordinary rise to eminence as one of the world's premier rice exporters during the latter part of the nineteenth century was a peasant reaction to a cash economy.[10] It may also be observed that since 1955 when agricultural data have been more specific, the volume of production of new crops has risen proportionately to availability of markets and increases in prices. This is graphically illustrated relative to sixteen "upland crops" which since the early 1950s have gained new and important status in the Thai economy. A growing Japanese de-

10. See below, p. 98, note 5.

mand for corn, for example, is reflected in a 250 per cent increase in the volume of corn exports between 1955 and 1960. A like trend can be discerned in the fifteen remaining crops. Jute production increased spectacularly from approximately 4,000 tons export volume in 1955 to 63,000 tons export volume in 1960.[11]

The means by which the peasant ascertains market demand and price changes are somewhat obscure and complex. Many diverse elements play a role. The response to world markets of individual trading agencies in Bangkok, mainly Chinese, is an obvious element. There is also an urban coterie comprised of bureaucrats and military officers, primarily the latter, who have relatively small land holdings as sideline enterprises but who keep a close watch on modern agricultural techniques as well as opportunities offered by the market. Then there is also a small but vital band of peasant entrepreneurs who seem to be well aware of the market, new crops, and what other groups in Thailand are doing.

One factor, however, is quite clear. The Thai government is generally an accessory *after* the event. The government usually renders limited assistance but comprehensive taxation after the diverse individual elements have initiated agricultural growth. But the Thai government seems also to have been wise enough not to tax to the degree where production becomes profitless. In any case, direct taxation would apply almost exclusively to urban-based producers and middlemen. The peasant producing a surplus has not as yet been caught up in the direct taxation process.[12]

In terms of deciding how large an area to cultivate to meet new agricultural opportunities, the peasant is guided by two criteria. Firstly, he is bound by a "land-power-climate ratio." Even if he had unrestricted access to land, which he has not,[13] the amount of

11. Gordon R. Sitton et al., "The Growing Importance of Upland Crops in the Foreign Trade of Thailand," *Kasetsart Economic Report No. 16* (Bangkok, Kasetsart University, November 1962, in Thai).

12. Human Relations Area Files, "Thailand," *Country Survey Series*, Thomas Fitzsimmons ed. (New Haven, HRAF Press, 1957), pp. 252–55.

13. For the nation as a whole, the average holding is about 6 acres. Only 10 per cent of farms are in excess of 25 acres. Restrictions as to the amount of land to be held by one person are fairly rigidly applied by the government through a series of laws dating back to the last century and before, resting upon ownership of all land by the monarch who could at will grant non-hereditary title to individuals.

land he can cultivate is limited by the power available for such work as well as certain time limitations. The power limitation is decided by the availability of buffalo and hands and this imposes the first restriction upon capacity to till land. A further, drastic time limitation is due to climate. At certain times, notably during the dry season, the soil is baked hard and buffalo-drawn plows cannot operate. The peasant can do nothing but wait for the rains to come and soften the ground. Thus the time available for cultivation is greatly shortened. The impact of these factors can be illustrated relative to rice culture. Not only must plowing wait for the rains but thereafter it must proceed at a rate which matches the filling of the rice fields with rain-disbursed water. With the power element limited to buffalo and hands, the area which can be cultivated in the time available is obviously restricted. At the same time, ensuing cultivation must match the rate of growth of rice seedlings, planted beforehand but which must reach a stage in their life cycle when they can be safely transferred into the field being tilled and which must by that time hold approximately the right amount of water. This land-power-climate ratio therefore, and the general attitude it engenders in a peasant's mind, sets quite distinct limitations, among other things, to the area a peasant family can cultivate.

A second criterion, namely the enterprise which prompts a peasant to cultivate new crops, is less easily defined especially where traditional crops are disbanded. Some crops which have boomed recently are traditional tropical crops but others are quite new, such as corn, cotton, jute, and ground nuts. It seems common among those who do not know peasantry to constantly underrate their agricultural ability in moving into new areas. The peasant's ability is limited more in the technological sense, in his capacity, for example, to handle the land-power-climate ratio, than it is in an agricultural sense. He has, for example, limited knowledge of chemical fertilizer, or scientific improvement of seeds or animals through application of genetics. He does not have agricultural machinery such as tractors which would enable him to break out of the confines of the land-power-climate ratio. Beyond this, however, he is a skilled agriculturalist with centuries of agricultural pragmatism behind him. The cultivation of a new crop as an exercise in agriculture does not especially frighten him. It is in an entrepreneurial sense that the peasant is much more likely to be cautious. If he seems reluctant to grow jute instead of rice, the reason is likely to be security. Full rice bins mean security. Sole reliance on jute means dependence on market prices. Like many other humans, the Thai peasant is often reluctant to throw certainty away and partake of risk.

The truly critical element in encouraging the peasant to accept risk is an adequate cash reward. The likelihood of a reasonably secure market and buoyant prices at the farm is the biggest and perhaps the only inducement for a peasant to try something new.[14]

Of all the areas of ignorance common to the United Nations, and the West generally, none was more pronounced or so related to fundamentals as ignorance of the dynamics of peasant agriculture, especially the impact of adequate cash returns. This is another study, but suffice it to say that the Thai farmer was aware of agricultural change and had demonstrated some expertise in meeting it. The impact of the export market and its interrelation with prices, issues of timing in marketing and the notion of risk in moving to new crops were but part of the peasant's ability to relate his lifeway to exterior events and to change. The peasant world was in fact a good deal more sophisticated than many imagined. This was to have important effects when theories advanced by the U.N. could not be related to cash in the peasant's pocket or, on a grander scale, to those UNESCO notions that the Thai peasant was malleable clay awaiting the firm touch of an alien potter.

It is not the purpose of this study to determine how far what is now generally termed "modernization" has permeated the Thai milieu. Rather it is to affirm that many of the material circumstances alleged to be stimulants of change had intruded into areas where the United Nations was to expend its efforts perhaps a century before that organization arrived, continued unabated while the U.N. was there, and are still active. But the degree of change, the nature of change, and the susceptibility of people to change are difficult to assess in meaningful terms, for there has been no large-scale research on this aspect of Thai life. It seemed clear that the impact was not observably traumatic. Rather the

14. See below, p. 74, note 57.

impression was of ready absorption of the material elements of modernization as a routine phenomenon, generally compatible with old values. The point to be made is that the notion of change was not completely alien to the rural Thai. He had observed the onset of the phenomenon and to some degree had participated in the process.

THE PROJECTS

The projects that are to receive examination in detail in this study were nominally concerned with education. They were the Pilot Project at Cha Cheong Sao and the TUFEC at Ubol. It must be emphasized, however, that these were not the only United Nations activities in Thailand. Over the past decade not only has the variety of United Nations projects been extensive but the capital city, Bangkok, has been the home of a number of United Nations regional and zone offices.[15] Many activities, however, were minor and of such a nature that evaluation in any concrete terms would be somewhat vacuous at this time. The Pilot Project and TUFEC are in a different category. They both offer distinct advantages for study and evaluation; and an assessment is facilitated by the fact that both projects are now ended.

They were by far the largest of the United Nations projects in Thailand. They involved the largest number of foreign personnel, who, as opposed to their colleagues in the regional and zone offices, did not work in an environment common to most bureaucrats in any big city. The Pilot Project and TUFEC were in the rural atmosphere of Ubol and Cha Cheong Sao, requiring personal contact with Thai and operations oriented toward that spectrum of life experienced by the great mass of the Thai population. As a routine matter, not only were project personnel in contact with national government officials, as were their fellows in Bangkok, but they joined forces with officials in the provinces—that is, where government reached the people. The governor and his staff, the district officer and his staff, as well as lesser officials in the lower echelons

15. An outline of overall United Nations organizations and activity in Thailand as of 1963 is given in Appendix I. Activity at this time was not too different from that undertaken during the preceding decade and the outline is therefore a reasonable approximation of United Nations activity over the period of this study.

of the rural hierarchy, were all points of contact for the United Nations. The village schoolteacher, the local doctor or public health nurse, the abbot at the wad, the headman at both commune and village level—all were important links. The daily routine brought the United Nations worker into close contact with Thai students, of both tender and mature years; and each United Nations worker was accompanied by at least one Thai counterpart with whom the very closest liaison was necessary. All these factors, together with the rural environment, its lack of Western style entertainment, and often fairly primitive living standards, combined to place workers in TUFEC and in the Pilot Project in a diffierent world from their fellows in Bangkok.

Perhaps the most important characteristic of the projects, however, especially from the point of view of accepting them as a basis for study, was that both had a beginning, a middle, and an ending and can be viewed as organic wholes.

INITIAL SURVEYS

Shortly after joining UNESCO in 1948, Thailand requested that a survey be conducted on Thai education by UNESCO specialists. In February and March of 1949 a two-man team visited the kingdom. Their report appeared in 1950.[16] Inevitably this team, because of the short duration of its visit, had to rely on data and statistics supplied by the Thai Ministry of Education. It is not surprising therefore that their report added little to what was already known about Thai education.[17] The recommendations of this Sargent–Orato report were very general and could be summarized as a familiar reiteration of standard Western ideas—the need for a centrally controlled, free, universal system of education designed to obtain effective literacy and "a command of the fundamental processes of reading, writing, arithmetic, language and similar skills."[18]

16. Sir John Sargent and Pedro Orato, *Report of the Mission to Thailand* (Paris, UNESCO, 1950).

17. Ministry of Education, *Report of Evaluation Committee Cha Cheong Sao Project* (Cha Cheong Sao, August 16, 1957), trans. from Thai by Smorn Gunatilaka (from the files, Ministry of Education, Bangkok), p. 2.

18. Sargent and Orato, pp. 35–42.

There was nothing particularly startling in this approach. In the Primary Education Act of October 1, 1921, the Thai government had introduced a national, compulsory, free education system. In education Thailand was, in fact, a pioneer in Southeast Asia. Apparently, however, "it took the Thai Government fourteen years [from 1921 to 1935] to put the law into effect in every village."[19] Even by 1963, while the majority of villages had schools and education was compulsory, the system provided only four years of schooling instead of the seven years intended under the act.[20]

There were certain material circumstances surrounding Thai education not shown in the Sargent–Orato report but of significance to any project aimed at educational improvement. Statistically, pertinent features of the national education system in Thailand at the time of the UNESCO investigation were as shown in Table 2, but some qualifications must be added to the data. The Thai educational infrastructure and organization had suffered some disruptions during the war. Between 1942 and the end of 1946 some 200 schools had been occupied, first by Japanese forces and then by the Allies. In Bangkok some 68 schools had been damaged by bombing. The total cost of repairing buildings in 1948 was $1,507,518 (Baht 30,150,373) or 31 per cent of that year's educational budget.[21]

The general picture must be further illuminated. There were few if any textbooks or classroom materials of even the most elementary type. In rural areas, a school building could be an open, thatched shelter, surrounded by a sea of mud in the rainy season and enveloped in swirling dust clouds in the dry months. Problems of nutrition and health also affected performance and attendance.

> Even in 1949, out of 1,033,112 primary school children in 15 provinces (in the North Eastern Region), 54,549 were naked to

19. M. L. Manich Jumsai, *Compulsory Education in Thailand* (Paris, UNESCO, 1951), p. 51.

20. Ministry of Education, *Report on an Investigation into Educational Conditions in Five Provinces in North East Thailand, 1955* (Bangkok, 1955), pp. 33–40.

21. An exchange rate of approximately 20 baht to one United States dollar has been used throughout this study. Thai currency remained consistently at about this figure over the duration of this study.

TABLE 2. EDUCATION IN THAILAND, 1908–1950*

Year	Per cent of national budget	Per cent of permanent school bldgs.	Per cent of children at school — Elementary	Secondary	Per cent of enrolled students completing Elementary (7 Years)	Secondary
1908	2.9					
1932	6.7		30		3.9	
1939	13.2		84		7.1	
1941	13.8	11.7	93.4	4.6	8.1	
1943	12.6	12.6	94.0	4.7	9.6	
1945	7.3	26.4	96.2	3.8	10.2	
1946	5.6	30.7	96.6	3.9		
1947	6.9	28.1	96.1	4.0		
1948	17.5	27.9	95.7	3.9	6.9	68.0
1949	19.6	28.6	96.2	4.3		
1950	22.1		96.0	5.3	8.0	60.0

*Where there are blanks in the table, data were unavailable. Statistics, especially in any orderly form, are difficult to come by in Thailand for periods preceding about 1960. Detailed census data from the new Statistical Bureau in the Ministry of National Development are coming to hand for the post-1960 period but, to date, the detailed data required for a table like the above have not been published.

Sources: Ministry of Education, Royal Thai Government, *A Report on an Investigation Into Educational Conditions in the North Eastern Region*, pp. 17–22, 34–36, 38; Jumsai, *Compulsory Education in Thailand*, pp. 60–61, 85; and Havananada and Charoon Vongsayaiha, *General Information on Education in Thailand* (Bangkok, Ministry of Education, 1954), pp. 34–35, 41.

the waist, 71,880 had no slates, 188,622 had no books, 55,399 had no exercise books and 43,712 had no pencils. It was also found that there were 28,438 cases of malaria, 20,887 cases of tracoma, 37,394 cases of skin eruptions and 44,166 cases of yaws as well as many other diseases.[22]

Also of critical importance was the teacher situation. By 1950 less than 20 per cent of the teachers in elementary schools had certificates, and sometimes the qualifications were distressingly

22. Jumsai, p. 86.

low. It was not uncommon in remote areas to find that the teacher himself had not had even the four-year education normally given. Very often his qualification was "a year at a school in the wad." It might also be observed that the application of the compulsory education act took the education of children away from the wad, where they could have benefited from the invariably greater learning of the teacher priests—all this being done in the name of modernity.[23]

In many other respects statistics only broadly indicate the real situation, especially with regard to variations in schools. Some schools, for example, particularly those in outlying areas, had the worst of everything: health facilities, material resources, and teachers. On the other hand, some schools in Bangkok would grace any nation's educational system.

Other factors did relieve the generally depressing picture. A scheme for national education had been established in Thailand. There was a national bureaucracy with a specific educational ministry that was not only relatively experienced in administration but also well motivated toward education generally. From the 1930s, if not earlier, there had been a small stream of Thai educators returning from abroad, mainly from the United Kingdom and France, who were well acquainted with modern educational processes and possessed distinctive skills.

Finally, in the immediate postwar era the nation at large was an oasis of calm relative to the rest of Southeast Asia. Apart from some official antipathy toward the Republic of China and toward Chinese nationals in the kingdom, foreigners were welcome and often the recipients of special courtesies and privileges.

This, then, was the general environment in which the Cha Cheong Sao Educational Pilot Project began. In 1951 the project was established by the Thai Ministry of Education and general aims were agreed upon between the Ministry and UNESCO as the sponsoring body. The purpose of the project was to

> set up on an experimental basis a prototype school system
> extending from the pre-primary classes through secondary

23. Article 63 of the Constitution Act of 1932 reads: "It is the duty of the State to promote and foster education. All institutions must be under the care of the State. Education is the responsibility of the State. Higher institutions of learning shall be under their own management."

and vocational education to teacher training and adult education. It sought to demonstrate:

(a) a type of school organization that would provide functional education for all children at various levels;
(b) improved methods of teaching that would enable the pupils to gain the maximum possible benefit from the education they were receiving;
(c) the responsibility of schools for the improvement of the life of all people in the community.[24]

During 1951–52 a further survey was undertaken by the United Nations in Thailand in an effort to establish the feasibility of creating a Fundamental Education Center. "Fundamental Education" was a popular term, especially within UNESCO where it was seen as a means of bridging the gap between skills required for modernization and the dearth of these skills within a community. The concept was later spelled out in some detail:

The term "Fundamental Education" was adopted by UNESCO at the first session of its General Conference in 1946 and has since been used widely, if loosely, throughout the world. To simplify and shorten the standard definition, fundamental education is "that kind of education that helps children and adults who have had little or no schooling to understand the problems of their daily life and their rights and duties as citizens and to get the knowledge and skills necessary for improving the living conditions of themselves and their community.[25]

To assess the possibility of implementing a project that might embrace the general concepts of fundamental education, UNESCO sent a distinguished sociologist to Thailand in 1951. In his lengthy report this investigator gave a somewhat glowing account of Thailand as a setting for the major changes that had to accompany a fundamental education project.

Thailand is a country in many ways ideally situated for a planned program of social change. There are no serious politi-

24. UNESCO, *The Work of the* UNESCO *Technical Assistance Mission in Thailand* (Bangkok, UNESCO Regional Office, n.d.), p. 1.
25. Internal memorandum, Chief of Mission, UNESCO Regional Office, Bangkok (from the files, UNESCO Regional Office, Bangkok, n.d.).

cal or religious divisions, no great gaps between rich and poor. There is a traditional belief in cooperation and willingness to accept guidance from a central authority. There has already been exceptional development in the field of primary education and a good start has been made in other fields. The country is orderly, peaceable and prosperous. It is practical good sense rather than a desperate internal situation that is leading Thailand now towards accelerated measures for planned social change.[26]

Whether Sir Charles Madge's report gave an accurate picture of conditions in the kingdom and the desires on the part of the government for change is, of course, highly debatable. Nevertheless, this was UNESCO's professed view, and it should be noted that other commentators arrived at similar conclusions.[27]

The emphasis of the Madge report was on "social change" with all the connotations and interpretations such a term might have for different audiences. The report did not look at economic factors involved, either internally or externally. It could be remarked also that the view that "there are no political divisions" was true only because at the village level (the target of the Madge survey), there were no nationally oriented politics. On the same theme, the report did not evaluate the existing administrative apparatus in the nation, through which the envisaged intensified "guidance from a central authority" would presumably be undertaken. The implications arising from the neglect of these issues will intrude massively later in the study and need not be pursued here. Similarly, the contention that the Thai hierarchy in fact wanted "change" can be disputed, as can the affirmation that the Thai village was the contented locale described in the report or that the villager was eagerly seeking alleviation of his lot along the lines proposed in a fundamental education program. But the lengthy Madge report set the tenor for the United Nations response.

On December 9, 1953, a formal agreement was signed between the Thai government, UNESCO, UNTAA, ILO, FAO, and WHO, where-

26. Charles Madge, *Survey before Development in Thai Villages* (Paris, ST/SAO/SER.o/25, March 1957).

27. James Morris, *The Road to Huddersfield* (New York, Pantheon Books, 1963), pp. 89–90.

by TUFEC came into existence. The expressed aims of TUFEC were: "(a) to study social and economic conditions in order to determine the needs and problems of the area and the country that can be solved by fundamental education (b) to train fundamental education specialists and field workers; (c) to produce educational materials such as books, posters, audio-visual and other instructional materials."[28] Although it was not specified in the agreement with the Thai government, the intention of studying the "needs and problems of the area" had its basis in the hope that TUFEC could ultimately become a training center for all of Southeast Asia.[29]

CONCEPTS OF OPERATION

It was planned that the Cha Cheong Sao Educational Pilot Project would be developed over a ten-year period and would embrace two phases: experimentation and development covering the period 1951–55; and extension of the results throughout the twelve education areas into which the kingdom was divided over the period 1955–60. Beyond this rather broad phasing it was further conceived that:

> According to the original plan [i.e. the phases given above] . . . the schools embraced at the beginning of the Project were ten primary schools (in two of which pre-primary classes were being started), two newly organized primary extension schools, two secondary schools, and a teachers' training college. Each successive year, during the five-year period, would see the Project extended to an additional quota of schools until, at the end of 1955, all of the approximately 250 schools in the province would be included.

Planning for the second phase, that of diffusion, was less precise. Here "the means whereby this extension was to be accomplished,

28. TUFEC, *Provisional Program of Study, 1954* (Bangkok, Chatra Press, April 1954), p. 1.
29. "Proposals for a Second International Centre," letter from the Director General, UNESCO, to Ministry of Education, Thailand, August 28, 1951 (from the files, UNESCO Regional Office, Bangkok).

in terms of the obviously large financial and personnel requirements, were not indicated."[30]

Considering the massive nature of the enterprise being attempted, the general concepts governing planning and operations
can at best be described as fairly loose. On the other hand, it could
be conceded that the lack of definition gave great flexibility to the
field operators—assuming, of course, that they possessed the knowledge and capabilities to exploit this freedom and that there was
to be an appropriate allocation of resources.

A corollary to this imprecise planning was the assembling at
Cha Cheong Sao of an international faculty with a wide spectrum
of skills.[31] There is no evidence of precise objectives being given
these persons either from the headquarters in Paris or from the
regional office in Bangkok. At best, therefore, the concept of operations in Cha Cheong Sao seems to have been based upon the prem-
ise that skills, if merely inducted into the Thai educational
system, would generate their own momentum and effect the desired
changes.

The concept of operations at TUFEC was better defined than
for its sister project. The Ubol Center was intended to train 71
teams of FEOs (Fundamental Education Organizers), one for each
of the 71 provinces in the kingdom. Each team was to consist of
five to seven persons with skills in "education, health, agriculture,
crafts, etc." who would "be trained as 'cultural missions' to return
to Government service in the district from which they came."[32]
A syllabus of training was drawn up, as was a general work program covering the production of materials, research, and general
project organization.[33] Foreign personnel were assembled.[34] Also
within the initial plan was the designation of a "laboratory area"
embracing four districts in the Ubol Province. It was here that the

30. Letter from Acting Chief of Mission to UNESCO Headquarters, Paris, on
the Diffusion of Cha Cheong Sao Pilot Project, August 1957 (from the files,
UNESCO Regional Office, Bangkok).

31. For a list of foreign personnel at the Pilot Project, see Appendix II.

32. Internal memorandum, UNESCO Regional Office, Bangkok, "Thailand
United Nations Fundamental Education Center, Draft Work Program" (Bangkok, n.d.) (from the files, UNESCO Regional Office, Bangkok), p. 3.

33. TUFEC, Provisional Program of Study.

34. For a list of foreign personnel at TUFEC, see Appendix III.

Center was to conduct much of its experimentation and research.

At this stage TUFEC was to "continue to operate for at least five years. It is also desirable that the international staff should be progressively withdrawn from the beginning of the fourth year, so that at the end of the fifth year the center will be run entirely by the Thai staff."[35]

Both the Cha Cheong Sao Pilot Project and TUFEC planned to include a large Fellowship Program in conjunction with each operation, with the hope that the returned Fellows would, in part at least, keep the projects going and perhaps become leaders within them. Sixty-seven Thai received fellowships from TUFEC and 21 in connection with the Pilot Project. Each member of the international staff was to have at least one Thai counterpart as an understudy. This was generally viewed as being perhaps the single most important adjunct to the foreign worker's efforts to transmit his particular skill. A last and, as it happened, a highly important factor in the general plan of operations was that both projects were linked with the Thai Ministry of Education.

AN OVERALL VIEW OF OPERATIONAL PLANS

In viewing the scope of United Nations operations in Thailand, several factors are noteworthy. Insofar as their own writing and commentary indicate, the United Nations planners did not foresee any major difficulties that might impede their programs. Indeed, as far as TUFEC was concerned, Thailand was viewed as something of an ideal milieu.

A further important aspect was the general magnitude of the programs contemplated, on the one hand, and the paucity of material resources, on the other. Whether this should be taken as a tribute to stout hearts in the United Nations or a lack of practical planning is, however, another question, which will be discussed later in this study.

There is a vagueness about the United Nations approach to the practical aspect of operations. The Pilot Project, if successfully implemented, would have imposed a standardized system of education over the varied regions and peoples of the kingdom. Yet

35. "TUFEC, Draft Work Program," p. 5.

at no time did the United Nations servants display any real concern for the implications inherent in their long-range concepts of the tremendously increased requirements in material and human resources that must arise if ever their programs were to develop to national dimensions. If, for example, the Pilot Project were to be diffused nationwide in ten years, it would be axiomatic that a massive training and building program should start with the initial program. In late 1954 another UNESCO mission visited Thailand and did attempt to estimate the costs involved in educational development. This mission concluded that:

> The estimate of costs of extending Compulsory Education by three years [i.e. to the seven-year cycle envisaged in the original Thai Education Act and later endorsed as a general UNESCO policy], excluding teacher training would be,
>
> An Additional Annual Recurring
> Cost of   Bt. 30,700,000
>   ($1,535,000)
> A Capital Cost of   Bt. 1,125,000,000
>   ($5,625,000)
> In addition, costs for providing Secondary Education for an additional 1,500,000 children would be,
> Annual Recurring Costs of   Bt. 92,100, 000
>   ($4,605,000)
> A Capital Cost of   Bt. 3,375,000,000[36]
>   ($168,750,000)

No estimate was made for related teacher training development, nor was any assessment made of the time factor involved. One Thai official stated that he thought UNESCO had greatly underestimated and that the figures should have been "four or five times as great."[37] Even so, all of these assessments were somewhat academic, for in 1955 the total public expenditure of the Thai government was only Baht 5,410,500,000 ($270,525,000).

36. Victor Clarke, *Report on Steps Being Taken to Improve and Extend Compulsory Education in Thailand Together with Some Suggestions for Further Development*, Paris, May 1954 (from the files, Ministry of Education, Bangkok), p. 35.

37. Interview at Ministry of Education, Bangkok, June 15, 1963.

No long-term financial estimates were made for the TUFEC program and indeed this was hardly practical. TUFEC, although it emphasized change, did not really define what that change was to be. In this regard, the program was something of an experiment. Fundamental education was the only concept that TUFEC had as its guide, together with the idea that a team of FEOs in each province in Thailand would somehow or other act as catalysts of change. Ultimately, these general goals would have to be translated into some form of action and objectives that would take account of the peasant environment, which after all was where change was to take place.

Nevertheless, whatever vagueness the modus operandi of these United Nations operations may have had, they did represent something unique in the relations that technologically advanced countries had had with Asia up until the postwar period. Here was a genuine desire to transfer skills thought necessary to promote the upsurge of material development. It now remains to see what disparity existed between this unique motivation, with its very generalized supporting concepts, and the practical implementation.

3

THE DYNAMICS OF
THE OPERATIONAL MILIEU

OPERATIONAL BACKGROUND

At some stage the aspirations for TUFEC and the Pilot Project had to be translated into work. The transition was not easy, but practical achievement would be the ultimate test of the United Nations enterprise in Thailand. There were, however, certain limitations and guide lines as to what the United Nations might do in the kingdom, and before examining the dynamics of the operations, it is necessary to trace briefly the general background.

Operations generally were conceived of as something separate from general national development. The Madge Report believed that social change could be planned and faced no national impediment.[1] The seemingly logical sequel of a formal integration of these planned operations into Thai national development was not, however, attempted during planning, or indeed even considered. Such an approach might, in fact, have proved impossible to implement. The general idea of planned economic development, such as seems to be the norm in the developing countries, was not present in the Thai approach to such problems. It was not until 1961 that Thailand formulated an economic plan, and even then the plan was not specific.[2]

The Thai reluctance to plan did not arise from any particular antipathy to planning, on the one hand, or because of adherence to free enterprise, on the other. It had simply never been necessary in Thailand to embark on economic planning. In the latter half

1. Madge, "Introduction," to *Survey before Development in Thai Villages.*
2. Eliezer Ayal, "Thailand's Six Year Development Plan," *Asia Survey, 3* (1963), 98–112.

of the nineteenth century the country was caught up in the increasing demand for rice exports. From an annual export of approximately 53,989 tons in 1857, there had been a near fourteenfold increase to approximately 868,235 tons in 1905. Along with Burma, Thailand had become the largest rice exporter in the world.[3] This massive increase involved expansion of the nation's traditional ecological modes, not introduction of new methods and systems with the disruptions that are normally attendant upon such changes. In the same period the nation's population approximately doubled, but this expansion too was easily absorbed (in fact, it aided increases in rice production) because of the ready availability of land. The density of population still remains low in Thailand, some 130 people per square mile, and there is still a farming "frontier" which continues to absorb population without too much change in the ecological pattern. Although these factors are sufficient to explain why economic planning was not actively espoused in Thailand, other elements in the Thai national character also inhibit this approach to life; some of these will be noted later.

While national economic development plans did not exist within which the United Nations planning might have been integrated, neither was the rural situation such that development was precluded. Processes of "natural" growth had in fact been taking place for a century or more. The two United Nations schemes had neither the advantages nor the disadvantages that some might view as concomitant with integration in a national economic planning scheme. Thus the United Nations projects were free to pursue their goals in accordance with the time factors and general objectives established during the original planning stages.

The Pilot Project

To support the Pilot Project at Cha Cheong Sao, Thailand originally requested that UNESCO supply "four education experts and 20 Fellowships per year and such specialist equipment as cannot be supplied by the Thai government," and the general tenor of negotiations was that the Thai government envisaged a fairly

3. James C. Ingram, *Economic Change in Thailand Since 1850* (Stanford, Stanford University Press, 1955), p. 38.

simple and small-scale operation.[4] In February 1951, a joint UNESCO/Thai commission was given the task of drawing up a comprehensive program.[5] Although details were not spelled out at that time, ten foreign experts were at work in Cha Cheong Sao by the latter half of 1951. It was not until between 1954 and 1956 that a completed curriculum appeared, embracing elementary and high schools, and teacher training institutions.[6] This sort of delay was to be expected. A very complex operation had been started and none of the foreign experts had had field experience in Thailand. Nevertheless, it must also be remembered that by 1956 diffusion of methods and techniques was to be initiated throughout the kingdom.

At this stage the project had just started to prepare its own detailed programs. Furthermore, the Pilot Project had greatly limited its scope of activity and was concentrating its entire effort on teacher training: elementary and high school teaching programs and techniques; activity associated with school and classroom management; and schemes such as in-service training for teachers, the latter aimed at raising standards of teaching outside of Cha Cheong Sao.

By 1958, when diffusion should have been well under way, schools within the town of Cha Cheong Sao itself had not, in fact, become either model or experimental as planned. The aim had been to produce "better than average schools" of the kind that could be imitated reasonably well in the rest of the country with the resources that Thailand was likely to have available.[7] Thus operations as originally planned had hardly begun before the concept of producing model schools through the advice and assistance of foreign experts appeared unworkable. Also the magnitude

4. Letter from the Ministry of Education to UNESCO Headquarters, Paris, November 6, 1950 (from the files, Ministry of Education, Bangkok).

5. Internal memorandum, UNESCO Regional Office, Bangkok, Ref. I.559, Annex VI, February 13, 1950 (from the files, UNESCO Regional Office, Bangkok).

6. UNESCO, UNESCO *Educational Program in Thailand* (Bangkok, December 1954) and Ministry of Education Order, 8/2499, on the 1955 Curriculum for Certification of Teachers, Ministry of Education, Bangkok, January 12, 1955 (from the files, Ministry of Education, Bangkok, in Thai).

7. Letter from the Chief of Mission, UNESCO Regional Office, Bangkok, to UNESCO Headquarters, Paris, Annex II, April 28, 1958 (from the files, UNESCO Headquarters, Paris).

of Thailand's educational problem was being revealed, in its basic form, as not so much a shortage of ideas and techniques as a shortage of appropriate material and human resources.

In 1957, sensing that all was not well at Cha Cheong Sao, the Thai Ministry of Education established an evaluation committee to examine the current status of the project. This full and comprehensive report asserted, among other things, that foreign experts should be withdrawn from the project between 1957 and 1959 and, where necessary to complete contracts, could be stationed in Bangkok, presumably either in the UNESCO Regional Office or within the Ministry of Education.[8]

Despite the foregoing, the process of spreading the work of the Pilot Project throughout the nation formally commenced early in 1958. Like most projects that adhere strictly to pre-planned schedules this process was mostly a paper exercise. What was to be diffused? Neither the workers in the field nor the UNESCO Regional Office could define the process, even in general terms. As a field worker noted: "The process of diffusion, which is supposed to be the second five year phase of the project according to agreement with UNESCO in 1951, started formally about a month ago. What is to be diffused, nobody knows clearly. How is it to be diffused? We are none the wiser."[9] The same issue was also being aired at different levels at about the same time by the Chief of Mission in Bangkok: "At meetings with various heads of the various sections at Cha Cheong Sao, when we have explained the new phases of diffusion and asked them to help identify the good results of the Project's work they say 'Yes—but we don't know what they are.' "[10]

By the end of 1958 all but three of the foreign staff had left Cha Cheong Sao, and by November 1959 United Nations participation had ceased. One summing up was given by the Chief of Mission:

8. Ministry of Education, *Report of Evaluation Committee Cha Cheong Sao Project* (Cha Cheong Sao, August 16, 1957), pp. 34–35, trans. from Thai by Smorn Gunatilaka (from the files, Ministry of Education, Bangkok).

9. Internal memorandum, UNESCO Headquarters, Paris, "Debriefing of Mr. Juul: Teacher Training Expert (Norway)," Paris, May 13, 1958 (from the files, UNESCO Regional Office, Bangkok), p. 3.

10. Letter from Chief of Mission, UNESCO Regional Office, Bangkok to Director of Education, UNESCO Headquarters, Paris, July 8, 1958 (from the files, UNESCO Regional Office, Bangkok), p. 1.

"I am of a sanguine temperament and I believe that something of value may yet be salvaged from Cha Cheong Sao; but it is unrealistic to look upon this as anything more than salvage work.[11]

Without fanfare, therefore, international support for the Pilot Project quietly subsided. During 1958 and 1959 UNESCO commissioned research with the object of evaluating the project. The 325-page document that resulted[12] was described as "not worth filing—just a summary of 26 experts' reports and no guide for diffusion."[13] Later a shorter report, in essence a synopsis of the larger one, was submitted.[14] Both reports stated that the project had been a success without specifying how.

Today the schools at Cha Cheong Sao, superficially at least, seem to operate much the same as do other schools in Thailand at similar localities. In the area of national planning, however, a new concept reigns. General improvement of education now falls under the GED Project (General Educational Development), which is supported by USOM (United States Operations Mission). In this project, activity is spread over all twelve educational regions and the objects are to: (1) improve education at all levels in rural areas; (2) conduct in-service and pre-service training; and (3) establish local supervisory centers and a general devolution of centralized control.[15]

Except for the very important issue of promoting decentralization, the general objectives are not dissimilar from those of the Pilot Project, but instead of creating a model which would be a pattern for the nation at large, account now is being taken of regional differences, and attempts made to tap energies inherent in local approaches in other countries.

Within the nation at large there is yet another education project which seems basic, even if a good deal more mundane than the

11. Ibid., p. 5.

12. Myrtle M. Imhoff, *The Cha Cheong Sao Pilot Project of Thailand 1949–59,* An evaluation study prepared for UNESCO, unpublished, undated (copy loaned by the Teachers' Training College, Prasarn Mitr, Bangkok).

13. "Cha Cheong Sao and TURTEP Projects," letter from Education Director, UNESCO Headquarters, Paris, to Chief of Mission, UNESCO Regional Office, Bangkok, December 16, 1959 (from the files, UNESCO Regional Office, Bangkok).

14. John Audriac, *Report on the UNESCO Thailand Cha Cheong Sao Pilot Project* (Paris, UNESCO/EPTA/THA/2 March 1962).

15. Interview, Ministry of Education, June 27, 1963.

projects sponsored from the outside. The object is to raise the period of compulsory schooling from the present four years to seven years. This is the same objective sought in the Education Act of 1921 and more recently sponsored by a series of worldwide education conferences held, interestingly enough, under UNESCO's aegis.[16] To attain this goal, UNESCO thought, would take up to twenty years. The Thai government has also subscribed to this estimate, although many Thai educators seem to consider twenty years far too short a time. The complexity of factors involved in providing basic services and infrastructure for such development has, among other things, curtailed the optimism of previous years. There is realization, at least on the part of the Thai educators, that there is no easy or quick solution to their problems, and that such solutions cannot be deftly and painlessly introduced from overseas. Enforcing this realization was the attack by the late prime minister, Field Marshal Sarit Thanarat, on the capabilities of the current education program with its four years of schooling. In an interview, the premier complained that some 600,000 Thai children out of a total school population of 3,000,000 failed to pass (or reach) the graduating standards compatible with the fourth (and final) year of their schooling. He went on to say that there was little point in the ministry pursuing grandiose development schemes (specifically mentioning the GED scheme), when even the current limited system was not working. Shortages of teachers and schools, he said, were the real inhibitors. He made a strong plea for private organizations to increase their already numerous educational programs, and he promised further increases in the educational budget.[17]

There can be little doubt that the Pilot Project failed to attain, either in quantitative or qualitative terms, the goals sought. Furthermore, there would seem to be a wide disparity between what the United Nations was trying to do and the real situation that existed in the kingdom. Some reasons for this disparity will appear later.

16. UNESCO, *Final Report of Ministers of Education of Asian States Participating in the Karachi Plan* (Bangkok, UNESCO/ED/192, Harry Frederick Printers, 1962), Chap. 2.

17. "Education, A Problem of Shortages?" *Siam Rath,* June 9, 1963, p. 17 (in Thai).

TUFEC

The operational background of TUFEC was somewhat different from that of the Pilot Project. On the surface, TUFEC had a more clearly defined mission as well as the autonomy that comes from the creation of a new and separate institution. But some issues were not resolved. From the beginning there were doubts as to what "fundamental education" really meant in terms of TUFEC's mission, and also doubts as to whether the enterprise should be directed toward community development.

> Community development is a term used to describe the processes by which a local community can raise its own standard of living, whereas Fundamental Education is that kind of minimum and general education which aims to help children and adults who do not have the advantages of formal education to understand the problems of their immediate environment and their rights and duties as citizens and individuals and to participate more effectively in the economic and social progress of the community.[18]

A further vital distinction was noted between community development and fundamental education, a distinction that was to have an important bearing on the TUFEC operation: "Effective programs to promote Community Development require the combination of assistance from outside the community with local self help and effort."[19]

The Center did not see itself involved in that sort of relationship, although even at this early and formative time it must have been difficult to see how any organization could become involved in rural Thailand without a working relationship with Thai provincial machinery. The rationale adopted by TUFEC to meet this obvious problem was interesting and of some significance to the Center's future. As the Center saw it: "TUFEC is not training

18. Minutes of the Second General Meeting of the Regional Education Officers Conference, Ubol, July 14, 1955 (from the files, UNESCO Regional Office, Bangkok), p. 2.

19. Ibid., p. 4.

specialists but is training its students in techniques that will help them *bridge the gap* between the Ministry officers (i.e. Ministry of Interior) and the level of knowledge and understanding in the villages."[20]

Disregarding the uncomplimentary inference concerning the relationships that provincial officials might have with their villagers, it seems that TUFEC saw itself possessing a sort of operational and institutional autonomy that would be advantageous to an organization viewing itself as a catalyst for change. Thus the Center adhered to its original concept of providing services for fundamental education. It also saw itself as highly autonomous. Both hypotheses were to have considerable significance as time went on.

By November 1955 TUFEC buildings included a large administration block, a student union building, several dormitories, five residences, a guest house, and a demonstration cottage. By 1958 thirty additional units had been added, mainly dormitories, staff houses, and demonstration rooms. A 180-acre farm was quickly established. Overall, by mid-1958 TUFEC was by Thai standards a large and impressive institution in its physical aspects.

The majority of recruits for TUFEC, not unexpectedly, came from the Ministry of Education. Most of them had been school teachers. There were a few representatives from other departments who, it seems, came without official encouragement from their departmental superiors. Initially a course for FEOs lasted two years; and, although there was some variation from time to time, basically the two-year period held good. In their course all students were expected to acquire a general knowledge in eight main areas of activity: agriculture, health, homemaking, village crafts, home construction, education, production of instructional materials, and social welfare. At an early stage each student was required to specialize in one subject and to become part of a team of from five to seven individuals who were expected to be collectively skilled in all of the subjects taught. About half of the training time was spent in the "laboratory area" outside of the Center, and it was here that the international experts were supposed to exercise supervision over training in field work.

20. Ibid., p. 6 (italics added).

On completion of training, teams were deployed at the pre-scribed ratio of one team per province, and by 1961 the planned total of 71 teams had been trained. An original TUFEC view was that a suitable locale in a province would be designated a TVC (Training Village Center) and would be the base area from which teams would conduct their operations. Officially the team was to come under the provincial education officer, an official of the Ministry of Education, but no record has been found of any clear directive ever being given to this official as to what he was to do with his new charges.

It was also intended that while in the field the teams would be "visited by TUFEC staff as often as possible," but, as it happened, "this was not very often."[21] No real machinery existed for either control or supervision by the Center after deployment of the teams, although many recognized the need. The disassociation was ex-plained: "There is a danger that if TUFEC's concern with the graduates is too close, they may well look to the Center for help and support in all their problems rather than work out their difficulties within the official framework of which they are a part."[22]

Whether in fact the teams were a part of the official structure proved to be a moot point, but at least TUFEC provided a rationale for severing association with the teams, and thereafter the Center was only dimly aware of the operational success or failure of the TUFEC trainees.

The international staff at the Center headed all training sections and held administrative posts up to and including deputy director. As the director proper (an official in the Ministry of Education) lived in Bangkok and made only periodic visits, the acting director was very much in command. One or more Thai worked with each international expert, and the intention was that, as soon as prac-tical, Thai should take over all posts of TUFEC. By early 1959 four sections were headed by Thai, and it was planned that by August 1959 all sections and services would be Thai-controlled, with the international staff acting in an advisory capacity. Structurally this

21. Letter from Chief of Mission, UNESCO Regional Office, Bangkok, to UNESCO Headquarters, Paris, April 28, 1958 (from the files, UNESCO Regional Office, Bangkok), p. 5.
22. Ibid., p. 6.

was achieved by the deadline, but not without serious misgivings on the part of the international staff:

> There is a widespread lack of academic background [i.e. of the Thai staff], a background which will be essential in handling the personnel of the in-service course. While members of the present staff can cope adequately with basic training up to FEO level, personnel dealing with group dynamics and human relations, with research and evaluation and with principles and practice of FE [Fundamental Education] and Community Development will need reinforcement.[23]

At the same time the commentator did not think that this reinforcement could, or should, come from international sources. He felt (quite incorrectly as it happened) that:

> The place of the Center in the national Community Development plan has been settled, the training pattern is established and I suspect that the appetite of the Thai staff at TUFEC for still more advice on principle and practice, curriculum building, methods, organization and administration is satiated.[24]

In December 1961 UNESCO withdrew from TUFEC according to plan; and on December 28, 1961, at a well publicized ceremony, the responsibility for training and all equipment at the Center passed into the control of the Ministry of Education. At this time TUFEC did not have a plan for future operations. The 71 teams had been trained and despatched, some vague views had been expressed about in-service training and short courses for district officials (some of which were undertaken), and hardly justifiable statements were made to the effect that TUFEC's "place in the national Community development plan had been settled."

In actuality nothing had been settled in any specific sense. The withdrawal of the United Nations under these circumstances was an end, not a beginning. Except for the short courses mentioned and the use of the buildings by Thai and United States military for another short course, major operations ceased. By 1963 most build-

23. *Final Report* of the Deputy Director, TUFEC to UNESCO Headquarters, Paris, August 1, 1959, p. 11 (from a photostat copy, supplied by Ministry of Interior, Bangkok).
24. Ibid., p. 12.

ings had been closed down. For all practical purposes by this time TUFEC had come to an end, at the time when it was supposed to have been proliferating throughout the nation. At the Center itself it appeared that any future for TUFEC was most uncertain, that the Center did not have a role, and that its activity did not interrelate with national community development in any direct sense. Clarification of this issue was sought from the director of the newly formed Department of National Community Development in Bangkok, who stated that TUFEC was not included in the national scheme and its experience had been largely discounted during the formulation of the national Community Development Plan.[25]

This was the reality of the TUFEC enterprise in the field. Despite the United Nations' confidence in its techniques and in the receptivity of the Thai milieu, TUFEC was unable to generate an operational dynamic that was self-sustaining, let alone a basis for future expansion. The same might also be said of the Pilot Project. An examination of field performance throws light on some issues concerning communication methods and raises basic questions about the validity of preconceived notions held by the United Nations (or indeed generally by the West) of peasant needs and aspirations in Thailand.

OPERATIONAL DYNAMICS

Much in the operations of both projects was routine. Activity in the classroom, workshop, and library did not differ too much from similar activity elsewhere. Other activities, however, highlighted the complexity of the task undertaken and especially illustrated the conceptual deficiencies of the international agencies involved, as well as the great gaps that existed between personal capabilities and requirements of the field environment. The typical activities selected here are presented not as criticism but as illustration of the magnitude of the task that the United Nations agencies had accepted with such slender and ill-adapted resources.

It is surprising at first sight that one of the initial activities of the Pilot Project was not education but an agricultural extension

25. Interview, Department of National Community Development, Bangkok, July 25, 1963.

—or, as some preferred to call it, a community development—project. In 1942 the Ministry of Interior had embarked upon a project of community development at the commune of Bangpakong, near Cha Cheong Sao. Apparently the Ministry's project failed to get properly started, but neither did it die. It still had some claim to life when the Pilot Project arrived. In 1952 the Project took over the scheme and announced its intention of developing a model rural community in conjunction with its educational activity. The Project stated that it would concentrate on many aspects of life: economic, social, cultural, educational, and, to be totally comprehensive, would not neglect the spiritual. The entire scheme was to be a backdrop to the development of education generally in the area.[26]

There was a strong element of chance in the pursuit of this particular activity by the Pilot Project. An FAO representative had been established within the Pilot Project and he sought an active role. The location and past history of Bangpakong provided an excellent oportunity for this; and the FAO Regional Office, recently established in Bangkok, gave strong support because it was seeking some means of getting agricultural activity started in Thailand. The written reports show that the initial activity at Bangpakong was very successful[27]—a view endorsed by one of Asia's foremost agricultural authorities.[28]

The project started with a valuable survey of the 89 families involved; and a detailed plan of agricultural extension was drawn up which in many respects stands as a model for the perceptive and particularistic assessment of a problem which later activity proved to be so necessary.[29] Arising from the study, a practical project was launched to solve the fundamental issue of providing adequate water on the farmers' fields at the right time. Research was conducted into water-lifting devices,[30] and a new canal was

26. Minutes of the First Meeting of the Bangpakong Committee, Bangpakong, July 2, 1952 (from the files, FAO Regional Office, Bangkok).

27. Frank Dickinson, *Report to the Government of Thailand on Agricultural Activities at Cha Cheong Sao* (Bangkok, FAO/ETAP/215, December 1963).

28. Interview at FAO Regional Office, Bangkok, May 31, 1963.

29. Frank Dickinson, *A Plan for Agricultural Development at Bangpakong*, July 1952 (from the files, FAO Regional Office, Bangkok).

30. See above, p. 20.

dug. It is reported that in the first year rice crops increased by 100 per cent.[31] But most remarkable of all was the means whereby this was achieved.

First, it should be noted that the peasant was involved in a process of extending his traditional ecology, dealing with not only familiar but congenial questions. Secondly, the survey conducted was specific and comprehensive, and, mainly because of the perception of the principals concerned, required action was reduced to a few simple and wholly attainable measures: 61 families asked for assistance with water-lifting devices such as portable power pumps or repair of their existing wind-driven pumps; 47 families wanted loans to buy buffalo; and 56 families required overall credit to repay moneylenders as well as to finance the purchase of buffalo.

While full financing was not available, solution of the water problem did go a long way toward giving the peasant the increase in cash income that enabled him to meet the other development needs. It would be unwise to read too much into this agricultural success in Bangpakong, but the peasant circumstances there seem so typical that it could well provide a good general view of the type of immediate problem facing Thai peasants elsewhere.[32]

The Bangpakong project, after starting with such promise, lasted only one year. The reasons for its demise are obscure, but it seems that it fell apart because of personal and bureaucratic frictions, none of which involved the peasants. The UNESCO Regional Office came to be less and less interested in agricultural work; the FAO representative withdrew and left Thailand after a very short stay. There was also friction between the Thai Ministry of Interior and the Ministry of Education. The former thought that the scheme was an unwarranted intrusion into its domain by another department which, administratively and functionally, should have had nothing to do with agriculture.

For the purpose of this study it is enlightening to contrast the methodology of the experiment at Bangpakong, brief as it was, with that of general TUFEC activity in the same field. In Bangpa-

31. Minutes of the Ninth Meeting of the Bangpakong Committee, Bangpakong, March 1953 (from the files, FAO Regional Office, Bangkok).

32. See also Chaiyong Chuchart, *Farm Success and Project Administration, Co-operative Land Settlement Projects: Part I* (Bangkok, Kasetsart University, November 1962), pp. 149–89.

kong the approach was particularistic; as a result, appropriate activity could be directed toward clearly defined problems in which specific research had indicated positive results could be attained. Not all peasant problems can be reduced to simple proportions, but many can if the requisite degree of attention is given them. But a TUFEC-FEO team could not approach its problems this way. One FEO team was spread out over the length and breadth of a province with, at a minimum, 400 villages, and possibly as many as 3,000. There was little chance, therefore, of an FEO team pinpointing activities along the lines of the Bangpakong project or, indeed, promoting any other project where a high degree of specific research was required. Neither would team mobility have solved the problem, as teams had to rely on local transport which greatly inhibited movement. Even the provision of personal transport would not have given the contact necessary. There are many areas in Thailand where travel between two villages may take a day when trails are dry, but during the monsoon, movement over vast areas becomes impossible for all practical purposes. After some five or six years had elapsed, TUFEC itself began to see the impracticality of the concept of "village workers" on the ratio of one team to a province. "There are 2,000 villages in Ubol *Changwad* [province] alone: even if 20 villages a year were activated the task would take a century."[33]

An even more basic contrast was that the Bangpakong project, despite its early aspirations, actually limited itself to impersonal activity such as water control and distribution, and ransoming of buffaloes. Improvements were in harmony with peasant life. TUFEC, however, aspired not only to change economic and educational patterns but also to impinge on social and personal life, hoping to give practical form to such phrases as "improved group dynamics and human relations," "activation of village social programs," or even the promotion of "a more enjoyable village social life." In Thailand where each village has a mutually understood, active, and full social pattern of its own, intrusions by TUFEC in this area were not only likely to be ineffectual but even harmful to

33. "Fundamental Education Situation: Organizers as Village Leaders," letter from Chief of Mission, UNESCO Regional Headquarters, Bangkok, to UNESCO Headquarters, Paris, November 16, 1959 (from the files, UNESCO Regional Office, Bangkok), p. 2.

practical programs. The Thai peasant may have had economic problems but his social and personal life was not commensurately deprived.[34] Differentiation of the areas open to TUFEC therapy was essential to successful operations. This, however, required a knowledge beyond TUFEC purview. There will be more discussion of this theme later, but at Bangpakong the effort was specifically economic and the peasant's personal life was left alone. TUFEC, on the other hand, increasingly seemed to see itself as an agent of total change.

Bangpakong did illustrate that, under certain circumstances, a United Nations agency in Thailand could activate a village in the direction of straightforward practical tasks. While it is probable that change and development relative to social, cultural, and spiritual objectives at Bangpakong would not have been feasible, there were impressive short-term results in the more practical field of agriculture. Even if TUFEC's activities had been confined to practicalities, they would still have been spread too thinly to have anything more than very local effects. The problem was never resolved nor, if UNESCO correspondence is to be taken as a guide, was it ever really faced.

In retrospect, solution to the problem can be seen in a variety of forms. Some proposals by Thai officials and field workers have been as follows: the initiation by teams of a specific pilot project in a province with the object of having it emulated by local leadership; a massive increase in personnel output from the Center; and the expansion and embellishment of the Center to make it an agricultural university concentrating heavily on research and development. It is not intended here to discuss the relative merits of these suggestions or what other courses might have been adopted. The point at issue is the physical limitations imposed upon the FEO teams by their lack of resources for the task conceived by the Center and the general inability of all, from the pinnacle of UNESCO Headquarters right through to the international workers in the field, to attain a balance between intentions and capabilities. There was a vacuous innocence, even in the realities of logistics, which alone doomed the prospects of any transmission of skills,

34. See below, pp. 71–72.

let alone ideas, to the Thai peasant. The specific impact of some operations best reveals the deficiencies of all.

"Felt Needs"

It was common jargon in the field of fundamental education to speak of "felt needs." To deal with a peasant's "felt need" was the most obvious way to establish common action between peasant and FEO. In the Northeast Region of Thailand, as has been noted, a shortage of water and an absence of water control had been the major obstacles to nearly all forms of agricultural activity. Water, therefore, was a "felt need"; TUFEC recognized this and proceeded to devise a simple well system which solved the curse of peasant wells—their rapid silting. It was not uncommon to find that peasant wells became useless within two or three years of digging. The TUFEC well greatly reduced the problem and was relatively simple to make and install. After some of these wells were constructed in villages, consideration was given at TUFEC to figuring out ways in which animal power might lift water from the wells, making them useful for agriculture as well as for family needs.[35]

In addition to the well program, some small dams were built by village labor under TUFEC leadership. During the 1950s the Thai government had initiated a major dam-building scheme. Twenty-seven hundred dams were planned, and although there is no information on how many have been built, the figure is probably not more than one or two hundred. The Thai government had planned to leave it to the villages to find ways of distributing water from the dams. This involved canal digging and building simple lock systems. Here was a project, closely allied to "felt needs," in which TUFEC could very aptly employ its concept of bridging the gap between government and people. Some limited efforts were made in this direction.

Overall, however, the impact of all these water projects was slight. Data are scarce, but it seems that perhaps not more than 100 TUFEC wells have been sunk in Thailand and perhaps fewer than 20 villages have been involved in "bridging the gap" operations

35. Donald K. Faris, *Technical Assistance Program, Community Development Training in Thailand* (TAO/THA/10, August 11, 1959).

using the dams.[36] Thus in attempting to meet a real "felt need," TUFEC's efforts were minimal, and there were good reasons for it. That a peasant felt something very strongly did not necessarily mean that a TUFEC-FEO team had a legitimate target. The "felt need" must first be translated into its practical dimensions, and the water problem illustrates this point.

For geographical reasons, in Thailand (as in most countries) water conservation, control, and distribution tend to be regional and not local issues.[37] Terrain and climate make it so, and as a result it is extraordinarily difficult, where operations are limited to village resources, to make any advance at all. Generally a new and better village well does little more than enhance standards of hygiene; any economic impact is slow and indirect. Even where more productive village wells can be harnessed for agriculture, such water resources again have a limited impact. Regional development is the key to water problems in Thailand, but this opens up an area well outside the concept of "village workers" unless they are integrated into a larger operation. During its lifetime TUFEC did not organize its activities so that it might play a role in Thai regional schemes, nor did it ever contemplate such a course. This factor alone condemned TUFEC action, at best, to sporadic small-scale efforts in the few villages where it could make contact and, at worst, to unfulfilled expectations.

Perhaps the single greatest activity spurred by TUFEC in the villages was road and bridge building, the latter to a somewhat lesser degree. There was a reason for this form of TUFEC activity:

> Road building . . . becomes of prime importance in the village economy. Between December and May of each year, the people have considerable time on their hands. Formerly much of this potential was wasted. The villagers are now finding an outlet for these slack periods in road building.[38]

Whether many Thai villagers would altogether approve of this utilitarian approach to their leisure hours is debatable, but there can be little doubt of the economic value, indeed of the necessity,

---

36. Estimate supplied by TUFEC, July 1963.

37. Ministry of Agriculture, Royal Irrigation Department, *The Greater Chao Phya Project* (Bangkok, Thai Watana Panich Printers, 1957), pp. 8–9.

38. Faris, p. 12.

for outlet roads in rural Thailand. A road is something that can be constructed fairly readily by hand labor in most areas in the kingdom, but an important additional ingredient is skilled supervision of the construction methods, especially provisions for drainage. The whole of the Southeast Asian peninsula abounds in so-called roads constructed by hand labor which revert to rutted tracks after one rainy season because of the omission of efficient drainage features. When the dry weather comes these roads are rehabilitated and used until the next rains.

There was some doubt as to whether the training given FEOs equipped them for the relatively complex supervisory task required in building and maintaining all-weather roads. It was noted that "in all development work technical knowledge was needed, in agriculture, irrigation, forestry, health, etc. and TUFEC was not competent technically to give the help needed but should seek this help from government officers who had technical knowledge." Road making was held up as a specific illustration of this point. "Road making was being tried in several villages" but "when these roads were made they were made slowly with no funds. However when Nai Amphur (the District Officer) also had made roads, in this case the work went along faster and the villagers were paid for their labor."[39] Thus in addition to the need for skilled supervision, the picture was further complicated in that the villagers, portraying a normal human tendency, preferred to be paid for utilization of this time potential which in other eyes was being wasted. Allied with this was the issue of coordination with provincial administration.

If the villager's efforts were not to be wasted and his faith in leadership weakened, a road project had to be sucessful. It is a fact of life that a badly built road demonstrates its faults to all concerned in an unmistakable way. There is no avoiding demonstration of success or failure. Where skills were not available, an FEO would have been wiser to leave the project alone. But this rarely happened. Instead, there was an attitude of "giving things a go," inspired by the Center but often somewhat misplaced on field projects. Of even more consequence was the absence of coordina-

39. Minutes of a meeting of a local committee with TUFEC staff, at Ubol, February 8, 1956 (from the files, TUFEC, Ubol).

tion between the FEOs and local officials. In a situation where
resources were minimal for all concerned, cooperation for utilitarian purposes would seem obvious. Perhaps an even more important lack was cooperation for planning purposes, linking TUFEC
with the provincial authority rather than having it unwittingly
become a competitor.

Satisfactory solution of a further problem concerned with building roads was mandatory to long-term success. A road can be constructed fairly readily with hand labor, but once it is built some
form of machine maintenance becomes imperative if it is to remain
usable by modern vehicles. Maintenance might take the simple
form of a grader locally constructed from heavy timbers with iron
flanges and drawn by an animal. But to construct and operate such
a machine at regular intervals is outside the capabilities of a
village. This maintenance operation even in a simple form requires the services of a larger administrative complex with some
sort of regular budget and a program.

"Indigenous Resources"

There is also a vitally important relationship between even the
simplest forms of development and technology. TUFEC abounded
in themes like "making use of indigenous resources" without, it is
suggested, having a very clear idea of just what could be achieved
with local materials alone. In Thailand, inland waterways carry
aproximately half of the nation's freight,[40] providing a low-cost
freight system for those who most need it—the nation's peasantry.
The vast majority of Thailand's canals were dug by hand labor,
some 1,300 miles in all, surely a labor-intensive project by any
standard. But the tremendous advantage of having many hands to
do this sort of thing lapses the day the canals are dug, for canals
require maintenance to keep their depth and the structure of their
clay banks. A machine dredge (the Royal Irrigation Department
has only a few) is the only practical way of keeping them at
depth.[41]

40. Ministry of Railways, *A Study on Transport and Communications in
Thailand* (Bangkok, March 1962), p. 32.

41. A traditional method of dredging canals was to drain them and then
redig, using hand labor. This method has not been used extensively in Thai-

Other basic forms of development require a mixture between the ancient and the modern, the hand and the machine. During September 1958, I was traveling between the village of Dansai and the town of Loeie in the northwest corner of the Northeast Region. Washed-out bridges and flooded trails frequently impeded the trip. Marooned at the tiny hamlet of Ban Muohy, I asked the headman why his village did not build a vehicular bridge so that some traffic might be maintained even when the monsoon was at its height. The only link this little village had with the outside world was a rickety bamboo catwalk crossing a water course which was a swift, treacherous torrent during the rainy season but was dry the remainder of the year. It was pointed out to the headman that there was ample heavy timber in the forest, the village had plenty of building skill as shown by their houses, and even had an elephant to do the heavy pulling. The headman's reply was simple. He said that his village did not really need access for the three or four months of the monsoon. The village's rice surplus went out before the rains came. The village was self-sufficient in the main essentials and in any case the ubiquitous peddler could always manage to get his wares across the catwalk.

This was the sort of village rationalization that one can meet anywhere in Thailand. Of more pertinence was the headman's explanation of what he thought was involved in building a vehicular bridge. The headman pointed out that the sort of heavy wooden structure that the village indeed had the skills to erect, while an excellent bridge under normal circumstances, did present problems during the monsoon. Massive maintenance would be required to keep the structure open. With this kind of construction bridge approaches constantly washed away. It was a constant village chore, which the headman had to organize, to have these inundated holes filled in. It was also common in a village-built bridge, under the constant scouring action of the flood, to have the piles loosen because they could not be sunk deeply enough with village resources. When piles loosened, the absence of iron clamps

---

land since before the demise of corvée labor at the turn of this century because it was based upon the rapid assembly of a large mass of laborers. Practically, therefore, the mechanical dredge remains as the solution to the problem.

and heavy bolts made the construction tenuous. In other words, bridging the water course, which was dry and easily traversable for most of the year, imposed burdens during the few months of the monsoon which simply were not worth the effort. When the headman was asked, "But supposing the village had a crop which had to be transported during the monsoon or found that it was essential for [villagers] to have intercourse with the outside, say, to work in the tobacco kiln nearby; what then?" If this remote possibility should arise, the village would have to acquire a bridge "like the ones they were building on the road between Loeie and Petchaboon." These bridges had concrete "shoulders" which resisted erosion even at the height of the monsoon. Furthermore, when this kind of bridge was built, the workers had "an American machine" which drove long, sharp concrete piles a great distance into the earth.

To build a bridge not using proper technology, then, was to dissipate one's energies for no good purpose. This was something that no sensible man would do: "So you ask me to do something, to build a bridge, which I know is a poor bridge and which might fall down unless we work day and night to keep it open. Why should we do a thing like that?"

In late 1962 the general idea of the village dilemma as illustrated above received publicity from a somewhat unrelated source. About this time, teams from the Royal Thai Army, the Ministry of Interior, and the United States Information Service started to move about in back areas, especially along the Mekong River. The objective was to gather information on the increasing Communist infiltration and assess their propaganda attack across the river from Laos. A common finding relative to the villagers' ability to fend for themselves arose from these investigations and was expressed as follows:

> Throughout the whole of the area visited, villagers seemed skilled enough to construct substantial homes depending on available material. They can make the necessary machinery to gin cotton, till their fields, weave their cloth and make a number of other machine-like objects necessary to village life. The problem of the villager is not the lack of skill in most cases, but the lack of manufactured materials which

are hard to obtain. In the case of village road construction it is the lack of steel nuts and bolts, angle iron braces and nails which prevents bridge construction necessary to all-weather roads, not the lack of timber or manpower.[42]

The basis of TUFEC's efforts, however, was not bringing "manufactured materials" to the villages but developing skills. TUFEC's themes, such as "helping the people to help themselves" and "exploiting the prolific natural resources that go to waste about villages," might be germane to specific situations, but they had little relevance as general theories. Bringing fundamental education to a village could mean very little if what the villager needed was not more information on how to make a thatch roof waterproof but the sheet iron which the average villager knew provided a much more practicable and efficient long-term solution. It might also be observed that the average villager does not need to be shown how to put sheet iron on his roof.

Little attention was paid to the radical effects the training programs might have had if TUFEC had realized that a general theory of education was not the solution to the villagers' needs. Only in one document was the warning sounded:

> As the team members [i.e. FEOS] become acquainted with the villagers, they begin to realize that work of various kinds has been going on in the villages long before their arrival, and they must learn to recognize and respect the considerable knowledge accumulated by the villagers themselves over the years. This sometimes necessitates a radical adjustment in the attitudes of the students before they are ready to work with people.[43]

It could be added that perhaps there was a need not only for the student to adjust to these rather basic revelations but for greater account to be taken of these factors by the sponsors of the organization. The concepts of felt needs and using indigenous resources could only have relevance when divorced from theory and related

42. Supreme Command Headquarters, *Report and Analysis of Communications Team II Assigned to Visit Remote Villages in Changwad Loeie, March 5 to April 3, 1962* (Bangkok, Ministry of Defense, 1962), p. 13.
43. Faris, p. 10.

to actual situations. In the event that such particular knowledge was not available, a recourse would have been to tap student experience. As will be observed, however, this type of adjustment was not part of the modus operandi.

Vocational Training

During the early stages of the Pilot Project and later in TUFEC considerable attention was given to the part that vocational or technical training could play in promoting general development. Both TUFEC and the Pilot Project embarked upon programs of vocational education.

During the early phases of the Pilot Project, an attempt was made to teach metalworking and automotive trades. Some metalworking machines were donated by Shell Oil (Thailand) and by USOM, and attempts were made to promote skills accordingly. Some machines were even distributed to schools outside of the town of Cha Cheong Sao proper. The Thai evaluation committee reported in 1958: "Metal working courses for boys are of no use, since work of this nature is practically non-existent in the localities concerned. Some schools have obtained a great number of metal work tools which have remained unused."[44]

But the reasons for the Thai lack of interest lay even deeper than the report indicates. For centuries most skilled trades in urban areas of Thailand have been in the hands of the Chinese minority. The Chinese have been regarded not only as being highly competent in trade skills but also as being prepared to work harder for less money than the Thai. In the Chinese trades system, skills and tools were family possessions, and both were handed down within the family group. There is much superficial evidence that this closely knit system is breaking down in Thailand, but visible evidence exists in every Thai town of the still extant strength and persistence of the long-established Chinese monopolies. To break into a trade like metalworking has in the past been difficult because it simply did not make sense to a Thai even to attempt entrance into an area where all the advantages lay with his competitors.

44. *Report of an Evaluation Committee, Cha Cheong Sao Project,* p. 34.

This reluctance to compete was powerfully reinforced by at least two additional factors. The question of status has always loomed large. The ability of the Chinese as tradesmen has usually evoked little envy. The common attitude is that of pity or even contempt for folk who had to work so hard for so little at what to the Thai seemed to be dirty and uninteresting jobs. Conversely, achievement of conspicuous success by the Chinese has often evoked envy and even fear. This general situation has pervaded the Thai scene at least since the end of the nineteenth century.[45]

Greatly influencing the Thai idea of status was another traditional view: if a Thai were not a rice farmer, the pattern of upward mobility was toward becoming a government official. This still represents the path to power and status.

Under these circumstances it was difficult to persuade a Thai peasant's son to compete in, say, the metal craft trades. Indeed it could be equally difficult to persuade a child of Chinese parentage to do likewise if his family were involved in some other calling. In other words, the general environment was still traditionally oriented in economic and social terms. The mobility that has come to be associated with modernization simply had not penetrated into the small towns where the United Nations expected to do its work.

On the other hand, it cannot be accepted—as has been inferred, as much by Thai as by foreign educators—that Thai young people lack some intrinsic quality that prevents them from becoming good technicians. Under different circumstances, elementary trade training has been very successful under foreign auspices. The military services, as one example, are by far the largest technical complex in the kingdom, and the Thai peasant has learned to service a wide variety of machines—jeeps, jet aircraft, medical equipment,

45. The overall issue of Thai-Chinese relationships in Thailand has been covered in numerous studies, the three most notable being: George William Skinner, *Chinese Society in Thailand: An Analytical History* (Ithaca, N.Y., Cornell University Press, 1957); George William Skinner, *Leadership and Power in the Chinese Community in Thailand* (Ithaca, N.Y., Cornell University Press, 1958); and Richard J. Coughlin, *Double Identity* (Oxford, Oxford University Press, 1960). For a short and comprehensive summary of relevant views held in the works above, see Richard J. Coughlin, "The Status of the Chinese Minority in Thailand," *Pacific Affairs, 25* (1952), 378–89.

radar. Those who trained overseas have stood up extremely well in comparison with their foreign colleagues, while at home foreign military instructors have had no more trouble teaching technical skills to their charges than would be normal anywhere.[46]

The Pilot Project failed in this field not because the machines supplied by USOM and Shell were too complicated, or because Thai youth was ineducable in these fields, but because the project did not assess the specifics of the local economic and cultural situation. UNESCO believed that there was a "universal hunger for education," whereas something to the contrary may have been true. At best, there may have been a very specific hunger for certain types of education where rewards were clear and where one was not called upon to transgress too many cultural boundaries.[47] The Pilot Project did not make prior evaluations of these matters.

There was also an attempt in vocational training, both at the Pilot Project and TUFEC, to induce Thai to make use of indigenous resources to satisfy what were assessed to be felt needs in the home. Early projects aimed at using bamboo to create utensils and furniture. Pilot Project authorities joined forces with the Ministry of Education to accomplish this. Indeed the Ministry complained:

> The creative work of boys and girls [i.e. at the Pilot Project] is not effective as the products are not in accordance with the needs of students or the community. There are many beautiful creative works with simple local resources, which reflect the skill of the clever makers, but they are of no practical value, only good as decorative pieces to be left in the classroom. This should be remedied.[48]

46. These views would also be strongly borne out by the Thai record in the SEATO Skilled Labor Project which now provides approximately 46 per cent of all technical training in Thailand and where Thai performance has been "normal," that is relative to the Western standard existing in SEATO schools.

47. An interesting and somewhat parallel view in Latin America, highlighting cultural resistance to education that brings about change, is given in: William S. Stokes, "The Drag of the Pensadores," *Foreign Aid Re-examined: A Critical Appraisal*, ed. James N. Wiggins and Helmut Schoek (Washington, D.C., Public Affairs Press, 1958), pp. 56–89.

48. *Report of Evaluation Committee Cha Cheong Sao Project*, p. 11.

Many Thai, as well as Thai-oriented foreigners, might lament that the Ministry should denigrate the Thai aptitude for the artistic and the beautiful and laud the utilitarian, but one project with very practical overtones had already been tried at Cha Cheong Sao and was also tried at TUFEC. This was the promotion of furniture-making from local bamboo, the objective being to take the peasant off the floor—where he habitually slept, ate, and relaxed—by showing him how to make his own furniture. It was also hoped at TUFEC that FEOs and other officials would attempt to enhance their personal comfort while living in rural areas by imitating some of the clever designs which the foreign experts devised and that this would be a further incentive to peasant emulation.

The idea of using bamboo functionally in Thailand was not new. For centuries the Thai have used bamboo for such utilitarian purposes as scaffolding, carrying poles, house construction, floatage on water, temporary containers for food, baskets, bells and other noise makers, fish traps, cages for animals and birds, childrens' toys, ornaments and musical instruments, and a host of other uses. The foliage of the bamboo is, of course, used as fodder for animals, and the shoots as food for man.

The attempt to extend the use of bamboo into making furniture was, however, unsuccessful. This was not the fault of the designs, some of which were ingenious, but because of nonutilitarian reasons. To be a peasant was to live on the floor, a custom which incidentally has its own merits and its own comforts. It was not conceivable for a peasant to have tables, chairs, and bedsteads and still remain a peasant. When a peasant became urbanized, he adopted among other things such appurtenances as furniture—possibly even bamboo furniture, bought from a store. But to a peasant in a village, furniture seemed not only unnecessary but alien. A pressure lamp, a transistor radio, or a permanent wave all had accepted and easily assessable values. Furniture did not. Furthermore, a discernible trait in Thai villages is not that of "keeping up with the Joneses" but rather of preventing the Joneses from getting above the accepted levels. It is not uncommon, at least initially, for the village to ostracize a peasant adding spectacularly to his worldly goods and even relieve him of a few possessions. Under these circumstances it was unlikely that bamboo furniture-making would be successful among the peasantry.

Furniture-making was only one of many features of handicraft or vocational activities sponsored by the Pilot Project and TUFEC. Nevertheless, if the typical list of activities in Appendix IV is noted, it will be seen that none of these projects was any more successful than furniture making. Again the point to be made is that a felt need must be carefully assessed. Sometimes it seems that the experts working for UNESCO cast a technician's eye over the resources that were obviously available at village level, used their skill and ingenuity to decide what could be made from those resources, and then assumed that these products could be fitted into the life of the people concerned, who of course were not consulted. That commendable expertise was involved was of no significance in the acceptance of ideas. Despite the Thai peasant's unfailing courtesy and apparently malleable character, he can be a stubborn opponent in resisting change which is of no interest to him. On the other hand, he is far from averse to change under circumstances where he perceives his real interests to be at stake.

Health Programs

In all of their activities the United Nations projects relied heavily on the impact value of expertise, and vocational training was not the only area where attempts were made to exploit this value. In health, for example, expertise was an obviously vital factor in producing sought-after ends. In 1949, predating the projects under study, WHO and UNICEF gave the Thai government assistance with projects in malaria control. In 1951 WHO and UNICEF withdrew their field support, and at that time it was estimated that some 77,000 people were enjoying some degree of immunity from the anopheles mosquito. By 1963, through continued activity of the Thai government with strong moral support and incidental grants from WHO and UNICEF, it is estimated that some 15 million people benefited from the spraying program. Malaria has declined as a cause of death from a mortality rate of 210 per 100,000 in 1949 to 33 per 100,000 in 1960. It is estimated that within the next six to eight years malaria will be wiped out as a significant cause of death in Thailand.[49] Nevertheless the

49. Ministry of Public Health, *Health Services of Thailand* (Bangkok, 1961), p. 12.

victory has not been quite so spectacular or produced quite the results that one UNESCO commentator envisaged when he said, "But in Thailand the clearing of the Northern Provinces from malaria means that the malaria-free peasant could produce a second crop and more than double the exports of rice."[50]

One feels that such an extraordinary increase in the culture of rice would involve a great deal more than a sudden increase in peasant health, but apart from such euphoric exaggerations a most significant advance was made, with United Nations assistance, against what was formerly the major single cause of death in the kingdom. Equally spectacular results have been attained in a campaign against yaws. Again the modus operandi has been WHO and UNICEF assistance to a Thai government campaign. As a widespread endemic disease, yaws has largely disappeared from all but the very remote areas of Thailand. The Director of the WHO zone office in Bangkok described the yaws campaign as "a fantastic job by the Thai government," noting, however, that the more difficult task now confronts all concerned of perfecting an organizational framework that will allow follow-up and prophylactic campaigns to be implemented and maintained over large areas.[51]

With the decline of deaths due to malaria, however, gastroenteritis and colitis became the primary causes of death, especially among the infant population.[52] The Pilot Project and TUFEC, particularly the latter, were deeply concerned with these so called "filth diseases." But the campaign was not an extension of the sort of action that so successfully combated malaria and yaws, even though the remedial plans all came under the same broad heading of health and all involved medical expertise.

In essence the antimalaria campaign involved an attack upon mosquitoes, and the yaws campaign produced spectacular and observable results with just one injection of penicillin. There was, however, no such direct linking of medical expertise and cure for the "filth diseases." Attack on these involved a change in the habits of all the peasants and a sizable proportion of the townspeople as

50. UNESCO, *Men Against Ignorance* (Paris, UNESCO Press, 1953), p. 37.

51. Interview, Local Office, WHO in Asia and the Far East, Bangkok, August 8, 1963.

52. *Health Services of Thailand*, p. 33.

well. Eating habits; preparing, storing, and disposing of food; defecation habits; the provision and use of drinking water, both on a community basis and in the home—these were some of the more obvious factors involved. The Thai peasant has almost an affection for injections and, had there been an injection curing and immunizing against dysentery, he would have accepted it gladly. But a mechanical type of solution to the problem did not exist. Instead, the onset of dysentery was associated with the peasant's personal, family, and community habits. In some instances I found that this association was known to peasants. Government posters, programs on the radio, and teaching in schools had given him some inkling of the cycle of intestinal disorders. The perhaps not so curious reaction of these more sophisticated people often was, "Well, why can't we have an injection? Malaria and other things are much more serious and these are fixed with an injection. Why not this?" The very efficacy of one campaign seemed to militate against the methods of another.

Most peasants are oblivious to the real causes of intestinal disorders. Being Thai they are fastidious about most aspects of personal hygiene and are reluctant to believe that disorders come from particular personal habits. Learning that only 6 per cent of the peasants in the laboratory villages used a latrine, TUFEC expended considerable effort in devising latrine systems. The only one that had any appeal was the water-sealed variety. As far as the peasant was concerned, all others smelled foul and were not as good as the open field.

Health problems are therefore not only concerned with change in habits but also bound up with aspects of modernization. Education, changes in material living standards, and permanent rather than sporadic contact with health services are some of the essential ingredients of curtailing the filth diseases. In Thailand changes of this nature could come only slowly. How long, for example, does it take to produce change through education—a generation or longer? This was one of the possibilities that any program in Thailand had to face. Does a gift of a latrine slab to a peasant family start the campaign against dysentery, or must a change of attitude be induced in the peasant's mind? The latter is more difficult than combating mosquitoes or a virus and is unlikely to produce the same spectacular, short-term results. The number of unused latrine slabs lying about villages in the Ubol area lends credence to this view.

Education

Operations in the area of education can be illustrated by the seemingly simple project of organizing a mobile library service. As has been noted, most Thai children had no opportunity to continue their schooling beyond a period of four years, and many did not get this far. The average postwar child was able to read, write, and undertake some elementary arithmetic. Perhaps he was vaguely aware that the world is round and, possibly, that Thailand is one of many nation-states. It was thought in TUFEC that an essential follow-up toward maintaining the rural Thai's slender hold on reading skills, and enhancing his sparse general knowledge of the world outside his village, would be to promote a library service by means of a mobile system.[53]

Initially, some 31 book boxes, each holding approximately 60 books, were circulated among villages in the laboratory area. With the arrival of another foreign librarian, the system was changed to that of distributing books by means of a pony cart. This did not succeed, and book boxes were reinstated. At present a rural library service does not exist under TUFEC auspices, but TURTEP (Thailand UNESCO Rural Teachers' Education Project), located just across the road, has started one, this time incorporating a system of reading rooms in villages.

Any scheme which endeavors to promote the UNESCO concepts of fundamental education inevitably inclines toward the active advancement of literacy skills. But even the reading process imposes certain practical demands. A survey of eleven villages—completed, unfortunately, as UNESCO support was being withdrawn from TUFEC—showed that 70 per cent of the houses had no illumination other than tiny lamps consisting of a bowl of

53. Mary Anglemeyer, *Report on the Pony Cart Travelling Library Service* (Ubol, November 9, 1957) (from the files, UNESCO Regional Office, Bangkok), pp. 1, 6.

vegetable oil and a fiber wick.[54] For all practical purposes reading after the day's work is impossible under these circumstances, and the conditions shown in the survey villages are undoubtedly similar to those existing elsewhere in the kingdom outside of the larger towns. The survey also indicated that probably fewer than 13 per cent of the people questioned were even exposed to reading as a pastime. TUFEC had pursued its library project with zeal, but lights and books go together. Again some minimum level of material development had to go hand in hand with education, or even precede it.

At the Cha Cheong Sao Pilot Project the same difficulty was manifested in other ways. All the foreign educational experts at the Pilot Project severely criticized the traditional Thai method of teaching by rote. The sound of Thai children reading—sometimes from a blackboard, more often merely imitating the teacher—is common enough throughout the nation. The system is well rooted, although most of the Thai educators at the higher levels, having learned modern educational methods long before the United Nations appeared on the scene, deplore the system. But the reasons for it are obvious—a dearth of textbooks, paper, and pencils. By 1960 UNESCO also came to recognize this factor, and by late 1962 a UNESCO worker was attached to the Ministry of Education to assist in producing children's textbooks. Again, it is only when this material condition is met and books begin to flow into Thai classrooms that changes can be effected in the system of learning by rote.

Recreation

Perhaps the most unusual sally into village activity, however, was in regard to recreation. The TUFEC activity of social welfare had the objective of "promoting a more enjoyable social life." Whatever else may or may not be a feature of Thai village life, nothing could be more apparent than its sociability. Most villages enjoy a variety of sporting events and various forms of gambling are still prevalent, even though banned in most instances by the gov-

54. C. J. L. Bertholet and Bencha Diswatt, *Housing and Food Patterns in Eleven Villages in Northeast Thailand* (Ubol, Research Section TUFEC, September 1959), p. 31.

ernment. Morning and evening worship in the temple, observance of the Buddhist sabbath, New Year festivals, the beginning of Buddhist Lent and the initiation of men into the monkhood, the end of Lent and presentations to the priests, birthday celebrations, funerals, marriages and confirmations, consecration of land, houses, and images, the light festival in November, even the beauty contest—all are highly social occasions and activities in which every village participates. There are also normal village social activities like the *ramwong*, a communal dance used to celebrate any extraordinary occurrence such as a visit by a stranger, and the *moh ram*, the traditional rhyming duets so popular in the Northeast Region.

Every ceremony is meant to be free and unrestrained. A traditional value is that life must be *sanuk*. This is a word with great breadth of meaning but can perhaps best be translated as enjoyment of every passing moment. The large number of ceremonies and the exuberant approach to participation give the Thai peasant more recreation and a greater degree of social activity than ordinary folk in the larger towns. It is surprising to read, therefore, that "recreation for both young and old is encouraged in the villages . . . [and] opportunities for a *larger outlet* in this field are being introduced by team members."[55] There are no data as to what, in fact, was being introduced, but it is doubtful if any material change in current patterns was brought about. The usual reason for unsociability in a Thai village is sickness or the extreme poverty of the village as a whole. Such villages were not, however, areas of concentration for the social welfare program. Even the most generous evaluation of the motives and methods of the social welfare program raises misgivings as to how well the devisers of the general enterprise knew the villages, which after all were a primary target for the entire operation.

Agriculture and Economics

In the end, TUFEC became primarily engaged in operations that had an economic motive. Although the term fundamental education (or community development) could be couched in a

---

55. Faris, p. 13 (italics added).

variety of forms and could have a variety of motives ascribed to it, a common motive, and perhaps its real goal, was to improve the peasant's economic lot. The most immediate and obvious target was agriculture. The objective of TUFEC's agricultural program was to stimulate increased production of crops. The organization, realizing the limitations on its resources, wisely avoided intruding into the complex and massive issue of rice production. It concentrated upon cash crops which could be grown by a family or a village.

Results were most disappointing. Despite some intensive efforts and sound agricultural advice, the peasants in the northeast were generally disinterested in what the TUFEC field workers proposed. In a "Grow More Food Campaign," for example, started in the immediate environs of TUFEC, peasant response was almost nil.[56] Why was this? At first glance it would seem natural for peasants to accept what was an extension of their indigenous work patterns. TUFEC found the answer itself:

> When increased production is discussed with villagers, a question frequently raised is: "where can we sell our products and how much can we get for them?" . . . farmers claimed that when they had increased their production of peanuts, loc, cassava and the like, in the past, markets were soon glutted.[57]

Here was the key issue. It was hardly a question of agricultural techniques but rather one of markets. To cite one example, Thai farmers showed in 1960 when there was a demand for jute, a new product, that they could without assistance from anyone respond rapidly to this opportunity.[58] Without assurance of markets, however, appeals and schemes to increase production were just irritants that made the proponents of such schemes seem foolish in the peasants' eyes. Some operators in TUFEC saw the fundamental aspects of the problem: "More comprehensive economic planning by the government is imperative. Programs designed to bring the

---

56. TUFEC, *Grow More Food Campaign: An Interim Report* (Ubol, TUFEC, October 1957), and attached appendix, "Report to Governor of Ubol on Food Shortages in Ubol Area," September 1957 (from the files, TUFEC, Ubol).

57. Faris, p. 20.

58. Gordon R. Sitton et al., p. 27, Fig. 9.

greatest benefit to the people must include all possible aspects of economic and social development."[59]

Whether the issue was one that could or should be attempted by the Thai government can remain outside this study. The point is that the entire question of agricultural development was outside the control of either TUFEC or the peasant. The factor of note is that TUFEC, in perhaps its key activity, became involved in an end which was unattainable and which could only damage its reputation among those whom it sought to help.

Summary

The foregoing describes some of the problems of the operational milieu, mainly as the foreign field workers in the United Nations agencies saw them and wrote about them. The theme of relating laudable intentions to attainable ends is an old issue that has bothered many organizations. It is, however, one of the more striking characteristics of the United Nations projects in Thailand as portrayed in the field of education and community development. Nor was UNESCO as sponsoring agency unaware of its generally unreal attitudes. As one field report from Ubol noted, "We are sometimes in danger of losing sight of the villagers' needs in a maze of theories and concepts."[60] The danger was real.

59. Faris, p. 20.
60. Letter from the Deputy Head, TUFEC, on the Influx of Theories and Theoreticians at TUFEC, to Chief of Mission, UNESCO Regional Office, Bangkok, June 20, 1958 (from the files, UNESCO Regional Office, Bangkok).

4

ROLES, PERSONNEL, AND
COMMUNICATION

The description of the dynamic aspects of the United Nations effort in Thailand serves as a background to a more particularistic examination of the overall United Nations approach in this venture, especially the key issue of personnel in the operational milieu.

DEFINITION OF ROLES

Records of the briefings given in Paris to nearly all United Nations experts proceeding to Thailand are not available. From the written reports of the experts after they reached the field, one can surmise that their roles were not clearly delineated. It seems, for example, that the health expert was briefed "to work in public health at the village level" or the librarian was told little more than that the task was "to organize rural library services."

If such loose phrasing undoubtedly permitted individual freedom, it also created confusion. The lack of role definition sometimes gave rise to schemes or projects dear to the heart of an expert but not otherwise important. Many stories are recounted by Thai who held executive positions at that time, the best known being that of the foreign teacher who decided that a drive against house flies was a legitimate aim.[1] Other experts expressed themselves in this vein: "In my observation during my short period of stay, I have come to the conclusion that it is the lack of definition of the objective that is the source of the apparent lack of co-ordinated efforts of the local staff as well as the UNESCO staff."[2]

1. Interview at TUFEC, Ubol, July 5, 1963.
2. Letter from Mr. R. Freznoza, Teacher Training Specialist, to Chief of Missions, UNESCO Regional Office, Bangkok, January 16, 1960 (from the files, UNESCO Regional Office, Bangkok).

This view was typical. The Cha Cheong Sao Evaluation Committee noted that "the overlapping of work carried out by the incoming and outgoing experts is quite a problem, because the Organization does not give them guidance. Therefore it causes confusion to the principals and prevents them from giving their best cooperation."[3] Amplification of the theme came from yet another source with an almost identical comment.[4]

Not only did lack of defined roles cause confusion and weakening of effort but it also caused personal friction. An expert sometimes tended to assume that he held greater responsibilities than he did and, as a result, either ignored or resisted contrary opinions, even when these came from administrative superiors. After all, if an expert saw his role as being to "(a) train our students to be competent to teach various school subjects in harmony with principles of modern education, and (b) improve the conditions of rural peoples through schools,"[5] it was likely that he would resist being transferred into a more mundane role like teaching a language or physical education. The urge toward grandiose activity was particularly strong, and many United Nations personnel saw their activity mainly in these terms. Apparently the lack of specific knowledge at Headquarters level of actual circumstances in the field allowed these general notions to persist until the expert came face to face with realities.

The friction between Thai and United Nations field operators created by undefined roles was a subtle issue, with some of its roots in Thai bureaucratic mores. It is common for Thai to be keenly aware of position and status in their own hierarchy. They were therefore vulnerable to what seemed like brashness on the part of foreigners but was, in fact, often a lack of appreciation of what to do and how. The foreigner was feeling his way, conscious that he was expected to display his expertise and be an activator. Neither were the Thai certain of what they were supposed to do, as their everyday roles were required to change in relation to their new foreign partners.

3. *Report of Evaluation Committee Cha Cheong Sao Project,* p. 13.

4. Interview at TURTEP, Ubol, August 1, 1963.

5. Letter from Mr. F. Urtim, Educator, to Chief of Mission, UNESCO Regional Office, Bangkok, December 23, 1957 (from the files, UNESCO Regional Office, Bangkok).

The Thai bureaucracy was also unable to define roles. Thai officials were mainly concerned with personal relationships within the bureaucracy, especially within the relatively restricted circles of provincial officialdom where the operations were being conducted. This attitude made Thai officials acutely conscious of being overshadowed by some newly arrived foreigner, sometimes younger than they and often a voluble exponent of some strange new idea. More interested in people than in jobs, every Thai coming in contact with a foreigner would first assess the way in which the worker conducted himself in relation to others, rather than how he carried out his duties. It was highly important, therefore, that both the foreign expert and all Thai who were concerned should at least know what the expert was supposed to do in a specific sense and where responsibilities lay. Above all, it was vital to know what official status was held by all functionaries. Without this degree of definition, contact was often dependent on the personal compatibility of persons of widely differing background and motivation.

It is not surprising that in the early stages projects were beset with the problems associated with poorly defined roles. The entire experience was unique, and it was probably necessary to play it by ear. But the most serious criticism must be leveled at the UNESCO Headquarters in Paris, which did little to reshape its concepts or translate information into better briefings for those proceeding to the field, even though data relating to role definition were available from field operators and Regional Headquarters. The project in Thailand was launched and the Paris Headquarters moved on to something else. Yet the experience being gained in the field was invaluable to almost everything that the organization would or might do in the future.

> Our personal affairs and equipment needs are taken care of admirably: in official matters we sometimes wonder whether anybody actually reads the quite voluminous correspondence and reporting materials we despatch to Paris. I must say frankly that the support we get from Headquarters, in the shape of answers to queries, action on requests and the supply of information is poor.

And this report went on to say that

> as experts passing through Paris on home leave stay only two
> days there, opportunities to see people at Headquarters and
> to raise matters affecting work in the field are restricted. We
> always leave Paris with a feeling that there is a very real
> interest in our work . . . but on the job we sometimes feel
> we deserve better support and advice.[6]

A feeling of neglect by a superior headquarters is not an uncommon complaint of operators in the field. A possible way out
is for field commanders to take matters into their own hands. The
degree of autonomy possessed by the regional offices in such matters was considerable, and at first glance it was surprising that it
was not exercised to a greater degree in delineating more specific
roles for their experts in the field. There were, however, other
factors besides poor role definition inhibiting the establishment of
clear and specific courses of action.

Language

Except for two American scholars who were associated with
TUFEC in its latter stages and who did have language skills, none
of the personnel employed by the United Nations spoke or read
the Thai language. Of 64 reports by field experts, more than 60
per cent raised the question of language deficiency and the immense barrier that this constituted in their daily tasks.

The medium of expression throughout all projects was English.
Fortunately English was the most widely known foreign language
in the kingdom. It could normally be expected that a high school
graduate would have a minimum of two and a maximum of six
years of English instruction. Nevertheless, the level of English
of such Thai graduates was completely inadequate for even routine
communications. There were not enough proficient interpreters,
even among the teaching staff at the Cha Cheong Sao Pilot Project.
For anything really important, often someone at the headmaster
level had to be persuaded to leave his duties and act as interpreter.

6. TUFEC, *Annual Report for* TUFEC *for the Year 1956* (in the files, UNESCO
Headquarters, Paris).

Numerous instances of friction arose from this system. The more senior Thai, those who had the best language skills, often resented being told to do this, or hold that, in front of a class of Thai students by a much younger foreign instructor. Sometimes the interpreter decided to give his own analysis of the foreign expert's views, although the reinterpretation may have been quite innocent. A distinguished Thai educator, commenting on what she called the "extraordinarily serious problem of language" at the Pilot Project, warned that one should not trust any Thai's English: "The words being used are often grossly misunderstood by the users [i.e. the Thai]. I learnt, as one example, that long after the Pilot Project was in being, the term 'modern education' connoted current education to most Thai and not a different concept of education."[7]

To improve the accuracy of lectures, some foreign instructors typed them in English, had them translated into written Thai, and then read to a class. Later, when TUFEC had started an English course for its students, the students were officially used as interpreters.[8] These measures, again inadequate, were mostly restricted to periods in the classroom.

The language problem extended far beyond these confines, into personal and village social contacts, administration, and research. In general, technical experts had fewer difficulties than the nontechnical, but the problem was never satisfactorily solved. In answer to the question "How can effective communication be made through interpreters?" it was stated:

> The only really practical solution is for instruction to be given in the mother language. This obviously involves much study and therefore a long term view of staffing. But I submit that where UNESCO cooperation with a national center is envisaged for a period as long as five years we should attempt to plan staffing on a three to five year basis: and even see that international staff are free during the first year to devote most of their time to language study.[9]

7. Interview at the Ministry of Education, Bangkok, June 24, 1963.

8. Minutes of the Third Meeting of TUFEC Operating Committee, Ubol, November 11, 1953 (from the files, TUFEC, Ubol), p. 6.

9. *Annual Report of the Deputy Director*, TUFEC, to UNESCO Headquarters, Paris, June 23, 1955 (from the files, UNESCO Headquarters, Paris), p. 8.

The true situation was more accurately revealed when at a later stage the same commentator observed in another annual report:

> There remains a weakness in the Thai counterpart staff although this tends to decrease with the passage of time as these staff members gather experience, learn from continuing contact with the foreign staff and improve their English, thereby improving communication with non-Thai staff. Most are making a creditable attempt to benefit from the facilities available for properly organized English studies.[10]

The onus was therefore on the Thai to acquire language skills. It had to be this way. Contact between a Thai and individual foreign experts was of short duration. A foreigner could thus always rationalize his failure to learn Thai on the ground that his brief tenure in the country did not make it worth while to embark on the long and tedious task of learning an exotic language.

Tenure

Contracts for service as experts with TUFEC or the Pilot Project were for one year's duration. Many experts stayed longer, but the average period of tenure for all experts was 1.65 years, with the longest single period for one individual being five years and the shortest some three months.

This short tenure affected almost every aspect of the experts' effectiveness in Thailand. The one-year contract system was an administrative arrangement within UNESCO; and the concept that a particular task might have an organic or "natural" life, and that tenure of participating experts should be geared to the circumstances of the task, seems not to have been considered. Quite often contrary considerations weighed with United Nations administrators. As one stated it: "If after two or three years an expert still wants to stay on, I have to look very carefully to see whether or not he has worked himself into an easy and comfortable living."[11]

Holding a major responsibility, as this official did, such caution was necessary, although he was quick to point out that he rarely

10. *Annual Report of the Deputy Director*, TUFEC, to UNESCO Headquarters, Paris, December 31, 1956 (from the files, UNESCO Headquarters, Paris), p. 1.
11. Interview at UNTAB, Bangkok, July 30, 1963.

found any substance for his fears. The same official was equally adamant, however, that a one-year contract was useless and that even two years seemed insufficient time for an expert to "get the feel of both job and country." As the Thai at Cha Cheong Sao put it: "Ah, the United Nations! Their trouble here was that they changed the jockey too often." And every time the "jockey" was changed, not only did rapport have to be reestablished but there was a strong tendency for the new incumbent to move off in a different direction.

MULTINATIONAL GROUPS

The field experts for the two projects came from seventeen different countries. Where solutions to problems are offered by many different nationalities, the recipient may take them "in such a way as to generate . . . a better solution."[12] In the minds of many United Nations officials this was exactly what they saw happening, especially at the Pilot Project. One official from the Paris UNESCO Headquarters commented:

> It was a pleasure to see evidence of contribution from various countries in the teaching methods employed by the teachers. I refer to the fact that one could see American influence in the unit and project method of teaching to which reference was constantly made. The British influence was also felt in some classes where the teachers were having group work and, at the same time, seeing to it that the pupils were working according to ability and interest. In the note books kept by the pupils and corrected religiously by the teachers, one could see the French influence even though there was no French expert sent there.[13]

The belief that a sharing of everyone's experience makes for a better end product has not been questioned, even though it may be

12. G. E. R. Burroughs, *Technique of Evaluation, Paper No. 12—Evaluation of Fundamental Education Projects* (Paris, UNESCO/SS/Eval/12, March 20, 1956), p. iii.

13. *Report on a Visit to Cha Cheong Sao Educational Pilot Project,* Head of Educational Section, UNESCO, Paris, February, 1957 (from the files, Ministry of Education, Bangkok).

that in a large majority of human ventures a single concentrated national approach has produced sounder and more spectacular results. Where the recipient has a sophisticated knowledge of a subject and communications are unrestricted, perhaps the variegated approach of a multinational group can add new dimensions and experience with profit to all. But when the subject matter is unfamiliar, the exact opposite can be the case. There are serious doubts under these circumstances whether a multinational approach helps recipients or confuses them. In Thailand two distinct aspects of the problem could be observed.

First, the issue of language, as we have noted, loomed large. Of the seventeen different nations represented, English was the native language of five; for the remainder, although English was a foreign language, it was the only one in which they could carry on communication with the Thai. Thus both Thai and the non-English speaking experts had to communicate in a foreign language. Every Thai interviewed for this study, as well as the Ministry of Education Evaluation Committee for Cha Cheong Sao, emphatically agreed that under these circumstances the language difficulty was greatly accentuated. The report cites an instance of one expert who was never understood during her whole tenure and, again because of difficulty with language, could not submit a written report.[14]

Despite the language difficulties, there was a good deal of "sensing" of what experts meant. The English language instructor at TUFEC, for example, noted that, "considering that TUFEC students are expected to listen to language spoken in all accents and on many subjects, I think many of them do surprisingly well."[15] Over all, however, language variance was one of the major inhibiting factors in the multinational group.

The second reason why the multinational approach was not successful was that there were differences in terminology and methods. When a fundamental term such as "model school" was used, it meant different things to different people. To a New Zealander a "model school" meant an experimental school, to a

14. *Report of Evaluation Committee Cha Cheong Sao Project*, p. 18.
15. John C. Allen, *Annual Report on the Teaching of English as an Aid to Training at* TUFEC, Ubol, December 31, 1956 (from the files, UNESCO Headquarters, Paris), p. 4.

Dane it meant a highly superior school. When differing conceptual backgrounds allowed for variety in interpretation, arguments arose. Differing interpretations confused the Thai recipients. The confusion increased in proportion to the language problem, and was further exacerbated by the rapid change of personnel. The Finnish approach to public health measures *and* the Finnish approach to the English language gave way to an Irish combination, or an American administrator was replaced by a Frenchman.

I do not suggest that differing national groups cannot work effectively together. Given clear direction and delineation of purpose, a little time, and sound day-to-day administration and control, multinational groups possibly may develop a viable approach.[16] If there had been more time, the difficulties might have been overcome.

Thai concern with the "change of jockey" thus took on added meaning when the variations inherent in the multinational group were added. At TUFEC, where there was a greater degree of institutional autonomy, the multinational problem was noticeably less apparent than at the Pilot Project, where, because the institutional framework was essentially that of the Thai Ministry of Education, the foreign experts had to integrate and operate in a Thai milieu. The problem was a very real one and the Thai felt the multinational group to be a major handicap. But according to one Thai, who incidentally was in a better position than most to sum up, professional failure did not destroy amicable relations:

> The advent of different national experts, with their different views and methods and their constant changing, was in a functional sense, a continuing burden we had to bear. Nevertheless we liked having these different people amongst us. While their project [i.e. the Pilot Project] accomplished little or nothing of what it set out to accomplish, I believe we parted from our foreign guests with good feelings all round.[17]

ORIENTATION TO MILIEU

Specialists were recruited for professional qualifications and without regard to their knowledge and attitudes toward foreign

16. See below, p. 173–74.
17. Interview at Ministry of Education, Bangkok, June 24, 1963.

cultural, social, and physical environments. The short briefing at UNESCO Headquarters in Paris was supposed to provide the acculturation. On the face of it, there may seem to be no overriding reasons why a particular professional goal can not be effectively attained regardless of environment. But many objections can be raised to this view.

The general problems encountered by the families of experts in adapting to an alien environment have been noted in another study,[18] and in Thailand many of the factors noted there were repeated. Major concerns were housing and children's schooling. The absence of non-Thai schools outside of Bangkok made it more desirable to limit recruitment to elderly persons or couples with very small children. Housing conditions were not so bad in either Ubol or Cha Cheong Sao, but they were markedly better in Bangkok. Compared to her sister in Bangkok, housing for the wife in the field was substantially less attractive. This tended to engender a feeling among the United Nations experts that there was an "in" and an "out" group.[19] Yet it was hardly practicable to be working closely with Thai colleagues in small provincial towns and also to be removed from them in living standards by emulating the munificence of foreigners in Bangkok.

The experts' professionalism also had to adapt to local conditions and knowledge. In experimenting with bamboo, for example, the handicrafts experts reported that when bamboo was left in water (in research concerned with devising a bamboo water pump), it "caused the water to smell objectionably." This information was relayed to the Thai government in a report.[20] It is hard to say how long this fact has been known to Asians at large but probably for at least a millennia or two. This is one reason for the development of lacquered bamboo.

Even the seemingly mechanistic problem of inoculating water buffalo against rinderpest could not be divorced from local dynamics. The Thai farmer had been accustomed to seeing suspect ani-

18. Walter R. Sharp, *Field Administration in the United Nations System* (New York, Frederick A. Praeger, 1961), pp. 141–45.

19. *Report of an Evaluation Committee, Cha Cheong Sao Project*, p. 34.

20. ILO, *Report to the Government of Thailand on Handicraft Activity at the Fundamental Education Centre in Ubol: Part I* (Geneva, ILO/TAP/RII, 1959), p. 14.

mals slaughtered during rinderpest epidemics. When Thai and
FAO officials appeared at the scene of one epidemic, even though
they were bearing nothing more lethal than a hypodermic needle,
the peasants hid animals which appeared to be sick, even borrowing healthy animals to replace them during the inspection. To the
peasant the issue was critical. Disregarding the sentiment he had
for his buffalo, the loss of its services just prior to the onset of the
rains (the season also for rinderpest) was a calamity. For just a few
weeks, when the earth has become sodden but before the water
rises too high, the soil has to be plowed and worked into a muddy
tilth. It was the buffaloes' efforts during that critical and inflexible
time period that made life possible for the peasant and his family
for the following year. Any risk was justified to avoid having his
buffalo's throat cut. The problem facing FAO with its newly developed rinderpest vaccine was therefore only indirectly that of
rinderpest. The real problem was how to communicate with the
peasant, to learn the grounds for his fears, and to reassure him
accordingly. Later, when cash grants were given for buffalo to be
slaughtered and the full impact of the new vaccine was explained,
the peasant eagerly sought vaccination for his animals. But the
problem of assessing the local situation was the key, and the ability
to do so could come only through an intimate orientation to the
local scene.[21]

All foreign experts were involved in what might be called local
diplomacy, and this was especially true of administrators. A knowledge of the bureaucratic mores of the Thai was at least as essential
to those in the regional office in Bangkok as it is to persons working with government in Whitehall, Canberra, or Washington.
None of the United Nations personnel had had previous experience in Thailand, and only 20 per cent of those involved had lived
outside their own countries. At UNESCO Headquarters in Paris
they were given two or three days of briefing, mainly about their
professional tasks, and sent on their way, with a small pamphlet
giving some hints about clothing, diseases, climate, and so on.
Orientation, a vital factor in the entire process of communicating

21. Another graphic description of the steps peasants will take to prevent
their buffalo from being slaughtered during rinderpest epidemics is given in
the novel: Kukrit Pramoj, *The Red Bamboo* (Bangkok, Akasarn Press, 1954),
pp. 137–47 (in Thai).

new skills and ideas, received only cursory treatment by the United Nations agencies. By and large, foreign experts were not well informed about the local milieu. The ramifications of the problem of orientation and the possibility of achieving effectiveness in this regard are important enough to warrant closer analysis in Chapter 9.

COUNTERPARTS

The Thai counterpart was a key factor in both UNESCO projects. The counterpart was to be not only the immediate catalyst for day-to-day activity of the foreign expert but one of those who would carry on the project when the United Nations finally withdrew. The successful indoctrination and training of counterparts was therefore of crucial importance.

It was intended that each foreign expert would have one or more counterparts. This was adhered to fairly well at TUFEC and to a lesser degree at the Pilot Project. Selection of counterparts was left up to the appropriate Thai authority, and no prerequisite was established other than that of speaking English. In practice not more than one or two of over a hundred counterparts ever really measured up to the language skills expected by their foreign mentors.

The Thai interviewed were nearly unanimous in saying that they did not like the counterpart system. Their reasons are as varied as might be expected, given the complexity of the human relationship. Nevertheless, some Thai who worked as counterparts stated that they had learned a great deal from the foreign experts. It was noticeable that the subject matter most readily assimilated was straightforward material not subject to argument and about which the foreign expert was indisputably an authority. In general, there was acceptance of (a) English language teaching, and (b) simple organizational skills such as library systems, program organization, textbook or pamphlet layout, conducting meetings, and such technical projects as methods of creating visual aids. Beyond this, however, ideas and concepts filtered through more or less fortuitously. There was no real guarantee of even limited transference except on a few occasions.

Generally, most of the problems already noted in this chapter tended to be concentrated within the counterpart/expert relationship. The expert's search for a specific role weakened counterpart faith. The combined problems of language, short tenure, multi-national variations, and general lack of orientation all seem to have come to a head at the counterpart level.

There were, of course, personality clashes, inevitable where there is an arbitrary matching of alien people who have never met before. The factors mentioned by the ex-counterparts as most irritating and disruptive to general transference can be summarized as follows:

1. The expert's manner seemed rude and overbearing, especially when operating with his counterpart in front of other Thai.
2. Counterparts did not understand the expert's language (and almost invariably these complaints were loudest from Thai who worked with non-English speaking experts).
3. The expert condescended to the Thai.
4. The expert soon lost interest when he did not get his own way.
5. The expert knew nothing about the Thai and would not learn.
6. The "expert" was not really expert.
7. The expert never listened to the Thai about anything, and when the subject matter was related to his profession, he would accept no advice.
8. Before both parties could become adjusted, the expert went home.

There is ample evidence to suggest that the complaints about language, tenure, and orientation voiced by Thai counterparts were just.

The experts seemed unaware of the antipathy that existed. This not insignificant level of antipathy arose through failure to establish communication between expert and counterpart. To a large degree both expert and counterpart were victims of the lack of recognition of the problems involved in the operations; consequently, there was failure to investigate what steps might be taken to heal the communications breach.

Even if the general problem of orientation of foreign experts could have been solved, difficulties would still have remained. Incompatibility would probably have been a disruptive factor in a small percentage of cases in any event. There are, however, some definable areas in the counterpart relationship which do offer prospects of improvement.

There must be some matching of skills. It is said that in Laos, for example, the "UNESCO experts just sit about," because that nation simply does not have enough people with the *minimum* level of skills to understand the experts' teaching.[22] On the other hand:

> It is useless for the expert to be of too high a level. Let us be quite clear, we don't want them at the Director level because here the foreigner is hopelessly out of touch with what goes on within our government organizations and in any case most of our Directors have a far better foreign education than the sort of people the United Nations send us. At the same time we don't want a philosophy major out in the field. We have nobody out there who can talk to this sort of person. Hands and tools are about all we can use.[23]

Without a doubt the matching of expert and counterpart at reasonably compatible levels of skills and knowledge is essential. Preliminary investigation must be done to ensure that differences in levels of knowledge between, say, a teacher and student can be bridged. Such was not the case in Thailand; and if attempts had been made along these lines, it is probable that the concept of transference through counterpart and expert would have been considered impractical. Thailand simply did not have sufficient people of the appropriate type.

Yet a further factor which may have had some bearing on the indifferent Thai counterpart relation was the background and motivation of the people recruited by UNESCO and the other agencies. To assess these factors is difficult. An attempt was made, therefore, to ascertain how the counterparts themselves categorized

22. Interview at UNESCO Regional Office, Bangkok, May 30, 1963.
23. Interview at Ministry of Education, Bangkok, June 5, 1963.

the experts. Based upon the views of 32 Thai counterparts, the United Nations personnel can be split into four main groups:

1. Ex-colonial civil servants, out of work as a result of the demise of colonialism (note the timing of the commencement of TUFEC and the Pilot Project).
2. Men who, caught up in the war, missed opportunities for extended education and the careers that they might legitimately have anticipated, and who found a substitute in the United Nations.
3. Younger persons who were interested in working for the United Nations in order to undertake research.
4. A tiny segment of idealists who wanted to serve their fellow men.

Only 10 per cent of the personnel involved had actually been colonial civil servants. These people tended to hold more senior and administrative positions, and their presence may therefore have been felt to a greater degree than their numbers would indicate. One United Nations official sympathized with Thai antipathy toward the ex-colonialists, describing them as having a "congenital inability to mix . . . probably the worst type of person the United Nations could possibly have recruited and not nearly worth the administrative skills that they undoubtedly brought."[24] Thai judgment relative to the other categories also had substance, although it must be noted that approximately 20 per cent of the personnel were women and could hardly have fallen under the category of those thwarted by World War II, at least not in any educational sense.

The problem of recruitment has long been a concern of the United Nations at large. General personnel shortcomings have been assessed from time to time by the United Nations, and these were applicable to the Thailand situation.[25] The point to be made, however, is that some of the persons were not compatible with either United Nations standards or the requirements of field work in Thailand.

24. Interview at Local Office WHO in Asia and the Far East, Bangkok, August 8, 1963.

25. UNESCO, *Records of the General Conference at Montevideo, 1954; Eighth Session, Resolutions* (Paris, UNESCO, 1955), pp. 51–59.

Conceptually, the counterpart system involved a highly personalized relationship, difficult enough under ideal circumstances. But to assess the experience in Thailand the relationship must be superimposed upon the shadowy role definition, a massive language barrier, the short tenure of experts, the peculiarities of the multinational group, and the appreciable deficiencies in orientation. Perhaps one should pay tribute to Thai and foreigners that a communication breakdown was not absolute.

EMPATHY OF FOREIGN EXPERTS

In an endeavor to sum up the general relationships at working levels between Thai and foreign experts, I attempted to discover how the Thai assessed the empathy of the foreign experts. It seemed to me that if the experts were empathetic with the Thai, they should have been able to transfer their expertise to their counterparts.

The term empathy, "the capacity to see oneself in the other fellow's situation," has been used in one major study in assessing the way traditionally oriented people looked at the modern world.[26] In the present study, however, the reverse approach has been used in order to see if the Thai thought the representatives of the modern world, the United Nations experts, attained empathy with the Thai milieu.

Twelve Thai were consulted in regard to 29 foreigners working at TUFEC. Included within the foreign group were two people who, though not part of the United Nations program, did work for TUFEC from time to time. The reason for their inclusion was that they had special skills in language and knowledge of Thailand, both having undertaken area studies on Southeast Asia, and Thailand in particular. It is not presumed that this survey should serve as a model or that it has validity outside the fairly narrow parameters of its setting. The factors raised in the survey came up spontaneously during association with the Thai consultants concerned. Details of the survey can be found in Appendix V.

In the minds of the Thai consulted, only four of the 29 foreign personnel were empathetic. Of these four, two were the area

26. Daniel Lerner, *The Passing of Traditional Society: Modernizing in the Middle East* (Glencoe, Ill., Free Press, 1958), p. 50.

specialists already referred to, and one other was an elderly Doctor of Divinity who had spent 24 years in China specializing in community development work. The fourth person, in the minds of the Thai, was *sanuk*.[27] It was *sanuk* to work with him, it was *sanuk* to go to a party with him or to visit a village with him. His handling of international staff members was *sanuk* also. It is suspected that this individual was atypical, assessed more on his capacity relative to the wonderful world of *sanuk* than as a foreign expert. He had the sort of rapport which made the Thai feel he was one of them and could see their point of view.

By whatever yardstick is used—whether one takes the views of Thai recipients or attempts a logical analysis of discernible factors involved—communications in their widest sense were poor in both projects. Yet for the type of organizations that had been established, adequate communication was the very lifeblood of the enterprises.

27. See p. 73.

PART 2. THE THÁI RESPONSE

5

THE THAI ELITE AND RURAL PROGRESS

Since the Constitutional Revolution of 1932, political power in Thailand has been the preserve of a small but distinct coterie. All but a tiny percentage of these have been either senior military commanders or senior bureaucrats. Between 1932 and 1960, for example, of the 200 men who served in 29 cabinets it is possible to identify 168 as coming from the military and civil services, whereas only 11 came from outside formal government institutions. Of the 168 identified, 90 were bureaucrats and 78 were military officers. The government of Field Marshal Luang Pibun Songkram held tenure from 1947 to 1958, that is for nearly the duration of the United Nations efforts under study. Field Marshal Sarit Thanarat attained the post of Prime Minister by a coup d'état in September 1958, but some 21 persons from the Pibun cabinet, all military men, continued as ministers in the new government. During the 1950s there was, as there always has been in Thailand, a high degree of continuity of persons and power at the decision-making level of government.

Reinforcing the concentration and continuity of power in the hands of a relatively tiny group is the fact that the general ecology of the nation has as yet not given rise to other groups with sufficient strength to compete for the fruits of power or indeed greatly influence policy or decision-making. In Thailand there is an absence of industry and organized labor, of groups such as banking or mining, where wealth can be highly concentrated. The single largest interest group in the nation, the Buddhist religious complex, derives at least some of its strength (and capacity for survival) by keeping apart from politics. In a similar way the king has recognized that the tenure of a constitutional monarch depends on maintaining a discreet gap between himself and day-to-day politics but—as has become increasingly the case in Thailand— reinforcing the government by cooperating with it in national ceremonies. Nevertheless, the position of the monarch is crucial relative to the rural scene. In the heart of every peasant the monarch *is* the government. It is common to find, for example, that while even 50 miles from the capital peasants had not heard of Field Marshal Sarit and were only vaguely interested in the post he held, all of them recognized and knew of the monarch and looked upon him as the architect and manipulator of power. But this situation at best represents only potential power. Since 1932 the monarchy in Thailand has had to struggle hard to maintain even symbolic status. Not only is its greater national participation in the ceremonies of state over the past five years or so a new role, but it appears to indicate acceptance of the function of all good constitutional monarchies—to reign but not to govern. The monarchy therefore reinforces the government, and this further accentuates the autonomy of the governing elite and the validity of treating it as the undisputed center of authority.

In addition, ecological centralism powerfully augments authority. Thailand is like a city-state. Outside of Bangkok there are no large urban centers. Bangkok has nearly two million inhabitants, but there are only six other centers with a population of between 25,000 and 50,000. Bangkok sets the standards for the nation in dress, behavior, architecture, art, education, social life, commerce, and technology. No Thai can expect to move to the top in any field outside of Bangkok. Coups d'état take place in Bangkok, not in the provinces. It is from Bangkok that the successful promoter of a coup exercises his authority. Furthermore, the development of all physical communications gravitates naturally toward Bangkok. Literally and metaphorically, all roads lead to the capital.

There is, nevertheless, a very small provincial elite, consisting in the main of provincial governors and their staffs. These coteries are widely dispersed, poorly linked to each other by communications, and entirely Bangkok-oriented. Their career prospects and their standards emanate from the capital. In their weak, isolated condition, rather than establishing rival centers, they conduct any criticism of the central government within the channels of administration and not outside them. Furthermore the concept of a centralized bureaucracy, dependent entirely upon the central authority for appointment, tenure, and reward, is old in Thailand dating at least as far back as the Ayudhyan period (about the fifteenth to the eighteenth centuries). The absence of hereditary titles and offices and large private landholdings also powerfully reinforces the general omnipotence of the capital and those in power at this locale.

The lack of opportunity for careers outside of the bureaucracy and, more recently, the military has led not only to the absence of multi-elites but to a very concentrated and easily identified decision-making group within the cabinet. The post of prime minister carries with it extraordinary executive powers, including wide control over finance. The prime minister normally has also held a top military appointment. The late Field Marshal Sarit was Supreme Commander, a post that gave him control of all policy facets of Thailand's military forces. The minister of defense is also a key person and usually holds command of the army in addition to his cabinet post, making him a central figure in deterring or promoting a coup d'état. Inside Thailand, the minister of interior holds vast powers: all provincial administration, including the control of the police force, is in his hands. Outside of these three posts and the immediate staff working close to these ministers (such as the chief of staff, Supreme Command, for example, who works very closely with the prime minister), many other ministerial appointments have been assigned only partially on the basis of competence as opposed to political or military affiliations, and especially personal loyalties. The post of minister of foreign affairs, for example, since World War II has always been filled by a distinguished professional. Nevertheless, reward and sinecure play a part in assigning minor posts. This procedure is not too different from that used elsewhere, with the exception that the "outer circle," as opposed to those few "inner" ministers (such as the prime minister and ministers of defense and interior), tends to lack authority for autonomous decision-making.

Two clear factors emerge. The first is that the decision-making group in Thailand is small and easily definable, and has sufficient autonomy to act with great freedom. Secondly, although little of moment can be done in Thailand without the approval of this group, obtaining their sanction gives one great freedom. Therefore, to obtain government support, one must be able to reach this circle.

PREVIOUS ATTEMPTS AT RURAL DEVELOPMENT

Since the reign of King Mongkut (1851–68) economic factors have prompted the central government to show interest in the affairs of the peasant, including his education. In 1855 King Mongkut negotiated a trade treaty with the British, the importance of which can hardly be overemphasized.[1] With the advent of this treaty (and others which followed), Thailand became a rice exporter of such dimensions that by about 1920—along with Burma —Thailand was one of the world's leading exporters of rice. There was a corresponding increase in the kingdom's other three main exports—rubber, teak, and tin. In common with other countries in the area, Thailand also experienced a population growth from an estimated 4.5 to 5 million in 1850,[2] to 8.3 million in 1911,[3] and thence to its current total of approximately 25 million.

The production of rice in particular has always tended to outstrip the growth in population, principally because of the availability of fertile virgin lands.[4] Through the energy of two remarkable monarchs, King Mongkut and his successor Chulalongkorn (1868–1910), the Thai peasant was encouraged in this activity in which, as one observer has noted, "the initiative came from individuals [i.e. peasants] . . . the extension of rice cultivation forms a notable exception to the general statements that the Thai left entrepreneurship to others and that change and reform were brought about from the top."[5] But the magnitude of the change in Thailand's general economic condition left the Thai government with little option other than to take note of the natural and human resources that were involved in such an eventful undertaking.

The previous major activities of the government toward rural development had been abolishing corvée labor and slavery, the

1. Sir John Bowring, *The Kingdom and People of Siam* (2 vols. London, John Parker and Son, 1857), 2, 217–20.

2. Ibid., *1*, 81–83.

3. Department of Statistics, *Statistical Year Book of Siam 1936, 19* (Bangkok, 1939), 48–50.

4. Ingram, Chap. 3.

5. Ibid., p. 43.

Consolidated Land Act of 1908, actions such as the abolishment of gambling shops by 1917, and various community development projects starting about World War II. The advent of educational reforms has already been noted.[6]

While the abolition of the corvée and slavery undoubtedly freed peasant labor for rice production and generally promoted greater peasant independence, the advent of a money economy together with increasing Chinese immigration made it obviously very inefficient to undertake public works by means of forced labor. Similarly, the Consolidated Land Act, which in its basic provisions limited an individual's landholdings to a maximum of 25 rai (approximately 10 acres), was part of Chulalongkorn's efforts to turn the Thai administrative system into a modern, centralized bureaucracy drawing salaries from a centralized authority. The Land Act formally abolished the ancient system of land grants given by the king commensurately with royal grants of rank. Large estates had been few, however, and the Land Act, rather than freeing the land for the peasants, had little effect since the surplus land already available was ample to meet peasant needs. The slow abolition of gambling shops, however, was directly aimed at the peasant. The literature stresses the amount of time and money taken from the peasant by the gambling shops and their contribution to a rise in the debts of the peasantry. The extraordinary extent of gambling is perhaps best revealed by noting that some 20 per cent of all state revenues came from taxes and rents emanating from the gambling shops. Chulalongkorn expressed his concern that immense peasant resources were preempted by gambling and this undoubtedly was one factor that caused him to give up this lucrative source of state revenue. No matter how one might speculate as to the motives of the Thai government in advancing these efforts, and no matter how many accolades might be awarded to the government relative to their concern for their peasantry, the measures were aimed at preserving the peasant, and thereby the elite, status quo rather than in promoting change.

The Thai elite was not necessarily cynical. The idea of some degree of elite responsibility and of elite action was a practical notion in Thailand and did not arise from the postwar intrusions.

6. See above, pp. 32–34.

The Thai elite may not have always been entirely effective when judged by theoretical (as yet unattained) standards of its Western mentors. But its members had recognized the existence of the peasants' problems.

CHANGE OR STATUS QUO?

A view expressed by the USOM Community Development Office was that the only objective of a community development program was to promote the growth of autonomous and self-governing institutions at the village level as precursors of the general development of democracy with a peasant base.

> If we are to use it [Community Development] as an instrument to foster and support the self growth of the nation . . . it will require a pattern set in terms of explanation, persuasion and training rather than decision from the top, ordering and inspection. Community Development . . . may prove to be the beginning of more adequate local institutions which the villagers of Thailand can use to carry out the functions of local self government.[7]

There is no evidence that the Thai elite shared these views. This is not to suggest, however, that the elite is or has been indifferent to peasant conditions:

> It is now accepted that the majority of the rural people are in a state of poverty, they are stricken with diseases, they are not developed (as urban people are). But they are the backbone of the country. So in developing our country it is necessary to attack the rural problems.[8]

The late prime minister then went on to discuss ameliorative possibilities, such as improved hygiene and schools and increased production.

7. Sheldon Turner, "Capacity for Self Growth Through Community Development," *Community Development Bulletin, 1* (Bangkok, November 1962), 32 (in Thai).

8. Field Marshal Sarit Thanarat, quoted by the Director General of the National Community Development Department in *Community Development Bulletin, 7* (Bangkok, September 1960), 11 (in Thai).

In a semiofficial editorial commenting on the National Community Development Plan and analyzing its objectives, no mention
was made of political objectives at all, except to note that "if
people get the idea of co-operating through Community Development they will soon learn to co-operate in other ways to their own
mutual advantage."[9] Indeed the great stress in this commentary
was on reinforcing ancient village values in recreation and spiritual
activities.

It is intended here not to judge the attitudes of the Thai elite
at the time of the United Nations operations but rather to assess
what they were.[10] While the politically minded Westerner may
see in rural development schemes generally a means of promoting
democracy, it seems certain that the Thai elite saw something
quite different. Amelioration of peasant problems was a means
of preserving the status quo. After all, what better way was there
of preserving the ancient Thai order of things than to have a

9. Director General of the National Community Development Program,
"Our New Community Development Program," *Community Development Bulletin, 1* (Bangkok, December 1962), 13 (in Thai).

10. The attitudes of some Thai elite were sought and it is largely their views
which have determined the general conclusions given. The Thai elites contacted were: an ex-premier who still leads a nominal opposition political party
but who in fact follows precisely the policies and patterns of the ruling authority; an ex-premier who holds an important international post; a royal prince
identified with the Free Thai movement during World War II and therefore
with the rebel Premier Pridi Bhanomyong currently in Red China; a major-
general, of the younger age group, who holds a high appointment in the
politico-military hierarchy; a young college professor who is an adviser in
administration to the National Community Development Department; a Thai
physician with connections both to the royal and political elite who has also
devoted considerable effort to the care of the indigent peasants newly arrived in
Bangkok; and a leading Thai industrialist and a member of the Privy Council.
Conversation was induced by two questions: "What do you think the Thai
government and educated people generally can do to help the Thai peasantry?";
and "What basic and fundamental changes do you think can and should be
induced in the peasants' way of life?" The first question evoked a far ranging,
not too articulate series of comments. Most considered that the peasant's life
was an enviable one but that improvements were necessary in health and
education. The second question received a flat "None"—the reason being
given when the questioner pressed was that if the peasant wants to change,
well, he can. It is noticeable however that "change" in this context meant
coming to Bangkok and being urbanized.

happy contented peasantry, with good health, an improved agriculture through application of science and technology, a developing school system, and a slow but steady rise in per capita income? If at the same time, Thai values regarding religion and monarchy and concepts of social status could be preserved, what better way could there be to avoid the stresses and general disruptions of more radical courses? To some Western minds this may seem to be the antithesis of the sort of approach that should be employed in Southeast Asia, an area which so many regard as revolutionary. Thus the Thai elite advanced an argument, not generally accepted, for slow development coming from above. When members of the elite were challenged, they readily admitted this position and in turn challenged the skeptic to offer an alternative.

The Thai peasant has ownership of his fields.[11] He has even had some opportunity for upward mobility into the elite through accumulation of wealth or successful entry into the bureaucracy, facing no opposition from the established hierarchy to persons rising from peasant stock. The expanding population in Thailand is counterbalanced by a land surplus. There is a strong sense of national homogeneity expressed by the mass practice of Therevada Buddhism and adherence to the monarchy, neither of which has been disrupted or broken by foreign invasion or colonial rule.

In this situation it must be assessed, therefore, what "change" it is that everyone is talking about.[12] Specifically, what kind of life is it that the promoters of "change" envisage for the peasant? While the basic ecology of the nation remains agricultural (and it is difficult to envisage major changes here), the national problem is, as one result, primarily one of markets and prices.[13] Within this

11. As an approximate assessment, 87 per cent of the Thai peasantry own their land: see Human Relations Area Files, *Thailand*, Country Survey Series, ed. Thomas Fitzsimmons (New Haven, HRAF Press, 1957), p. 305. This does not take account of liens relative to land titles. Data on this subject are not available but from observation it seems at least half of the peasantry have mortgaged their land to moneylenders.

12. As an example, of 84 final reports submitted by TUFEC personnel to UNESCO Headquarters, Paris, 44 contained one or more references to the promotion of "social and economic change."

13. It has been stated as a somewhat loose guideline that a 5 per cent fluctuation downward in rice prices on the international market would cancel out the

context, the peasant's immediate problem is less one of basic social or political change than of techniques, such as water control and distribution, low-cost loans, better communications systems, better seeds, cheap fertilizer, and, above all, more secure and higher cash returns for his crop. ——

Under these very practical conditions there was no incompatibility between the wholly generalized aims of the United Nations operations and the views of the elite. Insofar as the objectives of the United Nations operations could be translated into specific action, they seemed practical and utilitarian, far removed from such abstract goals as promoting democracy through improvement in the peasant's material lot. This highly sensitive goal of political ends through material gains was raised only by USOM. Political change was not part of the United Nations objective or inherent in their concept of operations. The "change" that the United Nations servants spoke of so frequently was material change, an amelioration of supposed peasant hardship and ignorance. As such, United Nations objectives bore a marked similarity to actions carried out by Thai elites over a substantial part of the nation's history. United Nations operations therefore seemed more likely to maintain the status quo than to disrupt it; and, insofar as the issue was investigated, the elite gave its blessing to the United Nations operations as a benign activity. ——

Nevertheless, the United Nations may have been indirectly a harbinger of minor political change. At Cha Cheong Sao, for example, one change unwittingly introduced by the United Nations was decentralized control,[14] but this was an ad hoc result, unplanned and unforeseen. It is possible, of course, that had the United Nations operations persisted for a longer period, changes of more or less unforeseen kinds would have occurred.

Perhaps the most significant impact upon the elite arising from the relative ineptness of the United Nations was the realization that rural development would have to be sponsored by Thailand itself. It became increasingly clear to Thai authority that no form

---

impact of foreign aid. Between 1953–57 prices varied as much as 20 per cent: ECAFE, *Economic Survey of Asia and the Far East, 1957* (Bangkok, March 1957), Chap. 5.

14. See below, pp. 128–29.

of magic coming from afar would quickly and effectively put things right. If this speculation is true—this may well have been the greatest return coming from the United Nations efforts.

THE DEVELOPMENT BOOM

A Thai outline of their own attempts to help themselves in the field of rural development in the era prior to the advent of the United Nations reads as follows:

1939: A program of levying local taxes for local reconstruction measures, such as health, roads, irrigation, agricultural extension services and public utilities. Nine "model" villages were created. The program however lapsed during World War II.

1942: The creation of rural improvement committees at local level, especially for the problem of marketing. This included short training courses for local leaders. This program was not continued after 1945.

1951: A Rural Reconstruction Program, again based upon the idea of Rural Improvement Committees. This program also did not develop.[15]

In 1956 a national program of community development was initiated, but action was negligible until the early 1960s, when with almost dramatic suddenness community development became something of a boom industry. In 1959 a National Community Development Plan was drawn up and endorsed by the cabinet. This plan was detailed and comprehensive.[16] Concurrently, a new Department was empowered to administer the Plan.[17] The Southeast Asia Treaty Organization also announced its intention of embarking on community development operations, and appropriate activity started in 1963, coincidentally just a mile or so away from

15. Ministry of Interior, "The Development of Community Development in Thailand," *Community Development Bulletin*, 2 (Bangkok, April 1960), 8, 40 (in Thai).

16. Ministry of Interior, *The Plan for National Community Development* (Bangkok, 1963) (in Thai).

17. "Act Transferring Affairs of the Re-organized Ministry of Interior," *Royal Thai Government Gazette*, 2 (Bangkok, October 7, 1962), 39–42.

the defunct TUFEC installations.[18] A further and highly significant development was that the Royal Thai Army entered the arena. It established a number of Mobile Development Units whose task was to initiate a short-range crash program of community development to precede the longer term national program.[19] The national plan and the army plan were both concentrated in two geographical areas, one along the Thai side of the Mekong River from the province of Loeie in the northwest to the Cambodian border in the southeast, and the other at the southern extremity of the kingdom in the three Moslem provinces adjoining Malaya.

The reasons for this community development boom are not hard to find. The de facto seizure of Laos by Communist forces caused a tremendous shock not only to the Thai government but to the public at large. The Mekong River, usually regarded by the orthodox military as a defense barrier, could be just that in the event of a conventional invasion, but at other times it is a great highway and connecting link, joining Laotians on the Laos side of the River with fellow Laotians on the Thai side. The area of Thailand along the west bank of the river was particularly vulnerable to Communist infiltration, which in fact had already started. Ethnic contiguity and the connecting link of the river are major factors, but the area along the Mekong also is heavily forested for great stretches, with few roads running to the Thai hinterland. The area is generally out of contact with the Thai administration.

The urgency with which Thailand viewed the relationship of events in Laos to their own Mekong River territories is best illustrated by the nature of the army intrusion into community development plans. The army's view was that any good that might arise from the National Community Development Plan would be too long in making an impact on the peasants in the Mekong area, and in the meantime Communist infiltration could make real inroads. The army's plan was to move in with such enterprises as

18. SEATO, *Operational Plan for Thai-SEATO Regional Community Development Technical Assistance Center,* Bangkok (Ministry of Interior, 1962) (in Thai).

19. Supreme Command Headquarters, *The National Security Organization and Conception for Countering Communist Activities in Thailand* (Bangkok, Ministry of Defense, May 29, 1962; released by Supreme Command Headquarters).

health services, schoolbuilding, and well-digging projects, all of which were expected to make a quick impact and demonstrate government presence. Villages were to be linked by radio to provincial or district centers, and a helicopter lift of commando troops was to be demonstrably available. The weakest part of the army plan was reliance on the Department of National Community Development to follow up immediately with sustained operations. Here, it seemed, lack of general resources, especially trained personnel, would gravely inhibit these measures. But based upon the areas selected for immediate operations, noting the vigor and speed with which Army operations were conducted and the avowed political objectives of the moves, there was little doubt that community development was arising not so much from the desire to supply the needs of the peasants as from the need to meet what the Thai government construed as a Communist challenge. This view was stated quite bluntly by one prominent Thai when he said, "We must have Community Development as a stopper against Communist insurgency."[20]

In the south along the Malayan border Thailand felt it faced a different problem. The three most southern provinces contained most of the approximately three quarters of a million Moslems in the kingdom. The fact that this minority is geographically concentrated has always improved its bargaining power with the Thai government. Evidence of this is that the Islamic group, as opposed to the much larger but widely dispersed and highly variegated Chinese minority, has had an "Islamic Adviser to the Thai Government" in Bangkok. Islamic schools, again in contradistinction to Chinese schools, have maintained their own cultural traditions, and Islam, like all other religions in Thailand, has generally enjoyed great freedom. There is no evidence that the emergence of Malaya as an independent Islamic state caused any apprehension among the Thai. Indeed, to be rid of the much more powerful British, with whom the Thai had disputed the area since the turn of the twentieth century, seemed to be a gain so far as control over their Islamic minority was concerned.

The advent of Malaysia, however, held two possibilities for the future. One was that in the long run the enhanced Chinese minor-

20. Interview at SEATO Headquarters, Bangkok, July 16, 1963.

ity in the new confederation might take over Malaysia and, like the British before them, would not be beyond using the excuse of defense of the Islamic faith as a pretext for bringing pressure on Thailand, pressure which could gain support from greater China to the Thai north. Of more immediate concern, however, was that Malaysia might become involved in a war with Indonesia, a war which, despite assurances of aid from the outside, Malaysia could lose. In this case Thailand would have a contiguous border with a vast Islamic empire, and an Islamic minority with a sense of grievance and located alongside their greater Islamic brethren could afford a pretext for all manner of pressures. These fears, and the reaction to them, are typical of the Thai—or perhaps of any small, independent state alongside a powerful neighbor whom it distrusts.

Superimposed upon the Islamic problem in the south is yet another issue. The hard-core remnants of the Communist insurrection in Malaya have been ensconced in the wild hilly regions on the Thai side of the Malaya-Thai border for some four or five years. There is increasing evidence that this coterie, numbering between 500 and 600 men, has been receiving arms and training more actively, concomitant with the increasing Communist successes in Laos and Vietnam. There has been clear evidence that propagandists from this Communist body have moved into many Islamic villages and other minor ethnic groups in the forests, in an intensified campaign to arouse the people there against the central government. Thus the long-standing Islamic problem is now complicated by the Communist problem. Of the five mobile development units created by the Thai Army for "shock" community development, two were assigned to the south, the rest to the northeast; the National Community Development Plan also assigned priority to these regions. It is from the threat to its security that Thailand sees that the community development boom derives its real impetus.

THE UNITED NATIONS AND ELITE OBJECTIVES

The question to be asked is how could a United Nations operation aimed at rural development and without political overtones fit into the framework of rural improvement as seen by the Thai elite? In the era preceding the development boom—that is, prior to about 1960—an unqualified answer is that the United Nations operation would fit very well. The United Nations agencies perhaps thought in a rather vague way that they were promoting change. But in the eyes of the elite they were not. Every fresh-water well that was dug, every young man or woman trained to go forth and work in villages, every school that received a better trained teacher, or every child who was taught to wash his hands before eating in actual fact helped preserve the structural concepts of the elite. A happy contented peasantry and a privileged but socially conscious elite—which, it must be remembered, did not impose social barriers to peasant mobility into its own ranks—seemed to have the best chance of structural survival when the peasant was helped to be cleaner, healthier, and more efficient in the fields. In this sense, therefore, the operations of the United Nations agencies and the attitudes of the Thai elite were in harmony.

In the urgency of the threat seen by the Thai government after the de facto Communist takeover in Laos, the situation changed. A national program, with some attempt to mobilize resources on a national scale, seemed essential if community development were to be employed "as a stopper against communist insurgency." Furthermore, the intrusion of the army, with its open political goals, made clear the immediate purpose of community development—to counter Communist infiltration. Thai planning and operations at this level ignored the United Nations. TUFEC was quietly allowed to phase out without comment; and the new National Community Development Plan ignored TUFEC methodology, material resources, and personnel. According to the last TUFEC report: "The Thai Government and UNESCO have together established an institution which is now capable of meeting the heavy demands that will be made upon it as the major Training Centre for a comprehensive programme devoted to the social, cultural and economic development and prosperity of the Thai countryside."[21] This was manifestly incorrect. As has already been noted, TUFEC virtually ceased operations after the United Nations left, and the National Development Plan does not bear any relationship to TUFEC doctrine.

21. TUFEC, *Final Report for 1959*, p. 12.

In answer to the question of how far TUFEC has influenced and intruded into the new Department of National Community Development, the Director of that Department said that as far as he was concerned TUFEC played no part at all, that TUFEC came under the Ministry of Education, and as far as he knew, the Ministry of Education had changed its program at TUFEC into one of providing in-service training for rural teachers.[22]

The difference in interpretation between the final report of the last United Nations Director at TUFEC and what in fact was actually happening leads to the last point to be made concerning relationships between a United Nations body and the Thai elite. It has already been noted that the TUFEC operation was assigned to the Ministry of Education. The consequence of this basic decision was that United Nations officials, regardless of level, simply did not have the ear of those who mattered. At best, the chief of mission might have reasonable access to the minister of education, but more probably to an undersecretary. As has been noted earlier in this chapter, this was not where power was located in the Thai hierarchy. The odds were very high that the average United Nations official would have only a hazy knowledge of what was happening at the decision-making level in the Thai government and still less chance of influencing these officials.

Those holding decision-making powers in Thailand did not actually place impediments in the way of United Nations operations. Although TUFEC appeared to be pushed aside by the new Department of Community Development, as well as by the army, it was more because of the onrush of external events than because TUFEC had fallen into disfavor. Along with the Cha Cheong Sao Project, as far as the Thai elite were concerned, TUFEC ended its mission with good feelings all round. At other levels of the government, however, the United Nations operations, and especially TUFEC, did not have easy passage. It is to the relations of the projects with officials at field levels that we now must turn.

22. Interview at Department of National Community Development.

6

THE BUREAUCRACY—RIVAL OR ALLY?

Although relations between the United Nations and the decision-making group in Thailand were always somewhat general, relations between Thai officials in the bureaucracy and the United Nations field operations were a day-to-day reality. Indeed, one of the critical areas of the entire mission was the viability of the working relationship established with officials in the field.

THE LINE OF AUTHORITY

TUFEC and the Pilot Project both worked with the administrative apparatus of the Ministry of Education. In the case of the Pilot Project the relationship was relatively straightforward. The operations at Cha Cheong Sao, after the agricultural project ceased, were solely educational, calling for integrating a certain number of foreign personnel within an existing structure, the Cha Cheong Sao school system. Furthermore, the local structure was directly linked with the policy-making and control authority represented by the Ministry of Education in Bangkok. The actual work conducted at Cha Cheong Sao was confined to this complex.

The relation of TUFEC to the Ministry, however, was not so straightforward. No doubt it could be argued that the work at the Center was "education" and therefore properly the concern of the Ministry of Education. But once TUFEC's activities extended to the villages and the farms, operations became more impracticable as they were without the support of the Ministry of Interior, the undisputed administrative authority in the provinces. All TUFEC operations nevertheless remained the responsibility of the Ministry of Education. This divorce from the recognized line of authority in the provinces inevitably had to be fatal to TUFEC's productive enterprises.

Thus while the Pilot Project faced problems of personnel relations and attitudes, TUFEC had not only these but a basic organizational difficulty. The consequences of working outside the line of authority had a fundamental impact.

The Consequences of Ignoring Established Institutions

Prior to the administrative reforms instituted by King Chulalongkorn near the end of the nineteenth century,[1] the kingdom had been divided into three *kroms* or departments. These kroms possessed a high degree of autonomy and, as far as administration of their domains was concerned, held absolute power over territory and people. The overall apparatus of the kroms merged into the new Ministry of Interior and the eventual organizational structure consisted of 71 provinces, with each province further divided into districts, roughly about five to ten districts per province; each district was further divided into communes, again about five to ten per district. At the bottom came the villages, with ten to twenty per commune. The Ministry of Interior has two great claims to authority and prestige. First, it still manipulates all levels of provincial administration. It appoints and dismisses heads of provinces and districts and is a de facto if not a controlling influence in the election of village headmen and the *kamnan,* the latter heading the commune and nominally the representative headman of the villages. The Ministry of Interior has the largest budget in the nation outside the Ministry of Defense and has more employees than any other ministry. Of even greater significance than its material power is its prestige. As has been noted, it has a continuity from antiquity to the present. In the provinces, representatives of, say, the ministries of agriculture and education are parvenus, those ministries having come into existence only in this century. At the peasant level (and virtually everyone in the provinces is a peasant), there has been no rival to the administrative omnipotence of the Ministry of Interior repre-

1. See James N. Mosel, "Thai Administrative Behavior," in *Toward the Comparative Study of Public Administration,* ed. William J. Siffin (Bloomington, Indiana University Press, 1957), pp. 292–300.

sentative. In the village the "big man" is the district officer. As
one observer of great experience noted:

> When one travels up-country [in the provinces] one cannot
> help but be struck by the all powerful role of the Ministry of
> Interior officials. The Governor, the District Officer and others
> of the Ministry of Interior are not mere figureheads. They
> hold the keys to effective action at the rural level. They cannot
> be sidestepped. Without their fullhearted co-operation no
> rural program can be successful.[2]

The same commentator in another place came close to assessing
the specific TUFEC problem:

> These FEOs at present under Ministry of Education's super-
> vision have found their position very difficult to maintain. In
> quite a few areas they have not been able to enlist the Gover-
> nor's and other officials' support. . . . Vis-à-vis the villagers,
> the FEOs have no real status especially if viewed against the
> prestige of those Ministry of Interior officials from the Gover-
> nor down. . . . The FEOs are not in the line of authority that
> the headman has been subject to. The Ministry of Interior
> officials are the ones who have the power, respect of the vil-
> lagers and a long history of contact with them. It is they who
> are responsible for the administration and the development
> of rural areas.[3]

In retrospect it seems extraordinary that the fundamental question of working within the line of authority in Thailand was not
at least discussed by the original United Nations survey groups.
Early records indicate that almost no thought was given to this
basic issue. But the error was not only one of omission. Early instructions issued to TUFEC students under the heading "Community Meetings" recommended the activation of village meetings

---

2. William Klausner, "A Memorandum on Ministry of Interior Community
Development Pilot Projects," Bangkok, May 4, 1959 (in the files, UNESCO Re-
gional Office, Bangkok), also published in *Community Development Bulletin, 2*
(Bangkok, February 1962), 38–46 (in Thai).

3. Ibid., p. 4.

on an organized and monthly basis, the controlling authority being the students.[4] To work in the provinces was one thing, but to establish one's own autonomous forum was another. Undoubtedly the idea was, at least theoretically, a move toward greater peasant control over his own affairs; but it was not this long-term prospect that TUFEC had in mind as much as bringing the workers and peasants together as a group. Although, in the long run, development of these or similar groups might have resulted in greater control by the peasant of his own affairs, the real issue was that to activate such groups was a blatant affront to existing administrative institutions. As a result, few if any of these village councils came into being. The TUFEC student was too well aware of Thai mores to embark upon such an alien activity.

During the formative stages TUFEC paid little attention to its relations with the Thai provincial bureaucracy other than in the most general way. A survey report made soon after TUFEC started training does not mention this isssue.[5] But as operations developed, the issue soon loomed as one of the major problems. Initially TUFEC looked upon the matter as something that could be solved by good public relations rather than by structural readjustment.

> One of the main indices of TUFEC's success will be the effectiveness with which our ex-trainees build up satisfactory working relations with official colleagues and gain acceptance from the provincial governor downwards. This necessitates the development at TUFEC of correct and cordial relations with the provincial administration so that the students can be given a good working pattern of official cooperation. This is not always easy as TUFEC's large and growing influence on the surrounding area sometimes gives rise to digestive troubles It is not always easy for TUFEC with its large international staff and its unfamiliar ideas of village participation to gain unqualified support; but the need to cooperate with and

4. Memorandum: "Plan for Village Work. Instructions to Students Working in the Villages," n.d. (from the files, UNESCO Regional Office, Bangkok), pp. 7–8.

5. Charles Madge, *A Progress Report to* UNESCO *Headquarters on Development of the* TUFEC *Program*, Ubol, June 1954 (from the files, UNESCO Headquarters, Paris).

involve the provincial government in our work is kept continuously in mind.[6]

By 1958 the problem had still not been resolved, but the key factor, structural configuration, was crystallizing:

> A major problem exists. . . . At present the teams [i.e. FEO teams] are under the administrative control of the Ministry of Education through the Provincial Education Officer but the vast majority of their work lies in the province of the local administration represented by the District Officer, the representative of the Governor of the Province.[7]

From about this time on, the objective of TUFEC appears to have been to have its trained personnel taken over by the Ministry of Interior, while the Center itself continued to be responsible for training under the Ministry of Education. An independent United Nations adviser, making a survey in Thailand for the Thai government on community development, confused the issue further by recommending that the entire TUFEC operation be taken over by a (then nonexistent) national community development agency.[8] This move was staunchly resisted by the UNESCO Regional Office in Bangkok.[9] In 1958 the Ministry of Interior itself intervened and dispatched a letter to some thirty governors who by this time had FEO teams working in their provinces. The letter followed the procedure of TUFEC and asked for cooperation "especially at district level," which was where the maximum contact arose between ministry officials and TUFEC personnel.[10] Finally, during 1959—as a result of further pressure, mainly from the Center itself

6. TUFEC, *Annual Report for 1956*, p. 6.

7. *Annual Report 1958 of the Deputy Director*, TUFEC, to UNESCO Headquarters, Paris, February 1959 (from the files, UNESCO Headquarters, Paris), p. 6.

8. Morris G. Fox, *Thailand: Community Development Programs, Part I: A Report by the Social Welfare Advisor to TAA*, Bangkok, June 26, 1957 (from the files, Ministry of Interior, Bangkok).

9. Conrad J. Opper, *Comments on Report of Mr. Morris G. Fox, United Nations Community Development Adviser in Thailand*, Bangkok, April 3, 1957 (from the files, UNESCO Regional Office, Bangkok), p. 1.

10. Letter from the Ministry of Interior to Governors, April 30, 1958 (translator unknown) (from the files, Ministry of Interior, Bangkok).

—all FEOs were transferred from the Ministry of Education to the Ministry of Interior.[11]

At about the same time the Ministry of Interior was becoming involved in the final organizational stages of its own community development program, which was to result in the establishment of the Department of National Community Development. TUFEC was included in the plans. In the role which the Ministry of Interior stated might be assigned to TUFEC, the most significant factor was the downgrading of the organization. It was to have no part in policy-making, research, or actual village work, and was to be limited to finishing its training program of providing some 71 FEO teams, completion being scheduled for the following year. It was thought that the Center "might then assist in the training of technical assistants and multi-purpose workers," but the nature of this training or its scale was never specified and this prospect came to naught.[12] For quite obscure reasons the Center itself was not transferred to the Ministry of Interior, nor was it given the training role in which the Ministry of Interior had professed interest. Instead, it remained in the hands of the Ministry of Education. It seems that by this time there was internal wrangling within the Thai bureaucracy in which the United Nations played no part.

IMPACT IN THE FIELD

During the period that has been reviewed—from the time the operation was initially surveyed until the United Nations finally withdrew—71 FEO teams involving some 426 individual workers were trained at the Center and dispatched to the field. The experience of these people reveals that the consequences of the failure, in human and productive terms, to understand and adjust to Thai provincial organization were far more serious than analysis of organizational structures would indicate.

11. Letter from the Ministry of Education to Ministry of Interior, November 1959 (from the files, Ministry of Education, Bangkok) (in Thai).

12. Ministry of Interior, Letter from Undersecretary to Chief of Mission UNESCO Regional Office on TUFEC's Role in Proposed National Development Program, May 23, 1959 (from the files of the Ministry of Interior, Bangkok).

The TUFEC students were victims of the failure to establish working relationships with the provincial bureaucracy. The first issue concerned student morale, especially its effects on performance. A second issue, of greater importance, at least from the point of view of the techniques and practice of aid operations, was the absence of an organizational structure which would have given assurance to the field workers.

Teams had not been deployed for long in the field before it became apparent, at least to the Thai staff at TUFEC, that there was a serious morale problem. In 1958 a survey was made of 27 FEO teams, involving 148 persons, to see if rumors of failing morale had any substance and, if so, for what reasons. It was discovered that while only 9 per cent of personnel had actually left field work, another 31 per cent stated that they wished to leave.[13] These data did not seem to worry the UNESCO Regional Office. "Only 14 FEOs lost in 2½ years. . . . We can conclude either the FEOs are on the whole content with their work, or that they are not allowed to leave except . . . for some very special dispensation."[14] But this was to disregard those who said they wanted to leave. All of the 31 per cent did leave, and more with them. By 1963 no FEO team was actually in operation in the kingdom. Some individual workers apparently still continued to function, but it proved impossible to discover how many.[15] It seems that some ex-FEOs had drifted back into teaching and combined their knowledge of rural development with their teaching role on an ad hoc basis. There may have been others working at various district offices as part of the Ministry of Interior staff. A few still administered the TUFEC establishment in Ubol while waiting to become instructors in rural teachers' in-service training courses. It was clear that at least by 1963 (and almost certainly a great deal earlier) the TUFEC-FEO teams had just quietly melted away as an identifiable field force.

13. Ministry of Education, *Report on the Results of an Enquiry into the Morale and Working Conditions of 27 FEO Teams in Thailand,* January 1959 (from the files, UNESCO Regional Office, Bangkok) (translated from Thai by M. R. Sermsri Kasemsri).

14. Conrad J. Opper, *Comments on the Results of an Enquiry into the Morale and the Working Conditions of 27 FEO Teams in Thailand,* Bangkok, February 1959 (from the files, UNESCO Regional Office, Bangkok).

15. This writer located only one field worker who still continued to operate, Mr. Udet Sookdhis at the village of Warin, Ubol province.

The reasons given in the 1958 inquiry by the FEOs for their generally low morale synthesize much that has already been noted, adding their dissatisfaction with their relations with provincial officialdom. In summary, the main problems as the field workers saw them were as follows:

1. Frustration in contact with other Thai officials in the field because of lack of clearly defined and realistic roles for TUFEC FEOs.
2. Indifference among officials, villagers, and general public relative to the work the FEOs were attempting to do.
3. Not enough status and recognition relative to the villagers or officialdom.
4. A lack of self-confidence on the part of FEOs arising from "deeply felt lack of knowledge and having the wrong knowledge."
5. No follow-up help and supervision by TUFEC.
6. Friction among team members.
7. Some provinces would not pay a per diem to teams.[16]

Specific criticism of professional training was simple and straightforward. The FEOs felt that their training was "vague and abstract and not really relevant to a Thai village" and that they had been confused by the "lack of consensus amongst all the foreign experts."

The breakdown in morale arose not only from factors such as ill-defined roles and nonperceptive training, but also from a basic organizational failure of TUFEC. In rural activity, it had embarked upon a course that required either integration within an existing provincial organizational structure, which in this case could only be the Ministry of Interior, or alternatively, creation of its own autonomous institution. UNESCO never quite saw the issue this way. Their orientation was toward education in the abstract. At all levels in UNESCO the vital issue of deciding what sort of machinery was necessary to transmit activity over area and over time seemed to be something outside the UNESCO purview. Yet without the use of some institutionalized structure, effective and sustained operations are impractical. Argument seems to center on why

16. *Report on the Results of an Enquiry into Morale,* p. 8.

UNESCO, as the sponsoring agency, should not get into the organizational field. It was recognized that "There has been a considerable loss of impetus through lack of firm direction and no adequate machinery has yet been established to provide a central policy for the teams or for their administrative welfare." But the report went on to say that

> The Center has resisted suggestions that it should assume some responsibility here. It is very pleasant to visit teams in the field in a spirit of mild paternalism, but there is a great danger of intrusions upon the responsibilities and problems of an established field force, the normal machinery of government and a short visit is not likely to reveal all the intricacies of difficult situations.[17]

These extracts show an understanding of the problem, but the action suggested is that of an administrator who attempts to sail only in smooth waters. It is not the view of a policy-maker who, having been presented with a problem, attempts to formulate solutions even if it means change.

Students feared that by becoming FEOs they had in fact become orphaned as far as a parent organization was concerned. What was the channel of promotion for a TUFEC worker, and where would promotion lead? Would the young teacher who became an FEO have the same opportunity to become, say, a headmaster as would a fellow teacher who stayed within the ministry's normal school system? In the end, it was this sort of question which led to the mass exodus of FEOs sometime between early 1959 and 1963. Again the lesson seems obvious. So basic an issue as the career prospects of personnel can only be solved, and some assurance given, within the framework of a known and viable institution.

INTERBUREAU COMMUNICATIONS

There are other, wider problems involved in working outside of established institutions, whether indigenous or foreign. If the United Nations has a message—either as simple as a new type of plow frame, or as complex as narcotics control—it has little alter-

17. TUFEC, *Annual Report for 1958*, p. 14.

native other than to work through existing institutions. The problem of simple communications assumes frightening proportions for the United Nations when the magnitude of the task is measured against the size of the United Nations staff involved, its skills, and its concepts.

> There are at least 80,000 fishermen in Thailand alone [commented one Regional Officer]. What am I to do in instructing them in some of the new and relatively simple fishing procedures which, if they wanted to, many could implement tomorrow? Must I go out and instruct every fisherman? And then what about the rest of my Region stretching from Japan to Iraq?

The same commentator went on to say that the task could obviously be done only through activation of government departments and perhaps through the hiring of private firms to undertake specific projects;[18] but he did not feel the task of selling ideas to governments was an expert's job. "I was hired as a fisheries expert and I am not a diplomat or a salesman."[19]

The same sentiments were echoed by FAO officers in the agricultural extension irrigation fields. The regional directors at UNICEF and WHO strongly intimated that this was the major problem that they too faced. The problem might be termed "interbureau communications," thus making it distinct from the planning and coordination of aid activity undertaken at a higher government level, where the issue is one of negotiating over selection and planning of aid projects, and their general structure, not the actual dissemination of information in the field. The problem was recognized by many in the field but no positive steps were ever taken to formulate a method for solution. It seems clear, however, that in general a solution could come only by integrating United Nations operators within Thai institutions or by creating autonomous institutions, with all the very important requirements either course implied.[20]

18. An operation sponsored by FAO in Thailand, and under way in 1963, was the hiring of units of a private German fishing firm complete with equipment to introduce new techniques to Thai fishermen. So far the program is said to be very successful.

19. Interview, Regional Office FAO, Bangkok, July 24, 1963.

20. See Chap. 9.

Perhaps the only way to avoid the issue of interbureau communications was given by the director of UNICEF, commenting on the success of the UNICEF yaws and malaria campaigns:

> One of the reasons why we functioned better was because we not only confined our attack to inanimate things like mosquitoes and viruses but we did not have to employ any quantity of experts. We were mainly concerned in manipulating equipment, and equipment neither talks back to its master or creates all those tensions inherent in people-to-people relationships.[21]

As far as TUFEC and the Pilot Project were concerned, however, people-to-people relationships at all levels were the very basis of their modus operandi. Specifically, relationships with the Thai bureaucracy constituted a vitally important link, and it seems that in TUFEC these relationships were such that the United Nations appeared more as a meddler than as an ally.

There were other, more wide-ranging examples of the problems of establishing viable relationships between the aid agencies, the real decision-making authority in Thailand, and the relevant departments of government. The example offered by Japan's rural development was much quoted within the FAO Bangkok Regional Office as a pattern for agricultural progress elsewhere in Asia. Japan is currently embarking upon another farm-development program with a threefold aim: (1) increased yields per unit area at reduced costs; (2) more nutritious foods for farm family consumption; and (3) stabilized prices and incentives. The overall objective of the Japanese program is to halt the steady drift to the towns on the part of the Japanese farmer.[22] Scrutiny of these aims, however —and especially (1) and (2)—reveals a requirement for action in areas so sensitive that they would affect policy at the highest levels of government as well as specific administration within several departments.

If it were assumed, therefore, that a program with the implications inherent in the Japanese venture was necessary in Thailand, the key factor, after having reduced the issue to specifics, would

---

21. Interview, UNICEF Zone Office, July 26, 1963.
22. Interview, Regional Office, FAO, Bangkok, July 25, 1963.

be detailed liaison between the aid agency and government. In Thailand, for example, the fiscal implications of a parallel to the Japanese program would require the blessing of the Prime Minister, and processing through appropriate government departments. Then, typically, this type of issue would be processed through the Cabinet. There is no evidence, however, that any United Nations agency in Thailand, least of all UNESCO, focused its planning and decision-making in this way. Even the Technical Assistance Board, which is charged with a good deal of program processing with the Thai government, deals with lower levels of the bureaucracy, usually at the level of routine administration rather than dynamic policies or programs.

On the other hand, the absence of perceptive working relationships with the bureaucracy and decision-making levels can sometimes lead not to inaction but to extraordinary action. Recently, by some means not yet clear, one person affiliated with the program of Technical Assistance did get the ear of the Prime Minister. As a result, the Prime Minister endorsed a program for an applied scientific research establishment for Thailand.[23] This organization was based upon an existing Australian establishment and was intended to spur development, mainly in agriculture, through applied research. When the existence of the agreement became known, it was resisted most strongly by FAO. But this resistance was intra-United Nations. At the time of writing the Thai Prime Minister not only was unaware of the scale and strength of opposition but, more importantly, was ignorant of the nature of the argument with which FAO opposed the "establishment of yet another operational Unit" which would "further isolate research from other development services . . . and which would not in any way be geared to meeting basic and well known problems in Thailand."[24] As the issue was explained to this writer, the Prime Minister saw so little of the United Nations that the appearance of a United Nations official presaged an important measure and one which on the surface seemed to have merit. Perhaps responsibility for briefing the Prime Minister lies outside the United Nations, but it

23. Frank G. Nichols, *The Development of Applied Scientific Research in Thailand: Stage One* (*Report No. 1* TAO/TAB, Bangkok, September 1962).

24. Letter from FAO Headquarters, Rome, to the Regional Office for Asia and the Far East, May 22, 1963.

seems that he simply did not know that FAO had been looking at similar problems for many years and had a totally different concept of how to stimulate development.

In a recent study C. P. Snow expressed a view that can be applied to the bureaucratic relationships of the United Nations:

> The politics of a chain of command, of the services, of a bureaucracy, of a large industry, on the surface seem very simple. Just get hold of the man at the top and the order will go down the line. So long as you have collected the boss, you have got nothing else to worry about. That is what people believe who are not used to hierarchies, particularly people who are cynical and unworldly, which is one of my least favourite combinations.

It has already been observed that in Thailand the United Nations had the ear not of the man at the top but of someone much farther down in the hierarchy. As Snow goes on to say:

> To get anything done in any highly articulated organization, you have to carry people at all sorts of levels. It is their decisions, their acquiescence or enthusiasm (above all, the absence of their passive resistance) which are going to decide whether a strategy goes through on time.[25]

Basically, therefore, TUFEC, as well as some of the supporting United Nations agencies in Thailand, faced three important and fundamental problems in their bureaucratic relationships. First, in one important instance they operated outside the line of authority; second, they never really faced up to the issue of either integrating within an existing institution or creating an autonomous institution so that their operations could be perpetuated over time and space; and last, without the capacity to communicate with and influence the working bureaucracy of the nation, general operational effectiveness was diminished. In Chapters 9 and 10 of this study some positive suggestions will be offered concerning the sort of measures necessary to communicate more effectively at various levels in Thailand. One further facet of United Nations relationships with the Thai bureaucracy, however, must be noted.

25. C. P. Snow, *Science and Government* (New York, Mentor Books, 1962), pp. 55–56.

INFORMAL ROLES

Although there might not have been a free flow of communications between United Nations workers and the Thai bureaucracy in a strictly functional sense, the United Nations presence was used within the Thai bureaucracy itself for various informal processes. There were at least four ways in which U.N. personnel served to further activity quite independent of the purposes of the international organization.

The transmission of unpleasant or sensitive messages from a lower to a higher echelon is not an eagerly sought-after task in any bureaucracy, and this is especially so in Thailand. Very often a United Nations official was the carrier of unhappy tidings—frequently, it seems, without ever being aware that he was so used. This process may well have given some much-needed lubrication to the upward passage of information. Furthermore, as was stated by one informant, the lower echelons were often agreeably surprised to find that the reaction from higher officialdom was less explosive than had been imagined. As a result, this particular informant was emboldened to press claims, pleasant or otherwise, long after the United Nations had left, presumably with some increase in the effectiveness of the bureaucratic machine. But with the United Nations present, it was so much easier to have the foreigner present the case, for he would always be received with courtesy and perhaps even at levels beyond those attainable by a Thai.

An embellishment to this informal communications process was the advantage that accrued to a Thai institution in the form of added money from the Thai government. All 17 Thai interviewees who had taken part in the Pilot Project were adamant that as far as their own government's generosity was concerned, the halcyon days were those when the United Nations was in partnership. By Thai standards their budget was lavish compared to fellow institutions and they did not suffer later cuts in annual estimates, an endemic process in the Thai bureaucratic system. Furthermore, any school that had United Nations participation obtained new equipment ahead of everyone else. Indeed one noticeable legacy still evident at two high schools and the one teacher training college at Cha Cheong Sao is that they are better equipped than other Thai provincial schools, even though most of this equipment was purchased by the Thai government.

A further informal role played by the United Nations, of which it was also unaware, was the use of the U.N.'s or a foreign expert's name. Here lack of language capabilities on the part of the foreigner distinctly favored the Thai. It was possible to declare fairly openly to a senior official or to a department that Mr. X from UNESCO needed something, or that the foreign staff had suggested that something should be done, thereby lending weight to an argument and avoiding identification with something that might not be too well received by higher authority.

Perhaps the most important informal function concerned the Fellowship Program. "TUFEC is too often considered as a stepping stone toward a Fellowship abroad and the resulting better job . . . but not a job with TUFEC."[26] To many Thai students of slender means, TUFEC's Pilot Project was a heaven-sent opportunity to obtain overseas training. An important adjunct was that in these projects, especially at TUFEC, one could learn English, a necessary prerequisite for most overseas training. That the returning Thai did not go back to work in TUFEC, or stay very long if he did, has already been noted.

It might also be observed that the fellowships offered by UNESCO were unique in that the students involved were in general from rural areas and under normal circumstances could hardly have expected to compete with the city Thai whose opportunities were so much greater. (If the United Nations or any other body wished to spread fellowship benefits more widely through all strata of Thai society rather than compounding the privileges of the privileged as at present, then a small rural seminar on English and some other basic associated subjects might be one way of doing this, as well as capitalizing on perhaps unrealized TUFEC experience.)

These informal roles assigned to the United Nations were in no sense sinister. Most bureaucratic structures develop them, and they are sometimes more important than formal and approved practices. Apparently the utilization of informal roles was more pro-

---

26. Jan Kinket, *Annual Report on Audio Visual Aid Section,* Ubol, December 1957 (from the files, UNESCO Headquarters, Paris).

nounced at the Pilot Project, where there was integration, as opposed to TUFEC, which was not so close to the bureaucracy generally.

Summary

The United Nations agencies did recognize the importance of relations with the Thai bureaucracy; but communications between Thai and foreign enterprises were still poor. The situation was, of course, unique. In Southeast Asia indigenous bureaucracies have generally been relegated to an inferior role in their relations with the "advanced" nations operating within their territories, even in noncolonial Thailand. But now the relationship attempted was a partnership. Where partners operate on a seemingly equal basis, each should be conscious of a modus operandi which is common to both and accepted by both. This was not achieved, and the Thai bureaucracy, while perhaps not falling entirely into the category of rival, certainly was not the ally that the United Nations agencies so badly needed.

The issue of the relationship of the United Nations in Thailand with the indigenous government and bureaucracy also raises another factor of more general concern to foreign aid projects generally. Foreign aid *is* interference by alien personnel with alien methods in the internal operations of a recipient nation. At the highest policy levels there may be agreement between donor and recipient about general lines of approach. At the working level, however, the situation changes. Some authority is needed to buttress even the most benign methods of persuasion. The more the alien donor strives for efficiency the more authority he must seek and impose. There is no alternative to this process other than to place entire responsibility upon the indigenes themselves to find and establish their own modus operandi. Perhaps this can be achieved by depersonalized assistance such as loans, equipment, or even training abroad for selected indigenous personnel. But when the donor provides personalized aid, with foreign experts and supervisors in the field, issues of interference must arise.

7

ACHIEVEMENT

It is difficult to assess the achievement of the United Nations field programs in Thailand. Purely quantitative data may accurately describe achievement when it is restricted to the number of cases of yaws treated and cured, the decrease in death rate from malaria, or the numbers of buffalo injected against rinderpest. Too often, however, the number of experts sent to a foreign country or, more especially, the amount of money spent or allocated tends to be taken as a measure of achievement; and the United Nations is by no means the only offender. The issue here was further complicated in that the United Nations did not have a means of evaluating its own projects in Thailand. A response to a request from Paris that "an accounting as it were, of Cha Cheong Sao, be made,"[1] noted that:

> One of our greatest difficulties was in fact identification of significant developments over a period of seven years wherein no less than 26 experts have come and gone and there was no "built in" machinery for continuous collection of records, of different experiences and continuous evaluation of new principles and methods as applied to the project's work.[2]

A year later, when the Pilot Project had ended, a further comment was that "it is normal for archaeologists or antiquarians to have to work with the minimum of data: but a project less than

1. Letter from Director of Education, UNESCO Headquarters, Paris, to Chief of Mission, Regional Office, Bangkok, April 16, 1958 (from the files, UNESCO Headquarters, Paris).
2. Letter from the Chief of Mission, UNESCO Regional Office, Bangkok, to UNESCO Headquarters, Paris, April 28, 1958 (from the files, UNESCO Regional Office, Bangkok).

ten years old should be better furnished with records."[3] The fact is that there was no evaluation of achievement at Cha Cheong Sao by the United Nations. The Thai Ministry of Education did undertake a survey,[4] but this was not so much an evaluation of achievement as an attempt to rectify failings midway through the organization's life.

At TUFEC the need for evaluation was again recognized but no overall assessment was made; there were some partial surveys. One study, coming at the end of United Nations participation in TUFEC, was detailed and valuable, revealing not only how little impact TUFEC had had but how little it knew about the village milieu in which it had been active for nearly nine years.[5] As is so often the case, this survey showed the need for more surveys. TUFEC did publish one small pamphlet to mark its closing ceremonies, but statements by the Thai staff in this document neither gave comfort to TUFEC nor specific examples of how its achievement might be evaluated.[6]

A great deal of reliance in assessing achievement must therefore be placed upon the writer's observations and his extensive contacts with Thai personnel and documents and with the United Nations agencies involved. While this is far from satisfactory, the failure of the United Nations to achieve very much does greatly simplify the task.

ACHIEVEMENT AT THE PILOT PROJECT

Achievement at the Pilot Project in the formal sense, relative to the stated aims of the enterprise, was to all intents negligible. The objectives of establishing a "prototype school system" from pre-primary grades to teacher training was not attained. Neither was it possible to discern achievement of other objectives such as "changes in school organization," "improved methods of teach-

3. Letter from the Chief of Mission, UNESCO Regional Office, Bangkok, to UNESCO Headquarters, Paris, November 5, 1959 (from the files, UNESCO Regional Office, Bangkok).

4. *Report of Evaluation Committee,* August 1957.

5. Bertholet.

6. TUFEC, *Eight Years of Cooperation Between* UNESCO *and Thailand* (Bangkok, Tung Mahamek Technical School Press, 1962) (in Thai).

ing," or demonstration of "responsibility of schools for improvement of the life of all people in the community." As a corollary
there could be no formal diffusion of any model system throughout
the kingdom, another stated objective. There were however some
smaller scale achievements, which should not be ignored for at
least two reasons. Primarily, the rather grim verdict of failure is far
too precise a term to use in operations of this sort. Secondly, there
is always a tendency for complex operations involving human be-
ings to have effects that were not intended or foreseen, and these
need not always be adverse. Some readily discernible positive returns arising out of the Pilot Project illustrate the point.

There is consensus among all the Thai participants in the Pilot
Project that the United Nations helped appreciably in four ways
to benefit Thai education. The first concerned a very simple classroom technique: participation in lesson discussion by pupils. It was
firmly held by the more senior Thai educators that, notwithstand-
ing the obvious value of classroom discussion as an educational
practice, it was not appropriate for Thailand. It was alleged that
Thai children simply would not participate. The practice was
frowned upon and was not an accepted educational technique
anywhere in the nation. With reinforcement by the United Nations
experts, Thai teachers at the Pilot Project broke with tradition,
brought their pupils into the discussion, and were amazed by the
results. It seems that Thai children were not too different from
children elsewhere—they enjoyed being heard.

It was also freely acknowledged that classroom layout and curriculum organization changed under the impulse of the foreign
experts. Here was an operation not requiring language skill, which
did not interfere with any particular habit or tradition, and which
was within local resources. These practices, although a relatively
minor achievement for a large foreign operation, were linked with
the substantially greater achievement of in-service training for
teachers. Indeed it was through this training that the new classroom practices were transmitted beyond Cha Cheong Sao.

The idea of in-service training was not part of the United
Nations program but was a concept held by many Thai educators,
who had seen the system working abroad and realized that this was
a cheap way of transmitting new methods to less experienced educators. At Cha Cheong Sao a large dormitory was erected complete

with social and classroom facilities, and rural teachers were brought in for short courses. As much an informal use of the United Nations presence by the local Thai teachers as anything else, the idea was accepted by the United Nations and given strong support. In-service training is still in use and is spreading to other areas in the kingdom with better developed school systems, which in turn can transmit ideas to less developed areas with practical results.

The last achievement was the impetus that the United Nations presence gave toward greater autonomy for provincial and district school systems. Compared with many countries, Thailand's educational system is still highly centralized. Cha Cheong Sao, however, is currently a notable exception to the general pattern. This autonomy did not arise from a specific effort by the United Nations. To have entered into such a sensitive area would have been impolitic for the international body, but its presence allowed the local teachers to take action which they could justify on the grounds that it was what the United Nations wanted, even though a certain amount of license was taken with United Nations aims. It is still too early to say whether the autonomy accorded Cha Cheong Sao education will spread, or will be curbed, but it was a change that could hardly have occurred without something like the United Nations presence.

In addition to the four more or less procedural changes noted, the efforts of particular individuals made notable contributions to the aid processes. The Thai Ministry of Education's evaluation report singled out the field of primary education extension as the one purely educational area where some excellent work had been done and a valuable influence exerted upon Thai teaching practice. This particular example was the work of a single individual who, as it happened, was not connected with the United Nations but was a United States Point Four employee. After five years at Cha Cheong Sao she became identified to such a degree with the Thai community and Thai education that today something of a legend surrounds her. While individual contributions of this magnitude were rare, they had an extraordinary impact, which colored local attitudes toward the entire operation.

Ultimately, the real measure of the Pilot Project's success should be judged according to what the Thai government feels remains to be done. It has already been observed that USOM is cooperating in a

General Educational Development Program, the objectives of which are in substance not too different from those of the Pilot Project, though methods may vary slightly. Similarly, it has been noted that in 1960 Thailand accepted the concept of providing seven years of education for all children in place of the current four years. This, in effect, seems to indicate that the situation is not much better than when the Pilot Project started, or indeed than 1921, when the first Thai education act espoused similar ends. And what of attainment of the real ends of the Pilot Project, the introduction of new educational techniques, theories, and organizational reforms? The final assessment of United Nations achievement and of the formidable task that remains was stated as follows:

> We Thai have difficulty in seeing our own problems not only in education but in many other fields as well. In Thai society everything overlaps, we do not have clear divisions in religion, in politics, in social status or even as a result of the great economic differences that exist. We see things only as shadows in the water. Then along came UNESCO who also did not see things very clearly. To them education was something between a theory and a mystique. It all had so little to do with our real problems. The problem was, and still is, essentially one of materials not theory. We required and still do for our educational development, money, construction, organization and a massive teacher training program. It was only when our tremendous shortfalls in these areas were reduced that we could talk about progress and achievement. But neither the United Nations nor we Thai would quite face up to this issue. We both hoped that there was some other, almost magical way of solving the problem.[7]

ACHIEVEMENT AT TUFEC

In TUFEC it becomes even more difficult to assess achievement in terms of the stated goals. One objective, for example, was to train field workers. This was done. Four hundred and twenty-six persons divided into 71 teams were trained and deployed, one team per province. Some educational materials were published but they

7. Interview at the Ministry of Education, August 11, 1963.

received a limited distribution.[8] As for TUFEC's further aim—
"studying the social and economic conditions of the people . . . and
the solutions that Fundamental Education could bring"—there is
an almost complete absence of any records indicating achievement.
TUFEC tried to assess the results of some of its efforts in a document
included in the pamphlet covering its closing ceremonies.[9] This
survey (see Appendix VI) covers only the villages of the laboratory
area, just a tiny fraction of rural Thailand. Scanning this list with
a generous rather than a critical eye, we notice that projects legitimately accredited to TUFEC are exceedingly small for eight years of
international effort. Such innovations, for example, as the spread
of bus services can hardly be counted, as the pattern is the same
throughout the nation.[10] Similarly, assigning to TUFEC sponsorship such things as use of cosmetics, newspaper reading, listening
to the radio, use of insecticides and medicines, and the greater
urge for children's education are all manifestly false. These are
national trends, and appear all over the kingdom, in areas where
TUFEC is completely unknown. In like manner, the claim that
TUFEC has stimulated the growth of cash crops evokes incredulity.
The great increase in cash crops and in crop diversity in Thailand
has been something of a phenomenon well beyond either the purview of TUFEC or the scale of its operations.[11] When critical analysis is made of TUFEC's own assessment of its achievement, all that
is left are the statistics on wells, latrines, and the like. Even for this
modest list TUFEC was not solely responsible. At the Center hand-
over ceremonies the Governor of Ubol province noted:

> I can assure you of the great changes in Ubol within this dec-
> ade but these derive from many factors . . . Ubol has been
> blessed with many kinds of development projects, such as the
> Rural Health Development Project, the Community Develop-

8. This program was planned as a series of short simple pamphlets in
Thai (The Bamboo Series) dealing with such basic issues as health, agriculture,
and so on. Ten separate issues were made. The criticism leveled against the
series was their lack of originality.

9. TUFEC, *Eight Years of Cooperation*, pp. 45–50.

10. Between 1954 and 1960, for example, motor registrations in the kingdom
increased from 52,361 to 129,604, a rise of approximately 145 per cent. Data
supplied by the Ministry of Transport, Bangkok.

11. See pp. 26–27.

ment Projects [Thai Government], the Project for Improvement of Nutrition in Rural Areas, the Rural Education Development Project for Higher Education.[12]

Perhaps the only person who was not bewildered by it all was the peasant, who, at least during the summer of 1963, seemed to be singularly unimpressed. After a two-year boom in jute prices, he was anxious about a possible slump in the market, and this seemed a good enough reason for his apparent disinterest in the little schemes that those outside his circle had been trying to weave about him.

The major achievement of TUFEC was the creation of a training center and its associated training pattern. Here the supreme accolade would have been acceptance into the national community development program. That did not happen—by and large because of UNESCO's failure to align itself with the right provincial authority, though some of the responsibility must be borne by the inflexibility of the Thai bureaucratic structure, where there was reluctance to make the interdepartmental adjustments necessary to give TUFEC a proper bureaucratic and functional home within the only power in the provinces, the Ministry of Interior.

The possibility that one major asset arose from both projects must be considered. The concluding remark of a commentator who had had an intimate and lengthy association with TUFEC in a senior position was: "Perhaps we have learned that there are not so many new ideas in Fundamental Education and Community Development after all."[13] This was another way of saying that skills and techniques brought by foreign experts provided no easy solution to the development problem, and that if there was to be development it would have to be by Thai efforts. When I suggested that she might at least have been persuaded to accept one of the most quoted United Nations statements—that a primary objective "is to help people to help themselves"—my informant admitted that this indeed might have been what she had really gained from her TUFEC experience. If her feeling was widespread, and there is some evidence that it was, this was an important gain. At times one could feel reaffirmation of an old Thai proverb which, freely trans-

12. TUFEC, *Eight Years of Cooperation,* p. 81.
13. Ibid., p. 23.

lated, says "one must be the mainstay of oneself."[14] The capacity of the Thai peasant to respond on his own initiative to new market opportunities is impressive, and the extraordinary spread of upland crops already noted was a case in point. One is sorely tempted to suggest that the whole spectrum of bureaucratic and international development programs was incidental to the real peasant interest and yearning. With assured and reasonably profitable new markets, the peasant might well have been able to take care of himself.

At the Pilot Project 22 Thai were given fellowships for overseas study. Some 67 persons were given fellowships under TUFEC auspices. It has become common in UNESCO writing to portray the fellowship program, in retrospect, as the single most significant achievement in Thailand. This may be so, but doubts can also be raised. Surely if overseas training was UNESCO's objective, then to sponsor it through TUFEC and the Pilot Project was a cumbersome, costly, and unnecessary procedure.

Fellowships represented a positive gain to individual Thai and presumably to the nation. It is especially important to note that fellowships, theoretically, allow the indigenous recipient to interpret the foreign skill in the local dynamic, something a foreign expert can rarely if ever accomplish. Here, in essence, is the difference between outside intrusion and indigenous determination of objectives, with local development of harmonious ways of operating. Accepting this notion, one is then moved to ask: if fellowships are the real contribution, could not even more have been granted if resources expended on the not too successful TUFEC and Pilot Projects had instead been used for fellowships? For this study, however, the point is that success in what was considered a minor activity, the fellowship program, does not mitigate the lack of success in primary objectives.

The drift of fellowship-trained personnel to Bangkok and away from the projects was a further problem. There was little UNESCO could do except ruminate upon the issue in its reports. Some practi-

14. During residence at TUFEC, July 4 through July 16, 1963.

cal steps might have been found of gaining a better return for the projects from the fellowship program. Making fellowship training conditional on a period of post-training service with the projects was one possibility, allowing for the training of personnel to fit specific project jobs.[15] Another possibility might have been the training of Thai overseas followed by their employment within their own country as United Nations officials. All this, however, bespeaks a long-term United Nations involvement, and that was not in the plan.

Summary

That neither the Pilot Project nor TUFEC fully achieved their stated objectives seems to be true, but it is incorrect to say that they failed completely. Some incidental and unplanned legacies were left behind, although their influence is hard to assess. Both TUFEC and the Pilot Project, with all their supporting United Nations agencies, conducted operations of appreciable dimensions. Relative to the overall United Nations effort they may seem small, but the work undertaken was important, because the idea of transmitting technologically advanced techniques to an underdeveloped society, more or less as a free will offering, was nearly unprecedented. Yet it is probable that a need for transference of skills and ideas to developing sectors of the world will continue for as far ahead as most enterprising persons can contemplate. Instead of making a final verdict, it seems better to accept the United Nations achievement as indeterminate and proceed to evaluate and classify some of those factors which, judged against the Thai case, might lead to improved performance in this unique task of consciously transmitting conceptions and methods from one culture to another.

15. When the issue was put to personnel at TUFEC, the reply was that this was always understood to be the idea of the fellowship program, but that in practice it was completely impossible because TUFEC's structure was constantly changing and no one was sure of long term objectives or methods. During residence at TUFEC July 4 through July 16, 1963.

8

THREE COMPARABLE OPERATIONS

A comparison, as yet not attempted, between United Nations aid projects and other bilateral national programs at government level would reveal very little; where comparisons are restricted to functional activity, there are only insignificant differences between one foreign participant and another. No particular national government project or international affiliation of governments confers special communication skills. In contradiction to the claims and counterclaims that one nation or international organization can do a better job than another, all face the same problems and show similar failings at the actual transmittal level. The basic involvement is one of technological, social, and cultural confrontation that cannot be negated by the waving of particular national or international banners.

In order to highlight certain aspects involved in the task of transferring ideas and skills from one society to another, we shall move away from the governmental plane and consider some private operations. The areas of investigation are three private firms engaged in the automobile trade, a special technical training institute, and the secular activity of Christian missions. Particular emphasis will be given to the mission activity, because the scale of its educational and medical endeavor dwarfs any like operation conducted in Thailand by any other body.

SKILL TRANSFERENCE IN THE AUTOMOBILE INDUSTRY

All automobiles in Thailand are imported from abroad—that is, from Europe, the United States, or Japan. The extraordinary increase in motor vehicles in Thailand over the past decade has already been noted.[1] Along with the increase has come a demand

1. See p. 131.

for skills not previously possessed by the Thai, and this demand has arisen within a fairly short period of time. The policy of all major automobile retailers in Thailand has been to train Thai mechanics to service their products. The training has been achieved partly by sending Thai abroad to parent factories but mainly by on-the-job training in Bangkok, supervised by foreign experts sent to the kingdom by the home firm. This practice has involved firms in a relationship not too different from that of Thai organizations with the United Nations and other unilateral aid projects. In one sense, however, the task of the automobile industry was simplified—it was not involved in national policies. Neither were the firms trammeled to the same degree by the complexities of working with government and bureaucracy. In running their operations they were very much their own masters, relatively unfettered by one-year contracts, diverse and often unclear policies, or unproven theories.

When a foreign instructor was brought into a firm, he was inducted into an institution that was a going concern, with practices already successful elsewhere in the world, with clear and distinct aims and purposes, and with experienced managers. The primary issue, therefore, was simply that of transferring skills and these were mainly technical.

In Bangkok I approached three firms whose executives were well known to me. One managing director was a Westerner with 30 years' experience in the Middle East and Asia. Another manager was a Chinese holding Thai citizenship, with 25 years of retailing and servicing industrial equipment in Asia. The third executive was a Thai who had lived in Europe and England as a young man, had moved in all strata of Thai society, from village to court, had experienced daring adventures as a British clandestine agent in World War II, and had been in the automobile trade for the past ten years. The three firms over the past decade or so had watched over the activities of four, seven, and nine foreign experts respectively, sent out to Thailand by parent companies. The responses of these informants showed a close similarity to the experience of the United Nations.

The executives were not particularly concerned with the sociological aspects of their jobs. Their concern was merely to teach Thai to service clients' vehicles in order to meet the high level of competition. Nevertheless, the sociological problem kept intruding, often disrupting plans. It was not a technical problem, for the expertise of the foreign instructor was never in question. Neither could bureaucratic controls, government apathy, local inefficiencies, lack of resources, poor management and direction, or the uniqueness of the technical aspects of the job be held responsible. It was the clash of one set of cultural habits with another that caused such trouble as ensued. As the managers saw it, the only way to reduce the problem was to minimize contact, as is done when foreign personnel are employed in high positions of management, or in relatively impersonal posts such as accounting or supervising machinery.

In discussing the performance of foreign personnel with the writer, the automobile managers made the following summarized observations:

> *Expertise.* The expertise of the foreign instructors was always good. No instructor trained by the parent firm ever failed for the lack of skills. The only criticism leveled against the experts was that sometimes they were too theoretical and could not "make do" with the more primitive equipment in Thailand.
>
> *Role Comprehension.* There was little difficulty in this regard. All instructors who had been trained by the parent firm understood their roles adequately, and there was little conflict with local management.
>
> *Language.* In a purely functional sense, language was not a real problem. The task was technical, and communication could be made adequately through demonstration. Furthermore, procedures were completely standardized and not open to varying interpretations.
>
> *"Environmental Adjustment."* Failure to adjust to general living and working conditions was high on the list as a cause of failure of instructors. This factor was especially critical during the first six months to a year. By then an instructor had either adjusted or been sent home. Typical factors inhibiting adjustment were: poor living conditions, as instructors were not paid very well while most other foreigners were (in a community where foreigners were few and easily identifiable,

this led to obvious loss of status); finding somewhere to have a non-indigenous lunch, although this problem has by now disappeared because of massive proliferation of Western-style restaurants; adjustment to the Thai disregard for time; health problems; and, the two most important issues of all, difficulties of families in adjusting and the reluctance of the foreign instructor to accept Thai as equals, not only on the job but also in the community at large.

"Evoking a Natural Response." Unless an instructor could evoke some sort of empathy from his students, he had to go home. In extreme cases Thai workmen approached higher executives and asked for the removal of instructors who were alleged to have, in the Thai view, such characteristics as "rudeness," "forcing Thai to stand at benches instead of squatting over their work on the floor," "shouting at people," "not understanding us," and having "a hot heart."[2] In two cases instructors were removed.

"Sympathy and Understanding." Again it seems that this rather nebulous quality was part of a search for empathy on the part of the foreigners involved. In the minds of the informants, "sympathy and understanding" were required relative to such issues as the intensely personalized relations that existed within a small factory; the avoidance of personal affronts;[3] giving the Thai credit where due rather than thinking them stupid because they did not agree with or perhaps understand the instructor; being able to mix with Thai on a personal level rather than as depersonalized instructors, and, above all, having a "cool heart."[4]

Tenure. The great healer and teacher seems to have been time on the job. In time, those who thought Thai food unbearable learned to take their lunch with the workers—a

2. To have a "hot heart" is to show a lack of equanimity, to show aggressiveness and ill temper.

3. As an example of this, one senior Thai educator who had worked at TUFEC recounted how, when interpreting a lesson for a young United Nations expert, he was passed an oily part of a machine to hold during a demonstration. Only the young foreign expert remained unmortified.

4. A "cool heart" denotes urbanity and calmness, especially when things are not going too well, perhaps best expressed if one could combine the two French terms, *sangfroid* and *savoir-faire*.

fifteen-cent bowl of noodles, meat, and vegetables or ten cents' worth of fried rice and chicken wrapped in a banana leaf. In time there could be an adjustment by most foreigners to most problems, indicating that the issue was basically acculturation. How much time was involved? Nobody was quite sure, but probably "several years."

Thus, even in the seemingly straightforward process of conducting a business, problems arose similar to those examined in the United Nations programs, especially when highly personalized relationships were involved. If anything can be learned from this brief look at the business community, it is that even if organizational problems are solved and foreign experts understand their roles, and even if functions are of a straightforward technical kind and are readily transmittable, there is still a cultural gap to be bridged. This gap becomes more formidable when one deals with ordinary folk rather than with those who have been exposed to a cultural background extending beyond local confines.

THE GERMAN JUNIOR TECHNICAL INSTITUTE

Government and international aid processes cannot often be reduced to the simplicity of straightforward business operations. In many instances the difficulties of institution-building at national levels or integration within existing national institutions will remain, and the operations themselves will encompass greater complexity of purpose and action and more widespread involvement. A German Junior Technical Institute, however, was one project which came close to the objective of building a national institution. It shows promise of success in its role and is therefore worthy of study.

In 1959 the German government established a technical training school in Thailand, working within the Ministry of Education. The purpose of the school was to train Thai youth in engineering skills to about the same level as would be held by a German technician who had undertaken apprenticeship in the engineering trade.

The school is small with a total student body of 250 boys who undertake either a three-year or five-year course. The annual output is about fifty boys, and so far the unofficial policy has been to assume responsibility for placing all graduates in employment with foreign firms or the Thai government. The school has stated unequivocally that it would never train more students than it was certain Thai industry could absorb.[5]

The equipment in the school is outstanding. The private German firms supplying it obtain special taxation exemptions from the German government, and the USOM Vocational Training Officer stated categorically that such an investment in training machinery would be "too expensive for the United States government to emulate in an aid mission."[6] The enterprise is German-controlled, and all instruction until very recently was given solely by Germans. At the present time some Thai educators are being employed as instructors in aspects of theory. The ultimate plan is that the school will become solely Thai; but, as was stated quite definitely by German teachers, there was no hurry about this changeover. Germans were prepared to stay as long as necessary, "even into the next generation if we are needed and wanted."[7]

Initially there was some difficulty in encouraging pupils to attend. In 1962, however, after three years of operation, some 1,000 applicants competed for 100 places. The Thai government has now asked the German government to duplicate the entire school at Khon Kaen, a provincial town in the northeast plateau, which is also to be the locale for the new Khon Kaen Institute of Technology.

By whatever yardstick is used, the German school is an extraordinarily smooth-running, efficient venture. It has already made its mark in the area that matters most—that is, it now has an ex-student body actually operating within Thai industry, rather than a disillusioned coterie of misemployed smarting under unfulfilled promises. To date relations with the Thai government and the Ministry of Education seem good, in that the school has been accorded the unusual honor of being asked to expand its activity.

The school has had its problems, of course, most of them con-

5. Interview at the Thai German Technical Institute, Bangson, in Bangkok, August 7, 1963.
6. Interview at USOM, Bangkok, June 20, 1963.
7. Interview at Thai German Technical Institute.

nected with German personnel. The first director was sent home because "he could not get along with the Thai." Unfortunate as this may have been, such a condition is far from uncommon, and the real test is whether such poor relations can be detected by the foreign authority and appropriate action taken. The school also found it difficult to persuade its German instructors with families to stay for more than two years because a German language school for their children was not available in Bangkok.

The biggest single problem has been language, and the current director felt strongly that in the future all instructors should take one year of language training before coming to Thailand. By and large, the language problem was more complicated than in the United Nations, since English was the school's only lingua franca. Book translation, for example, had to be in a German-English-Thai cycle. In general, however, it seemed that these more or less unavoidable stresses were fairly easily absorbed by the school, and there was certainly no impression that operations were being hampered in any appreciable degree. In particular it was noticeable that the turnover of instructors had small effect on the school program.

This seemingly smooth operation did not just happen. The German school is an autonomous institution with a modus operandi that is relatively stable and well known to all participants. The critical element is that the operation is based upon the use of machines that remain essentially unchanged, give continuity relative to operations, and demand certain fixed levels of knowledge which the German instructors have in full measure. Allied with this, institutional autonomy gives a skilled management not only day-to-day control over operations and personnel but also control over policy and the maintenance of continuity in policy and policy-making. The school does not betray that readily observable unsureness of where it is going, so marked in TUFEC. Neither does the "change of jockey" give rise to changes of direction in this machine-dominated operation. Equally striking is the absence of bureaucratic control and interference. The local German executives seem to have the autonomy normally associated with, say, a private business or private college in the United States. This was evident in the freedom, speed, and ease with which programs were adjusted to meet indigenous needs.

Above all, the operation of the school as a whole is related to the present needs of the Thai economy. It does not exceed demands or even seek at this time to stimulate them but merely to satisfy them, and perhaps provide concepts that might be emulated. A highly particularistic operation, it is also an exceedingly simple one not only in what it does in the Thai milieu but also in how it goes about its daily tasks. Its activity is not cluttered with theories of social and cultural change.

The German school is an example of autonomous institution-building within the Thai bureaucratic structure, is concerned with simple technical operations and is based upon the machine. A legitimate question, however, is how far can operations of this type be extended. At what stage, for example, does the relatively simple machine-dominated operation have to confront indigenous cultural or economic values which may conflict, or how far can an alien institution, even when highly successful, intrude into indigenous structures? The director of the school himself expressed doubts as to how far operations could expand. A very large-scale, effective, autonomous German operation (which, incidentally, is not contemplated) could hardly be assimilated by Thailand without undue German influence being applied at many levels, especially on the level of industrial development. On the other hand, small autonomous operations tend to exert small influence beyond their own fairly limited spheres. The director commented that already his small school "was like an alien island" within the Thai educational structure, and he was unsure if the school's influence extended very far beyond its annual output of pupils. If it were to extend its influence, at some time it would have to embark on a process of diffusion, like the original goal of the Pilot Project at Cha Cheong Sao. But the idea of German skills being integrated within the Thai educational structure en masse seemed to appall all six specialists at the German school. They felt there was insufficient demand for engineering capabilities in Thailand to prompt major growth, although they conceded that in a generation or two things might change. And would the output of the German school help bring these changes about? This "is something that is beyond the purview of this generation." To the German staff at the Institute the idea of creating a pilot project for an alien type of education and diffusing it over the entire educational system of the kingdom—all within, say, a period of ten years—seemed hardly worthy of discussion.

Insofar as one relatively small operation can be taken as an example, the German Institute highlights two important points. It illustrates the assets of institution-building but also the weaknesses of an alien enterprise which, no matter how successfully it functions, is limited in how far it can extend its operations and influence. At some stage the nation itself must pick up the ball and run.

Thus we return to the original concept of UNESCO, and indeed the United Nations at large, that the "task is to help people to help themselves." Does this mean that the quest must be continued for those properties that act as catalysts in transferring ideas from one culture to another, and are there distinct limitations to the content that can be transferred, especially over short periods of time? In other words, is the so-called "revolution of rising expectations" appreciably less universal, less demanding, less particular, and less prepared to pay the price to achieve material ends than is realized by those in the West who show so much concern?

MISSIONS AND MISSIONARIES

In all the United Nations literature devoted to their operations in Thailand, no reference was ever found to the secular work of the Christian missions in the kingdom. Yet the missions manage the largest nongovernmental educational enterprise in the country and provide substantial medical services. They have also conducted agricultural extension work. Their great contribution, however, has been in the field of education, that is, in the same area as the UNESCO-sponsored projects. The scale of the missions' educational enterprise is given in Table 3.

The Ecumenical Mission movement is supported by a combination of Protestant churches, principally the Presbyterian, Church of Christ, and Baptist denominations. Other Protestant faiths are also represented in Thailand. Some, like the Seventh Day Adventist and Overseas Missionary Fellowship, conduct large-scale secular activity, especially as regards medicine. There are many smaller denominations operating schools on an ad hoc basis. The schools listed in the table, which covers the vast preponder-

TABLE 3. EDUCATIONAL ACTIVITY OF CHRISTIAN
MISSIONS IN THAILAND

Mission	No. of Schools	Enrollment
Ecumenical Mission	36	21,493
Catholic	142	75,133
Total	178	96,626

Sources: Catholic Directory (Bangkok, Thai Publications Press, 1963), pp. E1–E56; "Report of Major Program Agencies to 173rd General Assembly of the United Presbyterian Church," Buffalo, New York, May 1961; and files of the Commission on the Ecumenical Mission and Relations of the United Presbyterian Church, Bangkok.

ance of Christian mission activity, are incorporated within the normal Thai educational pattern and recognized by the Ministry of Education. The range is from elementary or grade schools through high schools and special preparatory schools for students proceeding to a university. The Catholic Mission also operates a technical training school, with an enrollment of approximately 250 students.

Although there are numerous other private schools in Thailand,[8] the missions provide for approximately 4 per cent of the public and private school population. It is estimated, however, that they accommodate approximately 30 per cent of the student population at the high school level and above.

In the field of medicine the missions have provided ten major hospitals, approximately 10 per cent of the national total. The mission hospitals are recognized as leaders in the fields of nursing and nurses' training, hospital organization, and hygiene.

Virtually every Western country has sent missionaries to Thailand. Americans have predominated in the Protestant missions, while the Catholic missions have tended to be French-oriented.

8. There are approximately 1,800 private schools in Thailand. Mission schools, therefore, are only 10 per cent of this total. Islamic schools form 6 per cent, Chinese schools 21 per cent, and private Thai schools the remainder. Many of the Thai schools, however, are very small. Overall about a third of all children attending private schools attend mission schools.

Mission activity overall has been at least as international in its personnel as has the United Nations.

Catholic missionaries were in Thailand as early as 1555, but at this time they were not especially concerned with secular issues such as education and medicine. It was not until 1851 that the first mission school was opened, by the wife of the first United States Consul, Dr. Stephen Matoon; other schools soon followed. During the latter part of the nineteenth century, an influx of American medical missionaries established not only the first hospitals but the very concept of modern medical services. By the turn of the century mission hospitals and schools were preeminent in effort and quality. The missions themselves have acknowledged that in this decade "the mission schools have ceased to be unique in their excellence,"[9] and to a lesser degree this is also true for mission medical facilities. But the accolade for medical and educational pilot projects in Thailand must be awarded to these early mission enterprises.

The avowed aim of these secular activities was, of course, to promote spiritual ends. Here success was singularly lacking. In 1957 only .36 per cent of the total population of Thailand was listed as Christian and this total included non-Thai groups like hill tribes, Vietnamese refugees, and Chinese nationals. Perhaps it is lack of spiritual success, and the consequent absence of a threat to Thai lifeways, that has made the secular activity of the missions so acceptable. Nevertheless, the missions' primary objective did generate suspicion and must be considered a hindrance rather than a help in promoting secular activity. This was especially true of some of the smaller Christian sects which attempted to evangelize among the Thai, meeting considerable opposition that tended to be transferred to missions generally.[10] Overall, however, the Thai ability to resist Christianizing did cause the major missions to reexamine their approach, with important consequences for their methods of promoting nonreligious efforts.

9. W. G. Sinclair, "Integration of a Mission School System in Thailand" (unpublished M.A. thesis, Cornell University, 1950), p. 48.

10. For the opinion of one Thai commentator, which could be repeated in purport though not in sensitivity elsewhere in the kingdom, see Prajuab Tirabutana, *A Simple One: The Story of a Siamese Girlhood* (Ithaca, New York, Cornell University Data Paper, No. 30, 1958), pp. 20–25, 34–38.

There are differences in approach between Roman Catholic and Protestant missions. Catholics regarded their hospitals and schools as devices for bringing Thai into direct contact with the Church and for direct application of Christian teaching. An obvious corollary was that the better the school, the greater its propagandizing properties. While this view may have promoted the development of good schools and efficient hospitals, it did not have the intended end: the secular institutions prospered, religion did not. One of the most experienced of the Catholic missionaries in Thailand commented that Catholic schools are so good and so widely accepted in Thailand that the Church could double the size of its school system tomorrow and have the Thai authorities accept the increase with gratitude.[11] But even if it had the resources, the Church would be reluctant to do this because of the tiny returns from efforts to date.

Neither can the Church withdraw from education. In Bangkok, for example, three Catholic schools cater to approximately 6,000 boys and girls who come from Thailand's elite families. Royalty, the aristocracy, the military and political elite, all have their children educated at these schools as a matter of course, never fearing the religious consequences. In a sense, Bangkok without Mater Dei Girls School, Assumption College, and St. Joseph's would be like England without Eton and Harrow. Not only the scale but the excellence of Catholic educational activity makes it important to Thailand.

The Protestant missions rationalized their secular activity in a slightly different way. Realizing also that direct proselytizing was not paying dividends, the major Protestant groups settled down for a long pull. The directive of the Presbyterian Mission to Thailand was rewritten in 1910 with the aim to "establish self-governing, self-supporting and self-propagating national churches in Thailand," and here "churches" included schools, hospitals, and all secular activity "for the purpose of making Christian witness."[12] According to the current director of the Ecumenican Mission, the idea of propagating Christianity through "bearing Christian witness" still holds good, and is in fact the only sensible

11. Interview with priests of Society of Jesus, Xavier Hall, Bangkok, June 15, 1963.
12. Sinclair, p. 122.

method of bringing the Christian concept to the Thai.[13] As a practical issue, "bearing witness" not only meant the building of successful educational, medical, and other secular institutions but also was a caution to the missionary against expectation of attaining results within a humanly prescribed time schedule. Protestant missions, like their Catholic counterparts, were there to stay and to build just as long as the need existed.

Despite what might be called an ulterior motive on the part of the missions—subverting Therevada Buddhism and substituting Christianity—the acts of the missions established for them an honored place in the Thai social and administrative structure. The Thai monarchy and, later, the Thai government were generous in grants of land for churches, mission schools, and hospitals. In the reigns of Mongkut and Chulalongkorn the Palace drew heavily on the missionaries for language instruction, general education, and medical services. During the constitutional era after 1932, the Thai government continued accepting the missions for their secular value. In 1937 the Ministry of Education "adopted a policy of encouraging private schools to take over elementary education," and an annual subsidy was established to support this move, with mission schools sharing in the financial assistance.[14] When postwar inflationary pressures made virtual paupers of Thai teachers, the government established a Teachers Assistance Fund, and the indigenous mission teachers were included. In 1948 mission schools were classified as "public institutions" and exempted from taxes. To all intents and purposes the mission school system, like the mission medical services, was an integral part of the Thai scene.

The early missionaries brought new concepts to the Palace and the Thai elite, and had expanded this influence in education to include the peasantry. In the postwar era, as had happened with medicine several decades earlier, the increased influx of Thai educators back into the Thai educational system allowed them to shape their own concepts. There is little doubt, however, that in the early phases mission schools and mission teaching established

13. Interview at the Commission on Ecumenican Mission and Relations of the United Presbyterian Church in the U.S.A., Bangkok, June 2, 1963.

14. Tasniya Isarasena, "The Development of Elementary Education in Thailand" (unpublished Ph.D. dissertation, University of Wisconsin, 1953), p. 86.

not only methods of education but patterns of school organization and standards of excellence not common in Thailand.

If we accept the missions' role in medicine and education in Thailand as outstanding, truly a pilot project, an assessment of the factors that accounted for mission success, as well as of the obstacles faced, may be revealing in relation to U.N. activities.

The first and most obvious feature of mission performance is related to time. It is not enough to say that the missions had more than a hundred years to undertake their work and therefore have had time to multiply their activities and evolve ways of accomplishing their goals. From the earliest times the missions had some success; only lack of funds and trained personnel prevented their operations from being even larger.[15] They did, however, face many problems at the working level. It is alleged, for example, that the first mission school had to bribe its pupils to attend classes.[16] There are many accounts of the difficulties experienced because of the relative indifference of the Thai "man in the street" to mission endeavors, and because of the opposition of some Thai officials who were jealous of the favor the missions found with royalty or frightened at the prospects of erosion of Buddhism.[17] The relatively rapid success of the missions can best be ascribed, however, to the willingness with which they were accepted by the Palace, that is, by the real source of power and authority in the land at that time, combined with the undoubted fact that the missions were able to meet a currently felt need.

There is an obvious parallel between the ready acceptance of the missions and the equally ready acceptance of the United Nations with the same kind of goal a century later. Why then did the United Nations find its task so much harder? After the first decade of activity, mission education and medicine had become established, whereas the United Nations effort after the same period was faltering. One answer is that the missions could and did work in relatively virgin fields and did not have to take account of Thai institutions. The missions were standard bearers and as

15. George Bradley McFarland, *Historical Sketch of Protestant Missions in Siam, 1828–1928* (Bangkok, Bangkok Times Press, 1928), Chap. 8.

16. Ministry of Education, *A School History of Thailand*, 2 (Bangkok, Ministry of Education, 1952), 48 (in Thai).

17. Ibid., p. 46.

such had a degree of autonomy not possible with the United Nations. The United Nations, at least at the working level, looked upon itself as a standard bearer also. The continuous references, especially among UNESCO personnel, to the uniqueness of the United Nations mission permeate official documents, private letters, and speeches. In some world areas the arrival of a teacher or a doctor may indeed be a unique event. It was in Thailand in the mid-nineteenth century when the missionaries came, but not in the mid-twentieth century when the United Nations came. The United Nations faced the much more difficult task of endeavoring to be a torchbearer in a nation that was becoming more sophisticated and, it would seem, the U.N. failed to realize this. The ideas and methods of the U.N. workers may have been better than those held by many of the Thai, or may have been different in degree. But the United Nations did not offer totally new ideas and methods. Perhaps, therefore, the "selling" task of the United Nations in twentieth-century Thailand called for far greater finesse than did the "selling" task of the nineteenth-century missions. It could also be speculated that in the twentieth century the right "selling" formula might, with its more sophisticated audience, produce more spectacular results. As has been noted earlier, perhaps what was needed was not theories and concepts but the material appurtenances of education and other development. At this juncture, however, it is sufficient to observe that the difference between mission and United Nations efforts cannot be solely explained by the greater number of years of the mission operation or by different conditions at the time of initiation.

Closely allied with the longevity of the mission operation and its opportunity for independent activity was the issue of institution-building. The missions had to be autonomous in order to proselytize religion. Perhaps this idea of autonomy carried over into secular operations, or perhaps the absence of Thai educational and medical institutions at the time of the initial missionary intrusion allowed such independence. But the idea of an autonomous structure built by and sustained by missionary endeavor was a basic aspect of their operation. There was never any idea that the structure they were creating should be other than self-perpetuating and self-sustaining. The long life of their operation bears witness to this as does the continuity of purpose. While there were important elements of personnel policy aiding this sustenance of institutional structure, the factor of organization and general policy must also be noted. The policy was always clear. As the missionary in the field saw it, and as his home-based mission headquarters saw it, the task was to labor diligently as a teacher, a doctor, a nurse, a minister or priest, or an administrator, so as to lead people to well-defined Catholic, Presbyterian, or Baptist paths to God. Perhaps there could be argument about methods but never about ends or purposes. Those general terms (now so frequently used to describe activity in Southeast Asia and elsewhere) such as "ideology" or "dedication" may perhaps mean little more than this—that the Communist cell leader, the Jesuit father, the leader of a dissident minority, or the arrogantly rigid nationalist leader feels he knows where he is going.

Such a prop to institution-building was powerfully reinforced by institutional autonomy. Can this be said of the United Nations programs? At TUFEC, for example, there was the possibility of building an autonomous institution, but the concept and the implications involved were never really grasped. Instead, the idea was that a quick sally into the field of fundamental education combined with community development would then somehow or other generate a momentum and capacity for self-perpetuation. If institutions are to be created (and this is not necessarily the only modus operandi), one conclusion from the missions' experience is that clarity of policy at all levels and commitment of adequate time are vital starting points. But even these may be less important than the capabilities of personnel in the field. The success of the missions cannot be attributed solely to clear purpose, length of tenure, and the lucky chance of being genuinely unique at their commencement. The nature of the personnel involved lent the real substance to all mission efforts, and it is here that one sees the greatest contrast with United Nations attitudes and capabilities.

The term "dedication" springs most readily to mind as a description of the missionary's application to his role. The claim that missionaries were more dedicated than others needs substantiation. This can be given fairly simply by noting the practical areas of difference between missionary and other field workers that can be analyzed: tenure, language, and living habits.

It will be remembered that United Nations field workers spent relatively short periods of time in Thailand—in the TUFEC and Cha Cheong Sao projects the average tenure was 1.65 years. In the case of the United Presbyterian Mission, however, its director has already spent 24 years in the kingdom, and in five of the Roman Catholic vicarates in Thailand that are headed by foreigners, the average tenure of incumbents is 31 years. Many foreign priests have spent their lives in the kingdom; if asked "Where is your home?" they make the simple reply, "Here." This has been the pattern since missionaries first arrived.

Of greater importance than statistics is the concept, certainly held by the Roman Catholic and the major Protestant missions, that missionaries stay as long as they are wanted and while there is a job to be done. The implications of this practice are considerable. Acquiring language skill is an obvious need for someone who is to propagate religion in an alien area, but only a lengthy tenure in the country makes this practicable. As a group there can be little doubt that the missionaries stand supreme as linguists. The best Thai language school for foreigners is operated by the United Presbyterian Mission in Bangkok, the first Thai-English dictionary was compiled by a medical missionary and is still a standard reference.[18] The majority of missionaries can preach in Thai and most teachers conduct their classes in Thai.[19] Similarly the contribution of missionaries to English and French literature on Thailand has been notable. In regard to communications, therefore, the missionaries have surmounted the language barrier.

Along with tenure and language skill went a particular pattern of living, not so high that it elevated incumbents to unapproachable levels so far as the ordinary man was concerned, nor yet so low that standing was lost. For various reasons, mainly economic, missionaries usually avoided living in "status" areas when in the

18. S. G. McFarland in 1865 with a later version by his son George Bradley McFarland, also a medical missionary, *Thai-English Dictionary* (Stanford, Stanford University Press, 1944). This dictionary is a standard reference. In 1854 another dictionary was published by Bishop D. J. B. Pallegoix; it was basically a Thai-French dictionary but did include translation into English also. Many other dictionaries and glossaries were printed about the turn of the century, including a five-volume dictionary by the Rev. S. J. Smith published between 1899 and 1908.

19. At the present time, for example, one Jesuit priest, who holds a Ph.D. from the University of Chicago, teaches social anthropology at Chulalongkorn University exclusively in the Thai language.

larger towns. Many missionaries, especially those in remote areas or priests in residence in schools, lived on indigenous food and so broke down perhaps the most formidable of all barriers to social intercourse. Thus language, living patterns, and long tenure all interacted and produced an extraordinarily high ability to communicate. These factors gave substance to the missionaries' high motivation, an issue which must be accepted a priori but which by itself may well have meant very little.

Perhaps the most pertinent conclusion that can be gained from this brief survey of comparable foreign enterprises in Thailand is that the private automobile business, the German technical school, and the much vaster missionary enterprise all indicate that foreign-inspired educational projects can succeed in the kingdom. Success comes most readily when the learning process centers about machines. A second conclusion is that where persuasion is the only means of leverage, capabilities of personnel may transcend policy and organizational configurations, or indeed the type of organization represented. Here dedication or zeal is not enough. Specific personal skills, most of which can only be acquired over long tenure and by diligent application, become the substance of aspirations.

At the level where skills and ideas are actually transferred— that is, where the whole operation starts to justify itself—the recipient is less likely to be concerned with the banner borne by the field worker than with the field worker himself: how well the worker can perform in a particular situation and his capacity for effective communication in all its forms.

All evidence indicates that development of these qualities does not automatically follow from affiliation with a particular organization. The United Nations, as an organization, does not confer any greater capability upon its workers than any other body, national or international. Neither can one point to national representatives and say this nation performed better, or worse, than some other. The factors involved in communicating between cultures transcend these things. We in the West who are concerned must therefore be careful to differentiate. If we depend solely upon our national or international identity to provide the *point d'appui,* we may become guilty of dependence upon a shadow to the neglect of substance.

PART 3. THE COMMUNICATION BREAKDOWN

9

COMMUNICATION IN THE FIELD: SOME CRITERIA

THE STRUCTURE OF COMMUNICATIONS

Either aid projects must create institutions or field workers must integrate their operations within indigenous institutions. Except for relatively rare one-shot affairs, such as advising how a harbor might be deepened or surveying and mapping a territory, the absence of institutions usually means that when the foreign skilled workers depart, programs decrease or cease. Even gifts of equipment or the creation of transportation or irrigation systems require some sort of organizational structure if they are to be permanent.

The remarkable joint effort by WHO and the Thai government in curbing yaws in the kingdom has already been noted. Without denigrating efforts to date, I would suggest that in the aftermath of victory the most difficult task is yet to be done. To organize a system whereby all those carrying the visible evidence of yaws are given injections was relatively simple. The task now, however, is to organize "peripheral health services throughout the Kingdom, one of the objects of which would be to follow up the initial action on yaws and give further treatment to the minority who suffer recurrence and, at the same time, take immediate action against new cases." Only by these means can the disease be reduced to a state where the endemic conditions of the pre-1950s can no longer recur. WHO is only now coming to grips with the intricacies of making valid recommendations for the organization required. The WHO representative in Bangkok expressed the oft-repeated view of other United Nations officials that technical training was of slight value in meeting this problem. He noted that it was a shock for the expert to leave the relatively simple pursuit of his profession and come to grips with the Thai official beyond the issue of simple operations—to be confronted with "an organization which on paper says what officials are supposed to do but which bears no relationship with what they really do." Yet, as far as the WHO official was concerned, it was very clear that unless the organizational problem was solved, previous efforts of WHO in Thailand might be negated.[1] The tendency of activity to cease where there are no institutions to assist was described in the graphic phrase "cut flowers": "We give these people [in Asia generally] pretty things which wither and die just when they begin to like them, because our benefice has no roots."[2]

Establishing these roots is perhaps the most basic issue that confronts the United Nations or any other aid sponsor, and is the one which has been given the least attention in Thailand. It is easy to give the concept lip service. Evaluation of what it means, however, raises practical issues that bristle with difficulties which if grasped would of necessity substantially change a donor's views as to his capacities and methods. Key factors to be considered in formulating an organizational attitude toward communications include the length of the project, the tenure of individuals, and the significance of alien integration.

Length of the Project

If dispensing aid involves the issue of institution-building or working within existing institutions, a special concept of time is required. Where an aid operation is viewed in terms of its mechanics—e.g. time taken to apply DDT to a specific area or to train a certain number of people to do certain things—one may plan for a short operation. To create institutions or effect changes within institutions, however, calls for different timing. For example, the superintendent within the educational system sponsored by the Ecumenican Mission was a Thai woman. How long does it take to "create" a superintendent of education? A substantial part of a person's lifetime. How many superintendents or their equivalents were required after the first five years of the Cha Cheong Sao Pilot Project, when the diffusion process was to be carried into all re-

1. Interview, Local Office, WHO in Asia and the Far East, Bangkok, August 8, 1963.

2. Interview, Regional Office, FAO, May 31, 1963.

gions of the country? At that time a rapid rise in demand for super-intendents and a host of other skills and resources became crucial. At the Pilot Project, it was a matter of training not one super-intendent but many, of reorganizing not one classroom but thou-sands, and, on a more intangible plane, of building a storehouse of knowledge and experience to establish and sustain a method of operation that will create educators. And this was but one facet of the overall operation. UNESCO as the sponsoring body did not see the issue this way. Perhaps it was anticipated that a relatively quick United Nations sally into TUFEC and the Pilot Project would give the Thai educational system enough skills and general impetus to carry on with its own institution-building and reshaping. Ulti-mately the task had to become a Thai responsibility. What was required was not only to decide *when* the United Nations would be able to withdraw but also to have sufficient flexibility to con-tinue assistance required by new developments.

The need for flexibility imposes new requirements. If the invest-ment or degree of commitment undertaken by the donor is radi-cally altered, unanticipated difficulties in financing arise. Like many problems connected with aid, this one is not confined to the United Nations. Its ramifications, for example, affect the SEATO Community Development Center, so akin to TUFEC. Fears have been expressed that SEATO was creating an "orphan" in this enter-prise because member nations would be reluctant to take on the indeterminate commitments necessary to create viable institutions. Member nations are reluctant, if not unable, to commit themselves in advance to supply men and money for which no real definition has been given.[3] Yet for an establishment of this nature to have a chance of success, long-term effort must be available if required. The lesson to be drawn by the SEATO Community Development Center from its nearly defunct neighbor just across the road at Ubol, concerning time and flexibility, has been put aside.

Tenure of Individuals

Inextricably linked with the concept of length of the project is that of tenure of individuals. The significance of the "change of jockey" and orientation has already been stressed. At this juncture

3. Interview at SEATO Headquarters, Bangkok, June 17, 1963.

the question is how long, in general, an individual should stay if he is to become effective as a communicator in an alien culture. When this question was put to some 32 Thai officials who had either worked with or observed the work of United Nations field operators, the 21 who were prepared to make a positive reply believed five years was the minimum. All of those questioned, however—even those who did not specify a time period—qualified their response by saying that for some field operators any time was too long, and all those questioned were reticent about accepting people for five years without a probationary period of six months or so.

This five-year time factor applied only to field operators. In general, Thai officials had few opinions on United Nations officials stationed in the relatively detached environment of the regional and zone offices in Bangkok, reflecting in part the acute Thai awareness of personalized as opposed to impersonalized operations. It would seem then that the tenure of United Nations field operators in Thailand has generally been too short. This would certainly be the view of a substantial proportion of Thai co-workers; and the experience of the Christian missions further substantiates this view.

Alien Integration

Overriding all concepts of institution-building by aliens is the need for perception and knowledge of what is practical at a particular time and place, and this in turn calls for a degree of knowledge of a particular country and a degree of liaison within it which is rare among foreigners.

Institutions. An important question is whether indigenous institutions can be built by aliens. In Thailand, it has been practical to do so provided certain rather obvious limitations were observed. For example, it is likely that if the Buddhist religion in Thailand had been threatened by Christian doctrine, the same easy tolerance which has been so characteristic of the Thai-Christian relationship might not have prevailed. Similarly, activity which seems to threaten indigenous institutions or threaten to produce unassimilable changes would certainly be resisted. Institution-building cannot be undertaken entirely as a theoretical exercise. It must be related to and compatible with national interests and the rate of change which the nation feels it can accept. Although obvious, ascertaining the ideas of the nation concerned does not always provide a complete solution. Often high officials in Thailand were not certain themselves what their own institutions and personnel could take. More pertinently, however, there was a marked tendency for Thai to be dazzled with ends and to be little concerned with the ofttimes capricious pied piper of means, let alone the effort required in quantitative terms.

Personnel. The integration of foreign personnel within an indigenous bureaucracy imposes problems. These tend to be personal rather than structural. In Thailand the most important aspect of integration is related to the nature of the Thai bureaucracy. Although on the outside it appears highly formalized, in actuality it is highly personalized. The context of Thai public administration has been compared to that of Japan and Vietnam, and the considerable latitude and variation in Thai behavior in official as well as unofficial roles has been noted in several studies.[4] Thai attitudes have been well summed up:

> In a social system like the Thai, where social roles are only vaguely pre-determined and great latitude for personal idiosyncrasy is allowed, a person is by necessity an individualist and displays an almost determined lack of regularity and regimentation. The Thai seem to be motivated by . . . the desire to minimize environmental commitments, entanglements, and obligations which restrict individualism.[5]

In the workings of the bureaucracy such an attitude calls for highly personalized relationships and often subversion of the obligations consonant with the formal chain of command. Posts in the Thai bureaucracy tend not to be what they seem operationally. Power and influence are vested in the incumbent as well as the position, and it is in relations with the man that one is most likely to attain results. Quite extraordinary actions can be under-

4. Ruth Benedict, *Thai Culture and Behavior* (Ithaca, Cornell University, Southeast Asia Program, Data Paper No. 4, 1952) and John F. Embree, "Thailand—A Loosely Structured Social System," *American Anthropologist*, 52 (1950), 181–93.

5. Mosel, "Thai Administrative Behavior," p. 301.

taken for a friend and, conversely, poor personal relationships usually give rise to a hiatus in action. Obviously, very special talents are required of a foreigner if he is to integrate into this environment and play a dynamic role.[6]

The structural aspects of this situation impose extraordinary difficulties for a foreigner who comes to Thailand to utilize his technical or professional abilities and who is called upon to co-operate with the Thai bureaucracy. Short of acceptance of complete Thai direction, successful integration calls for some degree of specific knowledge about Thai bureaucratic mores unlikely to be held by foreigners in a technical field. Furthermore, such knowledge is unlikely to be acquired during the short periods of tenure common to United Nations appointments, especially as other issues of cultural and environmental adjustment also intrude. Nevertheless, without a high degree of intimacy and appreciable personalization of relationships, effective work by a foreigner, let alone any worthwhile degree of influence, becomes doubtful. Some United Nations personnel seemed to recognize the problem without being able to prescribe a remedy: "Still a matter for concern is how to establish and maintain closer relations with the provincial administrators . . . this must go beyond a disposition to collaborate: it must be a relationship that works in reality."[7]

One of the fruits of what was in fact an inability to achieve a "relationship that works" was unnecessary friction within U.N. organizations themselves, such as charges of Headquarters neglect relative to staffing and accusations of a "lack of understanding and a lack of consultation." This perhaps also led to more general charges of inefficiency on the part of the Thai bureaucracy, a charge generally made only by lower level United Nations officials. Perhaps the saddest reaction to Thai-foreign relationships, however, was of a type given in one field report: "There is nothing of any great importance that I can say with regard to our method of work, either relative to our Thai students or Thai staff. The main thing is to be very, very patient, smiling and friendly."[8]

6. See also pp. 167–72.

7. *Report of the Deputy Director of* TUFEC *for the quarter ending March 31, 1957* (from the files, UNESCO Headquarters, Paris).

8. *Report of an Advisor on Production Materials,* TUFEC, to UNESCO Headquarters, February 1955 (from the files, UNESCO Headquarters, Paris).

There undoubtedly were appreciable shortcomings within the Thai bureaucratic machinery generally, but this was to be expected. Indeed, it was why the United Nations was conducting operations in the kingdom. If the Thai bureaucracy and Thai officials had been as efficient and knowledgeable as some United Nations officials thought they should be, there would have been slight reason for the United Nations to be in Thailand at all. It is fortunate, however, that antipathy toward Thai officialdom was not widespread among U.N. officers generally. Such feelings did exist and this was at least one by-product of the lack of understanding of the Thai bureaucratic situation. Yet where "intimacy" was a requirement, such knowledge was essential for anyone charged with promoting change by persuasion.

Acceptance of Limits. Even the most perfectly oriented foreign expert working within an indigenous bureaucracy is likely to find that issues he can personally influence will be of fairly small dimension. One FAO officer in Bangkok, who had had wide foreign experience, observed that in his opinion a complete structural change was required within the Thai bureaucracy relative to the services it provided the farmer. In his view, there has been no real communication in Thailand among the policy-maker, the senior administrator, and the farmer, other than in matters of taxation. New means are required, in this expert's view, for the provision of advice on such matters as marketing, handling and storing of produce, investment and borrowing, and use of agricultural machinery.[9] Assuming that these views are valid, it might be asked whether a foreign expert can promote such changes even under the most ideal conditions. They would involve weeding out old officials and perhaps changing the provincial structure, with less power being accorded to the district officer and more to new officials such as the agricultural extension officer or his Thai equivalent. When these implications were discussed with the United Nations agricultural official in question, he agreed to the validity of the points even though he remained somewhat nonplused. He concluded that this was not a matter for the United Nations, that only the Thai themselves could institute changes with such wide ramifications.

9. Interview at Regional Office, FAO, Bangkok, July 25, 1963.

Many similar examples could be cited concerning change in other fields. It seems, therefore, that together with the recognition of possible structural measures to improve communications, cognizance must also be taken of limitations, even under theoretically ideal performance criteria. To know what is attainable has always been deemed an art, not only in politics but in most forms of human relations.

Particularism. A further factor implicit in building a communications structure is particularism. It has been noted elsewhere in this book that there was an extraordinary tendency on the part of United Nations personnel at all levels to generalize about operations in Thailand, when the real need was for specific evaluation of specific situations. This affected basic aims. TUFEC, for example, was envisaged as a center for the whole of Southeast Asia. "After the Center has been in operation for a year or so, reconsideration will have to be given to the possibilities of making it more truly international."[10] Perhaps the United Nations had little alternative but to cling to the idea that there were global solutions to problems. At the other end of the spectrum were such fantastic schemes as training at a Thai center those Annamite refugees from the Franco-Vietminh war who clustered along the Mekong River and were alleged to be highly skilled craftsmen.[11] In the minds of the Thai government these refugees were a "fifth column"; in 1959–60 this seemed to be substantiated when a segment of these refugees, some 40,000 strong, were finally repatriated and their destination was North, not South, Vietnam.

There were similar problems in the delineation of aims for most projects at TUFEC. Many field workers were prone to analyze problems rather than to work at them. For example, I found only one letter with specific requests from a foreign field worker for items of equipment (in this case stationery and writing materials), such as would inevitably occur in situations where field work was actually

10. Memorandum on "An Informal Discussion Held in the Fundamental Education Division, UNESCO Headquarters, Paris, with Incoming Head of TUFEC, January 8, 1953" (from the files, UNESCO Headquarters, Paris). Also note 29, p. 37.

11. Letter from the Fundamental Education Division, UNESCO Headquarters, Paris, October 17, 1952 (from the files, UNESCO Headquarters, Paris).

giving rise to participation by Thai recipients.[12] On the other hand, if foreign workers had stayed longer on the jobs, perhaps their analyses would have led to more actual operations. As TUFEC progressed, work at the Center did tend to be more specific and to be building up a store of knowledge related to real situations.[13]

Indeed, the whole question of particularism is to a considerable degree related to time, not only to the tenure of individuals but to the time span of the operation as a whole. Time, along with research, seems to be the essential ingredient in specifying the precise mechanics of doing things, and also what should be attempted.

Persuasion. The last important prerequisite in building a communications structure is to take note of the rather obvious but basic fact that, in general, aid operations must be advanced through persuasion. Many questions can be raised concerning persuasion as the mode of effecting change. It has already been noted in this study, for example, that the United Nations in Thailand was not reaching the top-level decision makers. Thus, at its peak of influence, the United Nations was limited to persuasion aimed at lower levels of the hierarchy. Where efforts are aimed at the level of the peasant, perhaps something beyond persuasion is required. One experienced observer, having noted that "the effective power to achieve action on the village level lies with the Ministry of Interior officials," went on to describe an indigenous effort at community development:

> The Governor ordered . . . officials to cooperate. The Governor feels that in the sphere of experimental field trials one

12. Florentino Freznoza, *Report for Period November 1959 to December 1961,* Ubol, January 1962 (from the files, UNESCO Regional Office, Bangkok).

13. As an example, by 1959 TUFEC had a small library of student theses on specific problems in the Thai countryside. Examples of some of the titles are: "Poultry: A Protein Increment"; "The Production and Marketing of Charcoal"; "Cement Jar Economics in Community Development"; "A Cow Dung Gas Plant"; "The Establishment of Village Libraries." On the other hand, a series of books (the Bamboo Series, see p. 131) written at the Center for guidance of the peasant on hygiene, diet, and so on were a failure because they were compiled by foreigners and had only academic relevance to the Thai countryside.

must, in the initial stages, use "pressure," "orders," "authority," etc., to assure that projects get under way. If one hesitated and applied theoretical self-help principles . . . a project would have never gotten off the ground.[14]

Similar views were expressed by the doyen of community development specialists at FAO.[15] Such coercion, however, is beyond the domain, if not the intentions, of United Nations field workers. They are limited to exerting their persuasive influence only on officials somewhere between the top levels of government and the recipient in farm or village. Opinion can vary as to whether in the long run persuasion, despite its apparent limitations, may not be the best method of effecting change. We cannot resolve the question. In the sphere of building a communications structure, however, persuasion is in fact the only real means that the United Nations can take and in the Thai case even the form that persuasion might take had quite distinct and limited dimensions.

THE COMMUNICATIONS CORE

The United Nations has long recognized in general that the quality of personnel recruited would be vital to operational achievement. The main concern, however, was with recruitment to the permanent positions in the Secretariat. An attempt was made to persuade member governments and private business to lend well-qualified personnel to the United Nations without penalty to their subsequent careers.[16] Yet there was no record that such measures were ever put into effect. In an immediate sense the United Nations was faced with the task of recruiting personnel with specialist knowledge in specific fields, and these were hired ad hoc on an annual basis, the United Nations having to take what it could get. In Thailand the recruits were a varied lot.[17]

14. Letter to the Chief of Mission, UNESCO Regional Office, Bangkok, from William Klausner, Rural Program Assistant, Asia Foundation, Bangkok, August 1959 (from private sources).

15. Interviews, Regional Office, FAO, June and July 1963.

16. UNESCO, *General Conference at Montevideo, 1954; Resolutions*, pp. 59, 62.

17. See also pp. 89–90.

The Pilot Project has not been particularly well served in the experts furnished by UNESCO. Few have left any real mark and some have lacked the professional qualifications and experience to be expected of consultants in a project of this sort. Their contribution has been diminished by poor living conditions and isolation, which have borne heavily on wives and families; by difficulties of communication with their Thai colleagues; by lack of opportunities to travel within Thailand; by blood clots within the administrative blood stream.[18]

Note has also been taken of the views of Thai who came into close contact with the foreign field workers.[19]

Such failings cannot be laid solely at the door of field personnel themselves. Poor briefing at UNESCO Headquarters in Paris has already been noted, as has the absence of clearly delineated roles either for the projects themselves or for the individuals operating within them, and the inadequate orientation of personnel to their locale. Superimposed upon these difficulties were the factors suggested above as being important to the building of a communications structure, which should presumably have been the responsibility of the regional and zone offices. Field workers were not given the kind of support which might have enabled them to identify their problems more easily, nor were they given the direction that might have assisted them to utilize their particular expertise more effectively. Neither should the impression be given that personal antipathies between Thai and foreigner were great. Of all Thai interviewed not one expressed personal dislike of foreign experts or failed to comment favorably on what he had learned from experts. Approximately half the Thai consulted said they would be happy to have experts back again, although all expressed some reservations about the role experts should play.

From the evidence assembled, it would seem that the function of an "adviser" is a very sensitive issue among the Thai. Reasons given for this were many. "The contribution of the senior expert was curtailed because, being an adviser, he had no responsibility

18. Letter from the Chief of Mission, UNESCO Regional Office, Bangkok, to Director of Education, UNESCO Headquarters, Paris, July 1958 (from the files, UNESCO Regional Office, Bangkok), p. 3.

19. See Appendix V.

and did not have to consult."[20] But the most repeated charge was that advisers knew nothing of the Thai environment and could not work within it, and that their advice was rarely relevant. As advisers were often quite senior officials in the United Nations, their counterparts were senior Thai officials who, while not necessarily being abreast of particular professional topics, had wide experience with their own bureaucracy and environment and therefore viewed the senior foreigners' necessarily superficial views on the Thai scene as being somewhat juvenile. On the other hand, all Thai interviewed said that the kingdom needed the assistance of technical experts, especially those who had a simple process to demonstrate. A portion of the interviewees said that they had had their interest whetted by some of the technical skills they had seen and would like to see more. By and large, it would seem that the technicians could be fitted in, but only if they met other personal requirements.

What sort of personnel is required in the ideal situation? What are the personal qualities needed to enable one to integrate successfully with a Thai institution and influence its methods, or to help build an autonomous institution acceptable to the Thai? How does one, assuming that he also clearly understands his role and has particularized it to the degree required by the local situation, acquire the personal attributes necessary to become a good communicator? There are four fields that might be explored in seeking an answer to what in the end must be the most important question of all, the personal qualities of field operators: orientation, physical and social mobility, personal adaptation, and personal relations.[21]

20. Mom Rajawong Sermsri Kasemsri, "The Evolution of the TUFEC Training Program," in TUFEC, *Eight Years of Cooperation*, p. 23.

21. These four fields were formulated by me after a number of years of living in Asia, particularly Southeast Asia, and were then used with success as the basis of orientation for military and academic personnel assigned for duty in Southeast Asia. While experience in the actual setting was regarded as the best and most essential element in building up a foreign operational capability, especially for living in rural areas, the enthusiastic response to the orientation was surprising, particularly the amount of practical knowledge absorbed, and the changed attitudes toward the local environment of the ordinary visitor to Asia.

Orientation

The orientation of personnel would seem to be the simplest of all requirements to meet. A general knowledge of the history, sociology, ecological patterns, religion, and political and administrative aspects of the country seems essential and can be fairly readily given. In addition careful orientation to one's specific purpose in a country is necessary. A clear understanding of what one is expected to achieve, the circumstances surrounding one's work—such as materials available for use, organizational factors, personnel involved, and, above all, some plan that incorporates timing—are essential. A detailed prognosis of what the field worker is expected to do together with a general summary of how he might go about the task is likely to be of benefit not only to the expert but also could be highly pertinent to headquarters' understanding of the problem. A switch from the generalities of two or three days of briefing in Paris to a detailed exposition on experts' roles would call for far greater analysis at, say, UNESCO headquarters than seems to have been the case up to now.

There is one other extremely important aspect of orientation which cannot be so readily provided. As an ideal, an indigenous language ability should be possessed by all foreign experts in both field and administrative headquarters posts in any country. We have already taken notice of the importance of language. But sometimes the ideal is not attainable. People who are fluent in a relatively exotic language, such as Thai, are unlikely to be recruited from the community at large.[22] A training period is involved, which could be lengthy. Several years are required to learn to speak Thai well enough, for instance, to conduct a very simple lesson with a class. A limited speaking ability can be ac-

22. At present there is no readily available compendium of Thai linguists in the United States. Consultation at Cornell and Yale Universities with area specialists indicates that up until the middle of 1961 not more than 100 students had accepted Thai language training, and it was thought the ability of most of these would be poor. Outside of the mission field, the available Thai linguists in the United States might not therefore number much more than a score or so. The possibility that returning Peace Corps personnel could greatly augment this estimate should be noted but they are likely to be speakers and not readers.

quired in a much shorter period, but to become effective further practice and study would be required in Thailand.[23] To read and write the language needs several years of study; and it should be remembered that unless the teacher can use the blackboard or read a Thai text, a speaking ability does not mean very much. There is little chance of reducing the time needed to reach a limited effectiveness, no matter what course is followed; and if even a limited language capability is a prerequisite, then a considerably longer contract period would be necessary, not only to acquire training but also to obtain returns from the greater investment that would have to be made.

Is there any way around the language problem? In certain circumstances it could be argued that a technical specialist might still be quite effective without the native language. A person engaged in medical research or even treatment, a person studying fishing techniques, a person bringing any highly technical skill, which in fact requires the recipient to learn its technical "language," probably can manage quite well without much language skill. It might also be argued that at the higher levels of administration in the capital, Thai language is not necessary, as most of the higher Thai officials can use English. But any worker in the field, having contact with the ordinary Thai both officially and unofficially, is sadly if not fatally handicapped without a sound knowledge of the language. The experience of the Christian missions attests to this fact.

Surprisingly, only once to this writer's knowledge did the UNESCO Regional Office in Bangkok ever seriously concern itself with the problem.[24] The most probable reason for such neglect was the short tenure of most officials. There were, however, in Bangkok at least seven United Nations officials holding very senior positions who had been in their posts for periods ranging from a minimum of seven years to a maximum of fifteen years, but none

23. The Peace Corps seems to reach minimal speaking standards in about four months (including general orientation), with the trainee improving his spoken language skill in the field, apparently with some rapidity. Nevertheless, the one Peace Corps Volunteer at TURTEP stated that after 18 months he still could not use the Thai language to any significant degree in his English language course.

24. See also pp. 79–81.

of them spoke or read Thai. This again seems reasonable, as all were regional officers with responsibilities in countries ranging from Japan to Iran. To them, Bangkok was only a place in which to live, and those who did have some contact with aid projects in Thailand had, if anything, as detached a view of it all as people at UNESCO headquarters in Paris. It seems that once again the wide-ranging global views of the United Nations exacted a toll—in trying to do the greater (i.e. serve all of Asia), the particular requirements of the lesser had to be neglected.

A general orientation to a particular local environment can, it is suggested, be relatively easily attained. But the virtual impossibility of experts acquiring the sort of specific orientation required by national operations if they also must cater to a region as diverse as Asia raises a formidable barrier to effectiveness. A dichotomy will exist, therefore, even in the most ideal situation between those with specific knowledge and those with general knowledge. This is far from unusual. The crucial issue is whether the parties concerned have the skill to cooperate on those issues where cooperation is necessary and to respect autonomy in other situations.

Physical and Social Mobility

The second factor, mobility, is complementary to orientation and cannot be divorced from it. Physical mobility means being able to move into any geographical environment necessary, and social mobility means the ability to work and live with various strata of society. Both kinds of mobility are essential if an individual worker is to acquire that vital "feel" for people and for the countryside so important to effective field operations. Without experiencing the reality of physical and social mobility, it probably would be just as sound to gain appreciation of a local situation from academic studies. Indeed the academic approach might be more reliable than the assumption, so often made, that an individual who has been physically, though statically, located in a country must have some special knowledge of that country. It can be questioned whether life in a small alien enclave—in, say, either the city of Bangkok or among fellow foreigners in a provincial town—gives an individual any significant degree of knowledge about the vast indigenous environment that lies beyond these extraordinarily restricted confines.

The importance of physical and social mobility is accentuated in a country like Thailand, where communications media, such as the press, radio and television, social groups, and the like, have very limited roles especially relative to the communications between town and country. The dearth of familiar Western aids to communication thus accentuates the importance of personal association with people and places: indeed there is usually no substitute.

The gamut of what must be learned through physical and social mobility runs from the simple and practical to the abstract and barely definable. Where flood statistics are nonexistent, the required size for drainage pipes is often best assessed by viewing the site and listening to local opinion. The observer in a village might ponder why a peasant prefers a picture or a carving on his new cart's tailboard rather than purchasing grease for its squeaking axle. The reason for promoting nicely balanced and well-integrated technical training programs comes under question after one observes a manifestation of centuries-old architectural and contruction skills being expended not in the utilitarian pursuit of higher living standards, but in the creation of a beautiful temple. The physical life of the peasant, so much the area of concern of the aid organizations, remains a theoretical obscurity until one has lived in peasant houses, eaten their food, observed work patterns, and understood their weltanschauung. From this kind of experience arises a new type of communication, one which involves feedback from the recipient and, hopefully, modification of the aid formula in the light of the recipient's own perspectives.

The alternative to two-way communication between donor and recipient is for the former to adopt a near-totalitarian stance, where it seems that his method is absolute, can be applied generally to all situations at any time and place, and need not be modified to meet local conditions. Catchwords such as "helping people to help themselves" are at best meaningless, and at worst deceitful, if, in fact, the lifeway of those to be helped is not understood as reality and aid formulas tested empirically, and adjusted, relative to that reality. Such a process, far from simple or readily discernible, can occur in a country like Thailand only if the donors of aid have the energy and capacity to be mobile enough in a physical and social sense to the degree where the recipient is regarded as a partner and not as an object. The essence of the process is physical and social mobility but other characteristics intrude which make the acquiring of such mobility less simple than it seems.

Personal Adaptation

Physical and social mobility are dependent upon another factor, extraordinarily simple and basic but absolutely vital to utilizing mobility. Personal adaptation to the living conditions away from the more developed centers is essential. Inadequate sleeping arrangements and hygienic facilities plus other risks to health and general comfort are all associated with travel in back-country Thailand, and indeed in Southeast Asia at large. At the worst these conditions have to be endured, and at the best accepted philosophically, if one is to move away from the confines of the foreign enclaves, let alone live for periods in the country as the rural Thai knows it.

Transcending the adaptation to general living conditions, however, is the ability to survive adequately on the local food. If this cannot be done, not only does travel become extremely difficult over any meaningful time or area, but so does getting along with Thai in other than highly Westernized strata. It has been the experience of this writer—based upon more than 50,000 miles of travel in back-country Thailand aggregating 436 days and 386 nights during 1956–60—that the biggest single problem for the foreigner is food. The most common reason for not adjusting to the local diet is fear of disease, despite the fact that the average foreigner is highly protected by modern medicines and usually has a fairly robust constitution. Though a foreigner who cannot eat the local diet may sustain himself on provisions carried along with him or survive on the monotonous fare of "safe" foods such as eggs, he can only endure this for limited periods. The most difficult time for such a person comes when he wishes to associate with Thai, which if done for any length of time must involve eating. Perhaps by careful selection a feast can be survived, but to live by this means for weeks or months among the Thai themselves becomes all but impossible. The irony of it is that Thai food, and the readily available Chinese food is delightfully palatable. It comes in an endless variety and is far from lethal. But fear of food-borne diseases tends to overwhelm the pleasure of taste to say nothing of the advantage of being able to mix in the native milieu because one can sustain oneself over time. The "Iron Curtain" has imposed its particular barriers to association, but the "Hygiene Curtain" makes for exclusiveness also.[25]

Personal Relations

The last factor is perhaps the most undefinable. By personal relations is meant the ability to make good friends among the Thai. It is these local friends with their capacity to act as catalysts between the foreigner and native who provide the ultimate link. Time spent by the foreigner sorting out a variety of indigenous methods and investigating aspects of daily living can be shortened considerably with explanations by good friends. Travel becomes simpler when undertaken in the company of a local resident with whom one is on intimate terms. Beyond these and other utilitarian aspects, there is an even greater value in having good friends. One has at his side informants ad infinitum. Even when the foreigner knows more about Thai history and politics than his Thai friends, he still requires, and through his knowledge can elicit, information on all manner of details and attitudes.

It goes without saying that to be party to such a free flow of information requires a relationship between Thai and foreigner

25. These problems are not the sole prerogative of the Westerner. On the maiden voyage of the "Sri Sukothai" in July 1963 (the vessel representing Thailand's first venture into international marine trade), a mutiny broke out and the ship put into the port of Houston, Texas. The complaints of the mutineers, who were all Thai, centered around the inability of their European officers to understand Thai ways and the Thai inability to eat European food. See Thammoon Mahapaurya, "Strike Hurts Thai Marine Reputation," *Bangkok World,* July 20, 1963. See also Hanson W. Baldwin, "Briton Rules Out Allied Navy Unit," *New York Times,* December 15, 1963. The core of the argument advanced against the practical operation of the NATO multinational nuclear fleet by Admiral G. T. S. Gray, Royal Navy, was that sailors of different nations could not work in the same ship because of different personal habits, food, etc.

beyond that gained at the cocktail party or during the routine associations of business. Real personal intimacy is required, and this takes time and perseverance as well as a readiness on the part of the foreigner to go along with a host of local habits and environmental conditions. Not only are the consequent professional rewards great but the personal associations are most pleasurable.

THE BROKEN REED OF EXPERTISE

The United Nations selected personnel for field operations primarily on the basis of technical expertise. Occasionally there was a fortuitous blending of expertise and orientation to the strange environment,[26] but in most instances all the foreign field worker had to fall back upon was his expertise. In those few cases where there was a happy combination of the technical knowledge of the expert and a complementary technical task in the field, expertise was enough. But in the vast majority of situations, where human contact was the core of the modus operandi, expertise alone was a poor prop. Indeed it is possible that this total reliance on expertise aggravated human relations. It was common to find Thai counterparts very critical of experts who

> claimed they knew everything about their field but who could not even relate it to the real conditions in this country and would not listen to us Thai when we tried to help them because we were not experts. But we did know what was possible in our country even if we were not sure of the details and how we might go about it.[27]

The aggravating aspects of complete reliance on expertise were viewed by another Thai from a totally different level:

> The trouble with experts who know nothing else than their particular calling is that they always have "solutions" and are sure they are right. One reason why the Peace Corps is doing so well in this country is not just because they are well

26. See Appendix V.
27. Interview at TUFEC, July 10, 1963.

oriented, but because they are not experts and do not have "solutions."[28]

If expertise is to be used effectively, sole reliance cannot be placed upon this attribute. Much more is required, including detailed orientation and time to translate it into a personal modus operandi in the field. The United Nations effort never came near meeting these requirements. The initial reaction of one field worker to arrival in Thailand could have been mirrored by many:

> This has for me been a most interesting period of time. Everything is so new and surprising. My feeling of wanting to learn all about everything at once is, I suppose, typical of everyone who goes for the first time to a completely different world. It is most frustrating to know that this is quite impossible.[29]

In less than a year after the above comments were made, this field worker had left the country. A similar spirit prevailed when field workers departed:

> Most of us are birds of passage, come from places where we have been well dug in. Field work in countries which seek assistance from UNESCO brings experience and makes demands for which we are not by any means wholly prepared.[30]

A communications breakdown at the field level between foreign workers and Thai co-workers was a root cause for the low achievement of the major projects upon which this study has focused. Communications broke down because of the lack of a structural conception aimed at ensuring an effective linking of operations over time and space, together with the lack of adequate field worker orientation.

A vital deficiency was the absence of a concept of institution-building or of what was involved in the alternative of integrating

---

28. Interview at National Community Development Department, Bangkok, August 1, 1963. Also interview at Ministry of Education, Bangkok, June 27, 1963.

29. Mabel Jesse, *Report on Rural Teacher Training*, Ubol, April 1957 (from the files, UNESCO Regional Office, Bangkok).

30. Harry H. Penny, *Report on Work Done at Cha Cheong Sao Teachers College*, Bangkok, January 1956 (from the files, UNESCO Headquarters, Paris).

within existing institutions. Allied with the situation was a failure to appreciate the extraordinary length of time required and the need for, and implications of, flexibility in methods of effecting change, especially in rural areas. Actions tended to be general rather than particular, and it would seem that the limitations of persuasion as a tool were not fully realized.

Personal adaptation of foreign field workers was especially important. Personal needs which could be obtained so readily in town or city such as food, hygienic living, medicine, transportation, a familiar language, social companionship, and entertainment were simply not available in the village in forms culturally acceptable to the foreigner. In the village one entered a new world, but it was about this world that knowledge had to be gained if the field operator was to do other than advance pre-set concepts which presumably the recipient was expected to accept without demur. In the event, there was little, if any, feedback from the recipient. Operations were therefore less a mutual contact than a process of alien ideas and practices being passed down from above. In many respects there was, at the field level, little difference between these actions and actions in former times by a colonial power. How deeply rooted were these shortcomings in the overall United Nations concept of aid operations, especially in UNESCO which carried the major responsibility for sponsoring the projects? A return to some specific policies at the headquarters level is necessary to see what roles these deficiencies played in the Thai experience.

10

A PERSPECTIVE AT
HEADQUARTERS LEVEL

In its relationships with operations in Thailand, UNESCO headquarters had one basic dilemma—relating very generalized objectives to the particular methods demanded by a local situation. The
dilemma is relevant for any organization with global goals. If we
can profit from the Thai experience we can conclude that just as
a high degree of rapport is needed between the United Nations
and local native problems, so too is intimacy required at the
diplomatic level between United Nations headquarters and national governments. At this diplomatic level, the need is not
only for new concepts but for more perceptive and knowledgeable
relationships between policy-makers and planners at the United
Nations as well as in the national governments.

NATIONAL PLANS AND UNITED NATIONS AID

On the assumption that material aid, nationally based, is necessary and desired by all parties, a simple schematic outline of an
ideal operation appears in Table 4.

The configuration given in Table 4 provides only general background to a more particular summary of operations at the local
level. Table 5 notes specifically the reemphases and changes which
might be applied from a headquarters point of view.

If the ideas summarized in Tables 4 and 5 are accepted as a basis
for discussion, it is apparent that United Nations aid operations
require a major theoretical change. Exclusive of the fundamental
issue of personnel discussed in the previous chapter, there is more
need to be concerned with particular and local problems than with
a search for general, global formulas. Nevertheless, there is little

TABLE 4. A SCHEMATIC OUTLINE OF AN AID OPERATION

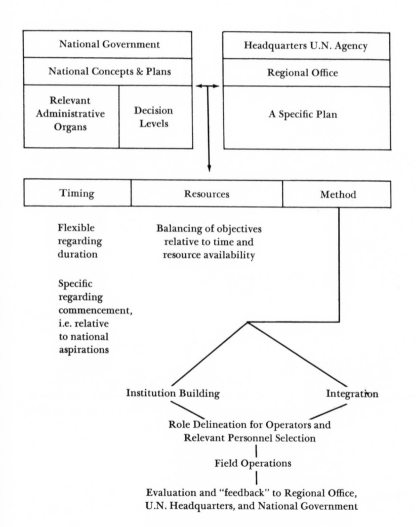

TABLE 5. CURRENT AID METHODS BASED UPON TUFEC AND THE
PILOT PROJECT, WITH SUGGESTED REEMPHASES

Distinction	Typologies Used in Aid Projects in Thailand	Notes on Typologies	Reemphasis Required
Objectives	General and New	Fundamental Education and Educational Development through pilot schemes.	Programs adapted to specific national needs rather than universalistic notions, calling for heightened United Nations and national perceptions.
Time	Precise	All programs had a specific lifetime. No activity directed toward "follow-up" but faith that local momentum would be generated.	No time limits for operations. Extended tenures for personnel and this measured relative to job requirements rather than administrative requirements.
Contractual Basis	Concerned with administrative matters only	Subject matter of contracts concerned personnel, equipment in use, etc. and did not concern responsibilities and activity relative to operations.	More detailed contracts required especially with regard to tenure and responsibilities of *indigenous* personnel, as well as a "spelling out" of nature and scale of indigenous bureaucratic support.
Project Autonomy	Potential for extremely high autonomy	Projects had very tenuous responsibilities to Paris Headquarters; this coupled with absence of defined relations with Thai bureaucracy gave potential for high autonomy but this did not eventuate—possibly because definition was too loose.	The provision of personnel at the executive level with ability and knowledge to take autonomous decisions plus better contractual definition.

Distinction	Typologies Used in Aid Projects in Thailand	Notes on Typologies	Reemphasis Required
Operational Method	Persuasion	No legal, economic, or political powers.	No change.
Resources	Only personnel skills and techniques of communication	Initially skills and communications were the only resources required.	Ultimately material resources would be an important determinant (i.e. if diffusion became a reality) and this would call for further contractual commitments by participating governments or organizations.
Experience	Highly specialized	Experience relative to an appropriate skill but little relative to the local milieu.	A build-up of a cadre of experienced personnel at the field level through creation of career service and renewal of tenures.
Cultural Values	Western or non-indigenous	The majority of personnel were ethnically Western and those who were not had been inculcated with Western skills and values.	A major reemphasis of personnel selection and training with provision of 1) orientation courses, 2) more perceptive use of fellowship programs to provide indigenous United Nations personnel and training for specific posts.

evidence that anything of substance has been learned from the Thai experience and most indications are that the search for wide-ranging solutions continues. Ultimately such solutions may yet be found; meanwhile, failure to capitalize on experience may betray other projects into going the way of TUFEC and Cha Cheong Sao.

THE "GRAND VIEW" AND PARTICULARISM

Remembering the overall attitudes of UNESCO toward world problems of education and related fields, it was not surprising that operations in Thailand should have had far-reaching objectives. A central feature of TUFEC and the Pilot Project, however, has been the wide disparity between what was intended and what happened. TUFEC was to become a Center for all of Southeast Asia. Somehow the Pilot Project was to spread new theories and methods throughout Thailand and even further. A system of education, based upon a four-year course with untrained teachers working in thatched open shelters, was to be transformed into a "vigorous modern system, embracing education in all its phases and which would at the same time set an example and act as a stimulus to the rest of Southeast Asia or even beyond."[1] In retrospect such concepts appear not only unrealistic but implausible.

Yet this ignorance of attainable goals is by no means restricted to TUFEC, the Pilot Project, or operations conceived during the nascent years of United Nations aid. UNESCO's newest theory regarding education in Asia has been included in the Karachi Plan. Under this plan, within a period of twenty years participating countries are to establish compulsory national education schemes based upon a seven-year curriculum.[2] It has been noted, however, that

> The most formidable obstacle for the implementation of this Plan is financial . . . the Plan involves a total expenditure of 56,217 millions of U.S. dollars in a period of 20 years and by 1980 the average expenditure on *primary* education is expected to rise about 4.3 U.S. dollars per head. Whence and how this money is to be found—that is the major problem which will have to be satisfactorily answered if the Plan is to be implemented.[3]

The sums of money involved might not seem large for a program of this magnitude. In actual cash, however, the money represents

1. Imhoff, "The Cha Cheong Sao Project," p. 301.
2. UNESCO, *Final Report of Ministers of Education of Asian States Participating in the Karachi Plan,* App. II. The countries involved are Afghanistan, Burma, Cambodia, Ceylon, India, Indonesia, Iran, the Republic of Korea, Laos, Malaya, Nepal, Pakistan, Philippines, Thailand, and the Republic of Vietnam. Neither Communist China nor the Republic of China is included.
3. UNESCO, "The Needs of Asia in Primary Education," *Education Studies and Documents No. 41* (Paris, UNESCO, 1961), p. 78.

more than a fivefold increase in expenditure currently made on *all* education in these countries. Obviously this additional money can come only from massive increases in foreign aid and/or through a rate of growth in national incomes as yet unrealized in Asia.

We can ask whether the Karachi Plan is in fact a plan, a statement of proceedings, or a highly detailed and voluminous reiteration of generalized ideas. Since prospects for even limited success seem poor, the plan can be read as a portent of a probable decline in educational levels in Asia *below* present levels. Launching the plan might well lead to useless dissipation of resources, that is, seeking not only what is unattainable but something which even if realized (for example, a universal seven-year education scheme) would not necessarily put nations on the road to modernity. Possibly available funds might more profitably be used to enhance and develop an educational elite with the hope that this elite would stimulate general economic development. Without such development, schemes like the Karachi Plan would seem to be illusions. When the plan was discussed with one prominent Thai educator in the upper echelons of the Ministry of Education, he stated unhesitatingly that the scheme could not be implemented as a state scheme in any Asian nation and that Thailand should not sacrifice its growing educational elite in an effort to produce a large semi-educated mass. The educator stated further that Thailand would proceed with its plans for compulsory education but it might be eighty years before the plans were effectively carried out. When asked why Thailand went along with the Karachi Plan, he explained that speaking against it would have seemed a hostile reaction resulting in ostracism from UNESCO circles.

There would seem to be great dangers for the policy-makers at headquarters levels in pursuing schemes like the Karachi Plan, which after all is really only the Pilot Project writ large. There is a possibility that agencies such as UNESCO will come to institutionalize generalities by according them a status that would normally be given actions. If those intimately concerned were persuaded that they were grappling with real solutions, when in fact they were undertaking little more than meaningless ritual, the ultimate effects on United Nations endeavors could be disastrous.

The dangers inherent in the grand view can be expressed in

other ways and relative to other contexts. One FAO official expressed the opinion that the mechanics of the United Nations task in Thailand and elsewhere had not been grappled with realistically because the organization was still generally caught up in an "emotional binge," characterized by the acceptance as stock in trade of clichés like "war against ignorance," "the abolition of poverty," and so on. These were alleged to be substitutes for specifics at United Nations conferences where delegations told each other about problems in a merry-go-round of such generalized phrases. Responsibility for this situation was assigned to headquarters' detachment from the field, an insufficient number of qualified headquarters personnel, and the limited feedback. Further perpetuating the "emotional binge" were the national delegations, which tended to be heavily overburdened with political figures who usually had an imperfect knowledge of actual situations and who for various reasons took refuge in platitudes.[4] Whether these views explain in its entirety the seeming predilection of such bodies as UNESCO to cling to the "grand view" at headquarters level is perhaps debatable. That the tendency exists, however, is undeniable.

A further indication of the general trend is the activity of publicity bodies in the United Nations agencies. As a typical example, the most recent FAO publicity pamphlet on Thai agriculture is couched in the most general terms. The booklet implies that agricultural production in Thailand (and indeed in the rest of Asia) is rapidly increasing and that somehow FAO is responsible.[5] Specific data on Thailand from other United Nations sources state that well-established crops such as rice and rubber actually have declining yields per unit area.[6] On the other hand, there have been several new "boom" crops in Thailand such as corn and jute, but these have had virtually nothing to do with FAO, representing instead a peasant response to cash inducements arising from new external markets. When the publicity officer at the FAO Regional

---

4. Interview FAO Regional Office, Bangkok, July 25, 1963.

5. FAO, FAO in Asia (Bangkok, Vichitrapsila Press, 1962).

6. ECAFE, Economic Survey of Asia and the Far East, 1961 (Bangkok, March 1962), p. 13 and Table 10, p. 175; and Ingram, Economic Change in Thailand, pp. 43–49.

Office in Bangkok was asked about the disparities between their booklet and data published by ECAFE, a sister organization in the same city, the reply was, "Well, FAO must be doing some good."

Many U.N. publicity documents tend to project a picture of continued success and mastery of problems, without supplying quantitative and qualitative data. Some documents reveal ignorance. One booklet, describing activity in the classrooms at Cha Cheong Sao, claimed that the teaching methods brought by the United Nations "emphasized the use of the children's imagination and the use of interesting and illustrative material," and went on to tell about a lesson in geography where the children "watched their country take shape in the sand tray with flour tipped mounds representing the *snow capped peaks of her northern mountains.*"[7] It is hoped that the publicity agent, not the teacher, so flagrantly misrepresented Thailand's climate. It is obvious that the absence of bona fide evaluations allows publicity writers a fairly free rein.

In short, the observed tendency of field workers to be generalized rather than particular in their approach is more than matched at the headquarters level. The problem is accentuated by the absence of real data from the field. The generalizing seems to compound and perpetuate itself, to be taken in fact as reality.

REGIONAL CONCEPTS AND NATIONAL STATES

Because a region faces common tasks expressed in terms like "raising per capita income" or "raising standards of literacy or health," it does not follow that solutions are identical in each of the national entities that make up a region. It does follow that solutions are to be found only within the framework of the national states with recognition of their administrative and functional roles. The development of working relations with particular members and relevant institutions seems to be an essential starting point. United Nations regional organizations, however, are not established this way. If the availability of personnel is taken as a basic starting point, the inability of regional offices and, at the ultimate level, the agency headquarters to establish such relation-

7. UNESCO, *They Can't Afford to Wait* (Paris, UNESCO, 1952), p. 22 (italics added).

ships becomes clear on the simple issue of numbers. There are simply not enough people available to handle the diversity of such vast regions. As one example, when the Chief, Asian Section, UNESCO Headquarters, visited Bangkok he, along with the Chief of Mission, "investigated and had discussions" on the following topics: TUFEC, TURTEP, the International Child Study Center, the fellowship program, technical education, primary education contingency fund request, scientific documentation under the National Research Council, a National Science Institute, social science teaching and research (Thammasat University), social science demonstration, preservation and restoration of mural painting, a library seminar, mass communications studies, the Mekong River project, the Thonburi Technical Institute, ECAFE liaison, pulp and paper manufacture. The visit occupied approximately four working days, and no Thai official who might have exerted real influence on decision-making was contacted.[8]

There are many examples in UNESCO headquarters files of like forays; and the physical evidence in the regional office in Bangkok of FAO officers covering agricultural complexes stretching from Japan to Iran, or a UNESCO chief of mission sitting atop the educational problems of a like area, is plain to see. Thus, even if the need for particularism were firmly felt, the physical resources are simply not available to cater to the wide-ranging interests that headquarters and the regional offices look upon as their raison d'être. The search for overall solutions, however, continues. At a recent major conference, for example, the following proposal was made:

> *Noting* the valuable pioneering research in cross culture in child development undertaken by the Child Development Institute in Bangkok,
>
> *Considering* that the research techniques of the center will yield information which must be used in the reconstruction of school curricula and the improvement of teaching methods

8. *Report on My Mission to Thailand May 13–20, 1960* (from the files, UNESCO Headquarters, Paris).

and instruction in the primary education programmes in Asia as recommended by the Karachi Conference,

Recommends to the National Commissions and Member States to co-operate closely with the Bangkok center and use of the results in the primary education programme of their countries and to invite UNESCO and the Government of Thailand to expand the research programme of the institute.[9]

It would be idle to predict what might come of an expansion of the Institute at the Prasarn Mitr Teachers Training College, Bangkok, referred to above. According to its director (one of two foreign staff members), the current activity is so small, so embryonic, and so limited to the local situation at present that the thought of a pan-Asian pilot project seems startling.[10] The Thai authorities, on the other hand, have a very utilitarian and parochial view of the Institute. They feel it can help materially in developing an elementary syllabus for Thailand.

This study does not suggest that there are no universal or even regional solutions to human problems in Southeast Asia and elsewhere. Such solutions may arise. The question is whether what appears to be the lesser and the more parochial is being neglected by the planners and the policy-makers as a source of solutions. Inadequate resources for seeking and solving particular problems encourage not only seeking refuge in generalities but even acceptance of them as a valid modus operandi. At this time, however, it does seem that there are specific problems, even though limited to one nation, on which outside assistance can be helpful. But in the background there is the pervasive thought that organizations such as UNESCO will always turn to the global rather than the local, even though the local situation might offer better prospects of achievement.

There need not be a real conflict between the general and the particular. The Christian missionaries, for example, feel that their message has universal application. This does not prevent

9. UNESCO, *Regional Conference of National Commissions for* UNESCO *in Asia on Primary Education, Resolution No. 6.6* (Karachi, January 1960).

10. Interview at Child Development Institute, Bangkok, June 4, 1963.

them from working with specific problems on a local basis. Perhaps through long experience they have learned that there are no formulas for transmitting ready-made solutions quickly and effectively everywhere. Instead there is only a long, patient grappling with smaller entities, which may seem insignificant when matched against the global problem. Perhaps the real lesson to be learned by those responsible for policy and planning is not how much needs to be done but how much cannot be done.

11

U.N. AID: THE NEW COLONIALISM?

Essentially this study has been microcosmic, whereas the United Nations, in its physical spread over the globe and in the universality of its aspirations, is a wide-ranging organizational complex. The reaction of one small Southeast Asian state to a segment of United Nations activity cannot be taken as an indicator of success or failure for overall United Nations aid operations. Indeed, it is not the intention of this study to pass final verdicts, even on the Thai experience. Such terms as "failure" are meaningless when measured against the enormity of the United Nations aspiration and the uniqueness of its methods. Nevertheless, there are trends that are reasonably clear and that offer some basis for prognosticating the future of aid processes, at least in Asia, and emphasize the need for United Nations agencies (and other aid organizations) to reevaluate these processes.

It can be assumed that United Nations groups in Thailand are representative of U.N. agencies in other areas. Similarly, it can be accepted that persuasion will remain as the field workers' general method of leverage and that the skills to be transferred will be related to Western technology. Personnel dispensing these skills will in the main be Western-acculturated and will be recruited on the basis of their expertise. It seems likely also that over any foreseeable period the headquarters levels in the United Nations, where general concepts and policy and plans are formulated, will retain views that are global and general rather than local and particularistic. In other words, there is no substantive evidence of any significant changes in United Nations aspirations or methods in the near future. And what of the other end of the process, the level of the recipients? Can general trends be discerned there?

There is no real evidence that the Asian milieu has changed during the postwar era in such a way as to make the communications task much easier. Indeed, the pessimist would say that the out-look has not only deteriorated but promises to deteriorate even further. The area certainly has not changed ecologically except for odd pockets of urbanization and industrialization here and there, and still remains almost wholly peasant-oriented. By general Western standards of development, with the exception of Thailand, the Philippines, and Malaya, ECAFE surveys indicate slow but steady economic deterioration in Southeast Asia. The same could also be said for South Asia. Similarly, in regard to features important to modernization such as advancement of literacy, there is strong evidence that in many countries illiteracy will increase in the near future.

This is not to suggest that Asia has in general been static: notable inroads have been made by medicine and the goods of mass production. But even here there is no visible sign that these have changed an essential Asian outlook on life so as to make those affected more receptive to the modes of Western aid technicians. Neither is it at all clear that the pockets of urbanization occurring in various parts of Asia are promoting the contentment and stability which the United Nations agencies and other bodies feel is consonant with this kind of development. Indeed, it could be contended that one major effect of urbanization is to produce a deracinated or rootless peasant who, in Malaya, Vietnam, Java and Sumatra, Burma, and the Central Luzon Plain, has shown a far stronger propensity for revolt than for orderly pursuit of economic development in accordance with Western formulas. It is not likely that the process of urbanization will cease; indeed both Asian leaders and many external influences (not excluding the United Nations) are urging even more rapid urbanization. On this count alone instability may well be accentuated.

The single greatest technological intrusion into Asia, especially postwar Southeast Asia, has been that associated with the creation of modern military forces. As an adjunct of political alignment to one or the other of the two great blocs, there has been a phenomenal advent of jet aircraft, radar, tracked vehicles, organizational concepts associated with logistics, national training programs, and large military complexes generally, just to mention some obvious features. Whether these military enterprises, unmatched by any other technological development, make the communications task easier is hard to say. The probability is that in an immediate sense they absorb the all too slender human resources available, to the detriment of more humanitarian pursuits.

Neither do political developments indicate that the situation is in line with Western concepts of orderly change. Generally political institutions are more unstable than in the past. The Communist bloc is attempting the physical conquest of the Southeast Asian peninsula. Furthermore, there is no evidence that the new leaders who soon must replace the original nationalist leaders—many of the latter being born of the revolt against colonialism—are any more willing or capable to assume the laborious and unspectacular task of social and economic development, in, say, the Keynesian or Marxist mode, than their predecessors have been in earlier decades. Some aspects of recent Western political trends, however, have been followed. With a few notable exceptions, current and potential leaders insist on state control, but it is a control which the principals are reluctant or unable to exercise in any specific sense. Again, the young elites, so many of whom have received Western education over this past decade, have shown no marked desire to take their skills to rural areas. As the United Nations at TUFEC discovered, and as the Peace Corps is discovering now, career prospects in the city and the higher levels of the bureaucracy and government are a stronger inducement than obscure service in a remote village. It would indeed be difficult to substantiate a claim that political evolution in Southeast Asia is moving toward a theoretical Western model.

Thus the pessimist could justifiably say that, with some exceptions in a few states and in a few fields of endeavor, the general milieu in Asia, especially Southeast Asia, has not materially changed and from a Western viewpoint has probably worsened. Even the most optimistic would have to admit that as far as transmitting aid skills through persuasion is concerned, the equation remains much as it was before. The factors involved in the technological, social, and cultural confrontation promise to exist as realities of formidable proportions for a long time.

Rather than devising more grandiose concepts, such as the Karachi Plan, the United Nations and other agencies might find it more practical to stop and take stock. An assessment of what can be done and also what cannot be done is required, with a decision regard-

ing the methods and the people needed to improve on past per-
formances. These are essentially practical issues. Lurking like a
phantom in the wings is yet another concern, more philosophical
and more abstract but equally basic. Foreign aid, especially personalized foreign aid, is interference in a nation's lifeways. In
reality it is as much a continuum of the technological confrontation, despite variations, as the implanting of Western techniques
on Asian societies by colonial powers.

Condemnation of colonialism has been made elsewhere, in
quantity and in depth. The stresses, the disruption, and the de-
bilitation have been graphically portrayed. Colonialism was cred-
ited with the introduction of the machine and its related techniques; the imposition of Western organizational methods and
commercial practice; and raising conflicts between Western and
Asian law. The personal activities of Western innovators have
been subjected to special criticism. A verdict of guilty has been
near unanimous on all counts. But why should virtually the same
techniques become nondisruptive when introduced by the United
Nations? A declaration of disinterested benignity in political matters does not substantially alter the scope of a technology and its
associated technique. Therefore, as well as concern over the practicalities of what can and cannot be done, there are also the more
abstract questions of what ought to be done, by whom, how fast,
and toward what end.

Of all United Nations agencies concerned, UNESCO was most
responsible for probing the abstract circumstances of aid processes.
Some tentative studies were made but not pursued.[1] As has been
noted already, any doubts entertained about UNESCO philosophy
were quickly overborne by practicalities. UNESCO failed to recognize itself as another actor in the continuing technological confrontation.

To be a conscious agent of technological change is one thing.
Marxism, for example, assumes this role and takes upon itself a
divine right to change people's lives. But to be an unconscious
agent of technological change is another issue and has its own

[1]: UNESCO, *Cultural Patterns and Technical Change*, ed. Margaret Mead
(Paris, 1953); and UNESCO, *Education in a Technological Society: A Preliminary
International Survey of the Nature and Efficiency of Technical Education*
(Paris, 1952).

hazards. Needs are not realistically seen. Methods are random and uncertain. Disappointment becomes part of both the donors' and the recipients' lives. The danger is that failure will promote greater zealotry by aid proponents—zealotry aimed toward a purely utilitarian end. One cannot but be impressed, for example, by the growing similarity between Marxism and Western liberalism concerning peasantry as a way of life. Both despise it. Neither can one but be impressed by the general similarity of material ends. Both Marxists and Western liberals see an industrialized, urbanized proletariat with a high standard of living as a laudable objective. Thus if the aid proponent seeks greater efficiency, prompted by past failures in his method of transmittal, he must always face the danger of being drawn into more absolutist methods, justified as attaining an end "known" by him to be good. Nonmaterial values can be obscured if not negated. In a recent study sponsored by the United Nations, a vivid example was given of this tendency. After describing (and indeed over-romanticizing), the charm and easy indolence of Thailand's people, the nonutilitarian beauty and the spiritual impact of its Buddhist temples, and the evident harmony between peasant, nature, and religion, the writer still concluded that modernization had to come to Thailand. "The transition is sure to be painful, sure to be unsightly, and the psychological impact will affect almost all of her citizens." But endure it Thailand must . . . "to get a better life."[2]

Most of the materially underdeveloped parts of the world are being assaulted by all kinds of agencies originally motivated by a concern for one's fellow man. In the affluent countries of the West this concern is most pronounced. At times it seems to take on the appearance of a vast psychic therapy, useful in countering guilt that the West should have so much while others have so little. But something more is required than trying to do penance through the cold practicalities of a more efficient technological confrontation—or, at the extreme, a technological totalitarianism. If any cultural integrity is to be left to an individual or group, the right of choice must be honored, especially the right to reject or the right to modify a given program. When change is sponsored by totalitarian systems, their certainty of being right both in

2. Morris, "The Road to Huddersfield," p. 134.

method and in ends can be understood. The United Nations is not such an organization. Along with what can be done and what cannot be done, the question of what ought to be done and toward what end needs to be raised.

In asking this question the United Nations, and the West in general, would by necessity have to examine its own value system: to query whether it possessed a universal solution, good for all men at all times, a cure for basic human ills. To raise this kind of question is not to be guilty of atavism—to resurrect the myth of the "noble savage" or to declaim the virtues of Rousseau's "natural man." Undoubtedly benefits can be gained by Southeast Asia from specific aspects of Western technology. The United Nations in Thailand could well be accorded an accolade for having attempted to bring some of these benefits. But to acknowledge that some aspects of Western technique are beneficial is a far cry from saying that anything Western will bring a better life to Southeast Asia. The issue of values has yet to be debated simply because the questions have not yet been raised.

This study has not intended to show that the twain of East and West shall never meet. On the contrary, they have met productively in a variety of pursuits. What UNESCO and its associated agencies experienced in Thailand was in one sense unique and new in international relations. They attempted to change aspects of a Southeast Asian society in accordance with Western values, using nothing more than the power of persuasion. That the results were less than the aspirations is not an indictment. The only place for reproach is where those concerned failed to take account of shortcomings, and, above all, failed to raise fundamental questions about the technological confrontation and its total meaning for all men.

APPENDICES

APPENDIX I

PART A

LIST OF UNITED NATIONS AGENCIES IN THAILAND

Headquarters
ECAFE (United Nations Economic Commission for Asia and Far East).

Regional Offices (for ECAFE Area)
FAO (Food and Agricultural Organization)
UNESCO (United Nations Educational, Scientific and Cultural Organization).
ICAO (International Civil Aviation Organization).
UNICEF (United Nations Children's Fund).

Regional Offices (for Thailand, Taiwan, Japan, and Hong Kong)
UNTAB (United Nations Technical Assistance Board)
United Nations Special Fund

Local Offices and Missions
WHO (World Health Organization)
ILO (International Labor Organization)
IAEA (International Atomic Energy Agency)
IBRD (International Bank for Reconstruction and Development)

Special Missions
Headquarters, Executive Agent of the Committee for the Coordination of Investigations of Lower Mekong River Basin.

Source: ECAFE, Special Feature, Series No. 7/Rev. 1, July 1963.

PART B

LIST OF AID PROJECTS, UNITED NATIONS IN THAILAND

Section 1. Projects for 1963–64

Serial	Function	Year	Experts M/M	Costs[a]	Fellows M/M	Costs	Total Cost[b]
1.	Industrial development and production	1963	1/12	$19,000	—	—	$19,000
2.	Pulp and paper	1963	1/12	19,000	1/12	$ 4,500	23,500
3.	Land settlement	1963 1964	1/12 1/12	18,000 18,000	— —	— —	18,000 18,000
4.	Natural resource survey	1964	1/6	8,700	—	—	8,700
5.	Geological investigation	1964	1/12	18,000	—	—	18,000
6.	Financial institutions	1963	1/12	18,000	—	—	18,000
7.	Public administration	1963 1964	— —	— —	7/84 6/72	32,000 27,000	32,000 27,000
8.	Statistics	1963 1964	— —	— —	1/12 1/12	4,500 4,500	4,500 4,500
9.	Prisoner clarification (civil prison)	1963	—	—	1/6	3,500	3,500
10.	Security system (civil prison)	1964	—	—	1/6	3,500	3,500

Sources: Development Assistance Committee Coordinating Group, *Compendium of Technical Assistance To Thailand 1963/64* (Bangkok, Thai-American Audio-Visual Services, May 1963); and Office of Technical Assistance Board, Bangkok.

a. M/M refers to man/months, that is the number of persons concerned and the total number of months to be worked, i.e. 2 experts working a full calendar year would appear as 2/24.

b. Equipment included in costs where applicable but not itemized.

Serial	Function	Year	Experts		Fellows		Total Cost
			M/M	Costs	M/M	Costs	
11.	Transport service training	1963	—	—	1/12	$ 4,500	$ 4,500
12.	Statistics (mapping)	1963	—	—	1/12	4,500	4,500

Section 2. Long Term Projects as of 1963–64

Serial	Function	Year	Experts		Fellows		Total Cost
			M/M	Costs	M/M	Costs	
1.	Advanced meteorological training	1961 1962 1963–64 1964–65	— — —	— — —	1/12 1/12 1/12	$ 4,500 4,500 4,500	$ 4,500 4,500 4,500
2.	Manpower assessment studies	1962 1963 1964 1965	1/3 1/12 1/12 1/9	$ 4,500 18,000 18,000 13,500	— — 1/12 —	— — 5,000 —	— — 23,000 13,500
3.	Labor administration	1963 1964 1965	1/12 1/12 1/9	18,000 18,000 9,000	— — —	— — —	18,000 18,000 9,000
4.	Industrial safety	1963 1964	1/6 1/6	9,000 9,000	— —	— —	9,000 9,000
5.	Handicraft design and marketing	1963 1964	1/12 1/4	18,000 6,000	— —	— —	18,000 6,000
6.	Labor economics	1963	— —	— —	2/24 2/24	1,000 1,000	1,000 1,000
7.	Nutrition	1961–62 1963–64 1964–65 1965–66 1966–67	1/12 1/12 1/12 1/12 1/12	16,800 16,800 16,800 16,800 16,800	— — — — —	— — — — —	16,800 16,800 16,800 16,800 16,800
8.	Animal production	1963 1964	1/12 1/12	18,000 18,000	2/12 2/12	6,000 6,000	24,000 24,000
9.	Land and water development, and soil survey	1963 1964	1/12 1/12	18,000 18,000	1/12 —	5,000 —	23,000 18,000
10.	Fisheries development	1963 1964	1/12 1/12	18,000 18,000	1/12 1/12	5,000 5,000	23,000 23,000

Serial	Function	Year	Experts M/M	Experts Costs	Fellows M/M	Fellows Costs	Total Cost
11.	Agricultural statistics	1963	1/9	$13,500	2/24	$10,000	$23,500
		1964	1/12	18,000	1/12	5,000	23,500
12.	Child Study Institute	1961	1/12	15,000	2/6	6,000	21,000
		1962	1/12	18,000	—	—	18,000
		1963	2/24	3,000	2/24	6,000	9,000
		1964	2/24	3,000	1/12	3,000	6,000
		1965	2/24	3,000	1/6	—	4,000
		1966	2/24	3,000	1/6	—	4,000
13.	Social science, teaching, and research	1962	1/12	—	—	—	—
		1963	1/12	3,000	1/12	3,000	6,000
		1964	—	—	1/12	3,000	3,000
		1965	1/12	18,000	1/12	3,000	21,000
		1966	1/12	—	1/12	3,000	3,000
		1967	1/12	—	1/12	3,000	3,000
		1968	1/12	—	1/12	3,000	3,000
14.	Documentation Center	1961	1/6	7,800	—	—	7,800
		1962	1/12	18,000	—	—	21,000
		1963	3/30	4,500	—	—	4,500
		1964	3/36	5,400	—	—	5,400
		1965	3/36	5,400	2/9	6,000	11,400
		1966	2/24	3,600	2/9	6,000	9,600
		1967	2/24	3,600	1/9	—	3,600
15.	TURTEP	1963	1/12	18,000	1/12	3,000	21,300
		1964	1/12	18,000	—	—	18,000
16.	Education	1963	—	—	2/24	6,000	6,000
17.	National Tuberculosis Program Pilot Project	1961	5/60	70,908	2/10	4,500	75,496
		1962	5/59	77,660	—	—	77,760
		1963	3/60	72,097	—	—	72,197
		1964	3/60	82,420	2/24	7,200	89,720
		1965	2/24	37,669	2/24	7,200	44,969
		1966	1/3	4,800	—	—	4,800
		1967	1/3	4,800	—	—	4,800
		1968	1/3	4,800	—	—	4,800
18.	Nursing Advisory Service	1961	2/18	26,234	—	—	26,755
		1962	2/18	17,700	—	—	18,200
		1963	4/48	47,119	—	—	47,619
		1964	4/48	47,486	1/12	3,600	51,086
		1965	4/48	48,151	—	—	48,651
19.	Yaws control	1963	3/36	45,278	—	—	45,378
		1964	2/24	33,195	—	—	33,295

Serial	Function	Year	Experts M/M	Costs	Fellows M/M	Costs	Total Cost
20.	Strengthening of health services	1963 1964	1/12 1/12	$15,513 15,347	— —	— —	$18,613 15,447
21.	Reactor physics	1963 1964	1/9 1/3	14,400 4,800	2/24 2/24	$8,000 8,000	25,900 12,800
22.	Electronic instrument techniques	1963 1964	1/6 1/6	9,600 9,600	— —	— —	17,100 9,600
23.	Mekong River Project, Hydrographic Survey	—	—	—	—	—	92,900
24.	Advisory services to National Economic Development Board	—	4/48	—	—	—	83,000
25.	Training, economic development	—	3/12	—	—	—	8,000

Approximate Total Costs $1,750,686

Section 3. Synopsis of Aid Given to Thailand in 1963 in Terms of Personnel and Man Hours

Donor Country	Expert (M/M)	Scholarships (M/M)	In Service Training (M/M)
Australia	32/242	8/64	28/252
France	19/168	59/477	4/180
Federal Republic of Germany	25/264	30/360	—
Japan	48/257	66/398	208/1256
Switzerland	1/24	7/84	—
United Kingdom	45/355	55/1246	40/32
United States (USOM & State Dept. only)	150/1509	229/1614	4847/2696
United Nations (incl. IBRD non-loan Mekong River survey)	100/1062	56/582	1717/1781

APPENDIX II

FOREIGN PERSONNEL AT THE CHA CHEONG SAO PILOT PROJECT

Nationality	*Field*	*Agency*	*Duration of Assignment*
United States	School health nurse	WHO	May 1954–March 1956
India	Visual aids	UNESCO	June 1956–Dec. 1958
United Kingdom	Secondary education	UNESCO	June 1956–Dec. 1959
United States	Rural primary education	UNESCO	June 1956–May 1957
United States	Secondary education	U.S. Point Four	May 1952–May 1953
United Kingdom	English teaching	UNESCO	Sept. 1952–Sept. 1959
United Kingdom	Vocational education	ILO	May 1953–Sept. 1956
Canada	Visual aids	UNESCO	March 1952–Aug. 1953
Canada	Agriculture	FAO	Dec. 1951–March 1953
United States	Vocational education	U.S. Point Four	Aug. 1951–July 1953
Norway	Science	UNESCO	Aug. 1954–July 1955
Sweden	Secondary education	UNESCO	Jan. 1954–June 1956
United States	Science	UNESCO	May 1952–April 1953
United States	Elementary science	U.S. Point Four	Aug. 1952–Aug. 1953
Denmark	Social sciences	UNESCO	April 1951–March 1952
Norway	Teacher education	UNESCO	May 1956–April 1958
Ceylon	School health physician	WHO	Feb. 1954–Jan. 1956
United States	Chief of Mission	UNESCO	April 1952–Dec. 1957
United States	Elementary education	U.S. Point Four	Oct. 1951–Oct. 1956
United States	Health education	U.S. Point Four	Oct. 1951–Oct. 1953
United States	Science	UNESCO	April 1951–May 1952
United States	Adult education	UNESCO	July 1952–May 1953
United Kingdom	Chief of Mission	UNESCO	Jan. 1958–continued beyond end of mission in 1959
Australia	Teacher education	UNESCO	Dec. 1953–Sept. 1954, May 1955–Jan. 1956
Denmark	Home economics	UNESCO	March 1955–Oct. 1955
United States	Elementary education	U.S. Point Four	Aug. 1951–May 1956
Canada	Adult education	UNESCO	Sept. 1953–Nov. 1958
United States	Teacher education	U.S. Point Four	Sept. 1951–June 1953
Japan	Handicrafts	ILO	Aug. 1954–June 1959
United States	Vocational education	UNESCO	May 1951–Sept. 1952
United Kingdom	Vocational education	ILO	Dec. 1951–Oct. 1954
New Zealand	Chief of Mission	UNESCO	Nov. 1950–June 1952

APPENDIX III

FOREIGN PERSONNEL AT TUFEC

Nationality	Field	Agency	Duration of Assignment
United Kingdom	Made preliminary survey of the Northeast region; took charge of social welfare section	UNTAA	1953–54
United States	Deputy Director, Agriculture	UNESCO	1953–56
United States	Agriculture (part time)	ICA	1953–56
Australia	Education	UNESCO	1954–55
United States	Library, research	UNESCO	1954–56
United States	Library service	UNESCO	1954–56
Netherlands	Audio-Visual Aids (AVA) & Production	UNESCO	1954–58
Netherlands	AVA & Production	UNESCO	1954–56
Finland	Health	WHO	1954–56
Canada	Education, training service	UNESCO	1955–58
Canada	Social welfare, agriculture	UNTAA	1955–59
United Kingdom	Village construction, crafts	ILO	1955–57
Netherlands	Research	Dutch Government	1958–60
Sweden	Research	UNESCO	1960
Denmark	Homemaking (part time)	FAO	1955
United Kingdom	English teaching	UNESCO	1956–57
United Kingdom	Deputy Director	UNESCO	1956–57
Denmark	Homemaking	UNESCO	1956–59
Ireland	Health	WHO	1956–57
United States	Library service	UNESCO	1956–57
France	Secretary to the Deputy Director	UNESCO	1957–58
United Kingdom	Deputy Director	UNESCO	1958–60
Canada	Agriculture	Colombo Plan	1957–58
Jordan	Library service	UNESCO	1958
United States	English teaching	Fulbright Fellowship	1958
France	Senior Advisor	UNESCO	1961
United Kingdom	AVA	UNESCO	1961
United States	Research	Ford Foundation	1955–56
United States	Research	Fulbright Fellowship	1951–61
United States	English teaching	Fulbright Fellowship	1958–59

APPENDIX IV

Activity	*Results*
Bamboo water pump	Unsuccessful (see p. 86)
Water sealed latrines	Not enough water—too much odor
Wooden winch	Not pursued
Potter's wheel	Not pursued
Improved well	Successful (see p. 57)
Village Persian wheel (for lifting water)	Not pursued
Cotton jenny	Not pursued. Locally built jennies are common in Thailand (see pp. 62–63); it was later discovered by TUFEC that there were 8,049 looms in Ubol province alone.
Wheelbarrow	Did not come into general use
Glazing of pottery	Not pursued; the local method was inferior but adequate for local needs. In any case, cheap Japanese crockery had a far greater attraction than a high quality local product which tended to be quite expensive.
Wood fire stove	Required a brick or wooden chimney and strengthened floor supports, all quite unrealistic in the average peasant house.
Pony cart library	(See pp. 71–72)
Wooden cog wheel	Not pursued
Adjusting screw device	For use with cog above; not pursued
Treadle lathe	Not pursued; no local use
Forge fan	Was more efficient as enabled a man to be dispensed with, but this was hardly necessary because labor was plentiful.
Model windmill	Not pursued (see p. 20)
Village work bench	Ten prototypes made and some interest shown
Bamboo artifacts	(See pp. 67–68)
Some homemade tools	Could not compete with imported variety

Source: United Nations, International Labor Organization, *Report to the Government of Thailand on Handicraft Activity at the Fundamental Education Center at Ubol: Part I* (Geneva, ILO/TAP/Thailand/R 11, 1959).

APPENDIX V

ACHIEVEMENT OF EMPATHY BY FOREIGN EXPERTS AT TUFEC—
A THAI VIEW

Part A: Survey Data

Foreign experts involved	Total: 29
Origin by region	Western: 28
	Middle East: 1
Tenure of foreign experts assessed in this section	Average: 1.15 years
	Longest tenure: 4 years
	Shortest tenure: 3 months
Thai involved as consultants	12 (all but one had functioned as counterparts)
Tenure of Thai as counterparts	Average: 3 years
	Longest: 8 years
	Shortest: 1 year

Part B: Synthesis of Thai Comment

Characteristics thought important by Thai consulted	Number of foreign experts assessed as receiving a positive response (out of 29)
Expertise:	
a. Knowledge generally	18
b. Relevance of knowledge to Thailand	14
c. Relevance of knowledge to TUFEC operations	14
Application of knowledge	13
Sincerity	
a. To his profession	13
b. To the job in TUFEC	10
Respected because of	
a. Age	4
b. Knowledge	6
c. Effectiveness at TUFEC	10
Induced sympathy because of	
a. Personal problems unconnected with TUFEC	4
b. Job difficulties	6
Indigenous orientation	
a. Held some knowledge of Thailand	2*
b. Learned something of Thailand	5
c. No orientation toward Thai milieu	17
d. Not long enough to judge	5
Communications	
a. Thai language spoken	2*
b. No language but a "feeling" for Thai attitudes	2
Empathy	
a. Full empathy	4*
b. Beginnings of empathy	7
c. No empathy	18

*Includes two area students.

APPENDIX VI

No. Items	10 Years Ago	"Nowadays" (1959/60)
A. Physical Changes		
1. Schools	Schools small and in poor condition	15 new permanent schools built by the people's contribution
2. Wells	Only temporary wells	104 wells constructed
3. Latrines	None	440 latrines made
4. Reading rooms	None	12 reading rooms
5. Roads	Very limited and rough	61,349 meters of road made by villagers
6. Farmers' Clubs	None	4 Farmers' Clubs (137 members)
7. Young Farmers' Clubs	None	4 Young Farmers' Clubs (105 members)
8. Interest groups	None	4 groups (180 members)
9. Fish ponds	None	12 fish ponds
10. Children's playgrounds	None	10 children's playgrounds
11. Community Centers	Some	4 new ones
B. Attitude Changes		
1. Communication	No bus	Buses from town to villages; and from villages to villages
		1. From Ubol to Nong Lai and Pa Oa villages
		2. From Ubol to Tungkunyai Tungkumnoi villages
		3. From Ubol to Kunyai Village
		4. From Ubol to HuaReur Village
		5. From Ubol to Nong Manoo, and Hua Kum villages
		6. From Ubol to Yangsalcapolum village
2. Agriculture	Villagers did not use fertilizer and did not grow other crops after harvest	Villagers use fertilizer and grow other crops after harvest

No.	Items	10 Years Ago	"Nowadays" (1959/60)
		They did not grow vegetables	They grow vegetables for Ubol market
		They did not use insecticides	They use insecticides
		They did not know how to caponize chicken	They know how to caponize chicken
		They did not grow field crops	They increase their income by growing field crops
3.	Education	They did not read newspapers	They like to read newspapers
		They seldom listened to radio	There are so many radio receiving sets in the villages
		They rarely sent their children to further their education	They send their children to town to further their education
		No school Co-operative store	There are now school Co-op. stores
		No school Board of Education in villages	They organized Boards of Education in villages
4.	Health	They liked old methods of treatment for diseases	They prefer scientific treatment to the old ones
		They believed in "Phi" or spirit: Phi Pop Phi Puta (spirits of their ancestors) and sorcery	Such beliefs are limited
		They used local midwife for delivering their babies	Most women go to clinics and hospitals for mother and child care, and for delivery of babies
5.	Social attitudes	They did not like to talk with strangers	They like to talk and share their views with strangers
		They wore old costume	They select suitable clothes and use cosmetics
		They did not consume their leisure time profitably	They seem to use their leisure time better than before. New games and new recreations can be found in villages
		They used to carry their commodities to town	They bring their commodities to town by buses
		They did not know how to conduct a business meeting and exchange ideas	They know how to conduct a business meeting. They discuss problems and share their ideas

Source: TUFEC, "Eight Years of Cooperation," pp. 40–44 (in Thai). No attempt was made by writer to adjust English syntax of the translation made at TUFEC.

BIBLIOGRÁPHY

PART I—PRIMARY SOURCES

United Nations Documents

ECONOMIC COMMISSION FOR ASIA AND THE FAR EAST

ECAFE, *Economic Survey of Asia and the Far East, 1957*, Bangkok, March 1958.

———, *Economic Survey of Asia and the Far East, 1961*, Bangkok, March 1962.

———, "Economic Theory and Practice and Under-Developed Countries of Asia and the Far East: An ECAFE Case," *ECAFE Special Feature Series, No. 2*, Rev. I, Bangkok, September 1961.

———, *Fields of Economic Development Handicapped by Lack of Trained Personnel in Certain Countries of Asia and the Far East*, Bangkok, II.F.6., 1951.

———, "Population Problems in the ECAFE Region," *ECAFE Special Feature Series, No. 4*, Rev. I, Bangkok, September 1961.

———, "The Quest of Asia's Economic Growth—The Role of Research and Planning," *Information Series* No. 2, Bangkok, September 1961.

———, "Regional Co-operation: ECAFE's Theme in 1962," *Press Release No. G/359*, Bangkok, December 31, 1962.

———, "Thailand and the United Nations," *ECAFE Special Feature Series, No. 9*, Bangkok, November 1961.

———, "United Nations Activity in Thailand," *ECAFE Special Feature Series, No. 7*, Rev. I, Bangkok, February 1963.

FOOD AND AGRICULTURE ORGANIZATION

Dickinson, Frank, *Report to Government of Thailand on Agricultural Activity at Cha Cheong Sao*, Bangkok, FAO/ETAP/215, December 1953.

FAO, Letter from Agricultural Research Section FAO Headquarters, Rome, to Director FAO Regional Office Bangkok, on Applied Scientific Research Corporation for Thailand, May 22, 1963.

———, *Report of the Mission for Siam*, Washington, FAO, September 1948.

Nichols, Frank G., *The Development of Applied Scientific Research in Thailand: Stage One* (Report No. 1 TAO/TAB), Bangkok, September 1962.

INTERNATIONAL LABOR ORGANIZATION

ILO, *Report on the Possibilities of Developing Small Scale Industries in the Ubol Area*, Geneva, ILO/TAP/Thailand/R1, 1954.

———, *Report to the Government of Thailand on Handicrafts Activity at the Fundamental Education Center at Ubol: Part I*, Geneva, ILO/TAP/Thailand/R11, 1959.

———, *Report to the Government of Thailand on Handicraft Activity at the Fundamental Research Center at Ubol: Part II*, Geneva, ILO/TAP/Thailand/R18, 1961.

UNITED NATIONS CHILDREN'S FUND

UNICEF, *Children of the Developing Countries*, New York, World Publishing Company, 1963.

———, *Digest of UNICEF Aid Projects in Asia*, New York, E/ICEF/464, March 1963.

———, *New Trends in UNICEF Policy*, New York, UNICEF/Misc. 33, 1961.

UNITED NATIONS EDUCATIONAL, SCIENTIFIC, AND CULTURAL ORGANIZATION

(Note: This section includes all documents, reports, etc., sponsored by UNESCO even if authors belonged to different U.N. agencies.)

Allen, John C., *Annual Report on the Teaching of English as an Aid to Training at TUFEC*, Ubol, December 31, 1956.

Anglemeyer, Mary, *Report on the Pony Cart Travelling Library Service*, Ubol, November 9, 1957.

Audriac, John, *Report on Secondary Education, Cha Cheong Sao*, Cha Cheong Sao, January 7, 1959.

———, *Report on the UNESCO Thailand Cha Cheong Sao Pilot Project*, Paris, UNESCO/EPTA/Tha/2, March 1962.

Bertholet, C. J. L., and Bencha Diswatt, *Housing and Food Patterns in Eleven Villages in Northeast Thailand*, Ubol, Research Section TUFEC, September 1959.

Bower, John, *The Use of Annamite Refugees as Craftsmen at TUFEC*, Paris, November 17, 1952.

Burroughs, G. E. R., *Technique of Evaluation, Paper No. 12–Evaluation of Fundamental Education Projects*, Paris, UNESCO/SS/EVAL/12, March 20, 1956.

Cha Cheong Sao Pilot Project, *Educational Development*, Bangkok, Prachacharng Printing, 1954 (in Thai).

———, *Primary Extension Schools in Cha Cheong Sao*, Cha Cheong Sao, Garn Chawit Press, 1959 (in Thai).

————, *Special Report on Handicrafts Section, Pilot Project,* Bangkok, November 1957.

Clarke, Victor, *Report on Steps Being Taken to Improve and Extend Compulsory Education Together With Some Suggestions for Further Development,* Paris, May 1954.

Couthcart-Burrow, H., *A Report on the Teaching of English in Thailand,* Bangkok, February 1956.

Ertem, Furzi, *A Report on Teacher Training and Rural Education,* Ubol, December 23, 1957.

————, *Final Report on Teacher Training at TURTEP,* Ubol, April 1960.

Faris, Donald K., *Progress Report to Chief, Office for Asia and the Far East, Technical Assistance Administration,* Ubol, April 15, 1956.

————, *Progress Report to Chief Program Division, TAA,* Ubol, undated.

————, *Technical Assistance Program, Community Development Training in Thailand* (TAO/THA/IO, August 11, 1959).

Flores, G. C., *Report on My Mission to Thailand, 13–20 May 1960, by Chief Asia Section, UNESCO,* Paris, July 1960.

Freznoza, Florentino, *First Report on Rural Teacher Training,* Ubol, November 21, 1959.

————, *Report for the Period November 1959–December 1961,* Ubol, January 1962.

Garraud, R., *Report to UNESCO on TUFEC and TURTEP,* Ubol, July 1961.

Gillet, R., *Report on Village Work for 1957 and Education in TUFEC,* Ubol, December 1957.

Halls, A. James, *Report on Education, TUFEC,* Ubol, August 1954.

————, *Annual Report on Education Section for 1954,* Ubol, undated.

————, *Annual Report for 1955,* Ubol, March 29, 1956.

————, *Final Report on Work Done at TUFEC in Elementary and Adult Education,* Ubol, undated.

Halonen, Marie, *The Health Program at TUFEC,* Ubol, July 1957.

Hayden, Howard, *Annual Report for 1957,* Ubol, January 12, 1959.

————, *Annual Report for 1958,* Ubol, January 12, 1959.

————, *Final Report,* Ubol, August 1, 1959.

————, *Annual Report for 1958—TURTEP,* Ubol, undated.

————, *Half Yearly Report: TUFEC,* Ubol, July 31, 1959.

Ingersoll, J., *Annual Report TUFEC Research and Library Section,* Ubol, March 12, 1954.

————, *Annual Report: TUFEC Research and Library Section,* Ubol, mid-1955.

——, *Annual Report: TUFEC Research and Library Section*, Ubol, mid-1956.

Jarland, Stig, *Progress Reports Nos. 1–3 on Cottage and Small Industries by UN Industrial Planning Expert*, Bangkok, April 15, 1958.

Jesse, Mabel, *Report on Rural Teacher Training*, Ubol, April 1957.

——, *Annual Report for 1957*, Ubol, December 31, 1957.

——, *Final Report on My Efforts at TURTEP*, Ubol, December 1958.

Juul, Peter M., *Report by the Teacher Training Expert*, Cha Cheong Sao, December 31, 1957.

——, *Annual Report on Teacher Training and Syllabus for Secondary Education*, Cha Cheong Sao, January 16, 1958.

Kinket, Jan, *Bi-Monthly Report on Production of Educational Materials*, Ubol, October 1954.

——, *Annual Report on Production of Educational Materials*, Ubol, February 1955.

——, *Bi-Monthly Report on Production of Educational Materials*, Ubol, December 1955.

——, *Annual Report on the Production of Instructional Materials*, Ubol, February 7, 1956.

——, *Annual Report on Audio Visual Aid Section*, Ubol, December 1957.

Klausner, William, *Memorandum on a Visit to Udorn*, Bangkok, August 30, 1958.

——, *Memorandum on Ministry of Interior Community Development Pilot Project*, Bangkok, May 4, 1959.

Madge, Sir Charles, *Progress Report to UNESCO Headquarters Paris on Development of TUFEC Programme*, Ubol, May 1954.

——, *Progress Report to UNESCO Headquarters Paris on Development of TUFEC Program*, Ubol, June 1954.

——, *Survey Before Development in Thai Villages*, Paris, ST/SAO/ SER. 0/25, March 1957.

Marshall, Kendric, *Observations and Recommendations Concerning the Re-organization of the Cha Cheong Sao Educational Pilot Project*, Bangkok, August 1957.

Nichols, Frank, *The Development of Applied Scientific Research in Thailand: Stage One (Report No. 1 TAO/TAB)*, Bangkok, September 1962.

Opper, Conrad J., *Comment on the TUFEC Annual Report, 1954*, Bangkok, June 17, 1955.

——, *Annual Report for 1956*, Ubol, December 31, 1956.

——, *Annual Report for 1957 on TURTEP*, Ubol, February 8, 1957.

——, *Progress Report for Quarter Ending March 1957*, Ubol, March 1957.

——, *Comments on Report of Mr. Morris G. Fox, United Nations*

Community Development Advisor in Thailand, Bangkok, August 15, 1957.

———, *The Second Phase of the Cha Cheong Sao Educational Pilot Project,* Bangkok, April 3, 1958.

———, *Comments on the UNESCO Headquarters Request for an Accounting of the Pilot Project,* Bangkok, April 28, 1958.

———, *An Evaluation of the Pilot Project,* Bangkok, July 8, 1958.

———, *Comments on the Results of the Enquiry into The Morale and Working Conditions of Twenty-Seven F.E. Teams in Thailand,* Bangkok, February 1959.

———, *Half Yearly Report on the UNESCO Technical Assistance Mission to Thailand,* Ubol, June 30, 1959.

———, *Fundamental Educational Organizers as Trainers of Village Leaders,* Bangkok, November 16, 1959.

———, *The Technical Assistance Mission to Thailand: Annual Report for 1959,* Bangkok, January 1960.

———, *Report of the Chief of Mission for the Half Year Ending June 30, 1960,* Bangkok, July 1960.

———, *A Report on TUFEC,* Bangkok, undated.

Opper, Hayden et al., *Recent Developments in the TURTEP Project,* Bangkok, September 24, 1958.

Orato, Pedro, *Report on a Visit to Cha Cheong Sao Educational Pilot Project,* Head Educational Section, UNESCO, Paris, February 1957.

———, *Report on Follow-up Mission to Thailand: Outline of Proposals to Chief of Mission,* Paris, undated.

Pederson, Inger-Marie, *Report of the Home Economist, TUFEC,* Ubol, December 31, 1956.

Penny, Harry H., *Report on Work Done in Cha Cheong Sao Teachers College,* Bangkok, January 1956.

Silversten, D. A., *Report on Rural Teacher Training,* Ubol, October 1960.

Smith, David, *Annual Report on Education and Training Services at TUFEC,* Ubol, February 15, 1956.

———, *Report to UNESCO Headquarters on Education Materials Production, UNESCO in Thailand,* Bangkok, February 5, 1962.

Tacchi, H., *Report on Rural Teacher Training for July 1959 to December 1961,* Ubol, March 1962.

Takaki, Matsuro, *Bamboo Work,* Ubol, Audio-Visual Section, 1961 (in Thai).

Tisinger, R. M., *Annual Report for 1953,* Ubol, February 15, 1954.

———, *Progress Report on TUFEC,* Ubol, October 1954.

———, *Annual Report for 1954,* Ubol, March 1, 1955.

TUFEC Publications

Draft of Revised Work Programme, Bangkok, May 1954.

Draft of The Course for Training Supervisors in Community Development, Ubol, TUFEC, September 1957.

Eight Years of Cooperation Between UNESCO and Thailand, Bangkok, Tung Mahamek Technical School Press, 1962 (in Thai).

Grow More Food Campaign: An Interim Report, Ubol, October 1957.

A Manual for Agricultural Workers, Bangkok, Tung Mahamek Technical School Press, 1960 (in Thai).

Minutes of the First and Second Meetings, TUFEC Executive Committee, held at the Ministry of Education, Bangkok, May 23, 1953, and February 18, 1955.

Minutes of the First through the Third Meetings of the Regional Education Officers Conference, TUFEC, Ubol, July 12 to July 15, 1955.

Minutes of the First through the Twenty-Third Meetings of the TUFEC Operating Committee, TUFEC, Ubol, June 1953 to March 1956.

Minutes of the First and Second Meetings of the TUFEC-TURTEP Joint Committee, Ubol, TURTEP, July 1959.

Minutes of a Meeting on Field Evaluation Methods in Technical Assistance, UNESCO Regional Office, Bangkok, October 5–9, 1959.

A New Look at TURTEP; A Report by the Working Party, Ubol, March 1960.

Notes on Training—A Manual for Community Development Workers, Ubol, TUFEC, 1958.

The Optimum Use of Fundamental Education Teams, Ubol, March 6, 1959.

Plan for Village Work, Ubol, undated.

Provisional Programme of Study, 1954, Bangkok, Chatra Press, April 1954.

Provisional Programme of Study, 1958, Bangkok, Chatra Press, 1958.

First Report of the Co-ordinators on the Progress of Village Training and Other Matters Related to Village Work, Ubol, undated.

Second Report: Village Co-ordinators, Ubol, July 12, 1958.

TUFEC News (Issues I–7 January–June 1960), Ubol, TUFEC (in Thai).

Working With People—A Manual for FEO's, Ubol, TUFEC, 1957 (in Thai).

TURTEP, *Report of the TURTEP Working Party,* Ubol, January 29, 1960.

UNESCO, *Appraisal of UNESCO's Programmes for the Economic and Social Council,* Paris, IIC/12, 1960.

———, "Education as a Basic Factor in Economic and Social Development," *Educational Planning Documents, No. I*, Bangkok, UNESCO, January 1963.

————, "Educational Statistics Needed in Asia and Oceania," *Educational Planning Documents No. 4*, Bangkok, UNESCO, February 1963.

————, "Educational Planning in Three Continents," *Educational Planning Documents No. 5*, Bangkok, UNESCO, March 1963.

————, "Essential School Statistics for Educational Planning," *Basic Statistics*, Bangkok, UNESCO, October 1962.

————, *Final Report of Ministers of Education of Asian States Participating in the Karachi Plan*, Bangkok, UNESCO, Harry Frederick Printers, 1962.

————, "Incidence of Literacy in a Country," *Statistical Study No. 1*, Bangkok, UNESCO, September 17, 1962.

————, "The Needs of Asia in Primary Education," *UNESCO Educational Studies and Documents No. 41*, Paris, UNESCO, 1961.

————, "Population, Labor, and Educational Statistics in National Planning," *Educational Planning Documents No. 3*, Bangkok, UNESCO, February 1963.

————, *Records of The General Conference at Montevideo 1954—Eighth Session—Resolutions*, Paris, 1955.

————, *Regional Conference of National Commissions for UNESCO in Asia on Primary Education, Resolution No. 6.6*, Karachi, January 1960.

————, "Social Factors in Educational Plans," *Educational Planning Documents No. 7*, Bangkok, UNESCO, April 1963.

————, *UNESCO Educational Programme in Thailand*, Bangkok, 1954.

————, *The Work of the UNESCO Technical Assistance Mission in Thailand*, Bangkok, undated.

UNESCO Headquarters, Letters, etc., Internal Memorandum by the Director General UNESCO on Second International Fundamental Education Center (TUFEC), August 28, 1951.

————, Internal Memorandum by Director General, UNESCO on Policy for Second International Fundamental Education Center (TUFEC), February 19,1952.

————, Notes on an Informal Discussion Between Fundamental Education Division, UNESCO and New Deputy Director TUFEC, January 8, 1953.

————, Director General UNESCO to Under Secretary for Education Thailand, on Support Policy for TUFEC, March 4, 1953.

————, Telegram of Assent and Agreement for Conditions in Setting up TUFEC, from Thai Government, October 13, 1953.

————, Internal Memorandum by Fundamental Education Division UNESCO (R. Attagalya), Commenting on Annual Report for 1954, TUFEC, June 17, 1955.

————, Fundamental Education Division UNESCO (Pedro Orato) to Chief of Mission, Bangkok, on Evaluation Procedures, December 16, 1959.

UNESCO Regional Office Bangkok, Letters, etc.

Ministry of Education to Chief of Mission, Commenting on UNESCO syllabus for Pilot Project, February 13, 1951.

Ministry of Education to Chief of Mission Establishing a Supplementary Agreement Relative to Services at TUFEC, March 13, 1953.

Chief of Mission to UNESCO HQ on the need for Agricultural Specialists to be sent to TUFEC, February 16, 1956.

Chief of Mission to Deputy Director TUFEC on Need for Integrated TUFEC Program, February 16, 1956.

Teacher Training Expert, Pilot Project, to Executive Committee, Pilot Project, on the Demonstration School, October 10, 1956.

Chief of Mission to Ministry of Education on Diffusion of Cha Cheong Sao Pilot Project, November 6, 1956.

Teacher Training Expert, Pilot Project, to Chief of Mission on Basic Curricula at the Pilot Project, February 1957.

Chief of Mission to UNESCO Headquarters on Shortages of Suitable Personnel at TUFEC, June 17, 1957.

Teacher Training Expert, Pilot Project, to Executive Committee, Pilot Project, on Co-ordination within the Pilot Project, June 4, 1957.

Chief of Mission to UNESCO Headquarters on Shortages of Appropriate Personnel for TUFEC and TURTEP, June 25, 1957.

Chief of Mission, on Personnel Strains at TUFEC, December 1, 1957.

Acting Chief of Mission to UNESCO Headquarters, Paris, on Diffusion of Cha Cheong Sao Pilot Project, August 1957.

Director, Department of Education, UNESCO Headquarters, to Chief of Mission on Need for and Problems associated with Evaluation of Pilot Project, April 16, 1958.

Chief of Mission (reply to above), April 28, 1958.

Ministry of Interior to Thirty Provincial Governors Regarding Their Relations with FEOs, April 30, 1958.

Teacher Training Expert, Pilot Project, to Chief of Mission on Teacher Training Program, January 18, 1958.

Handicrafts Expert to Head, Fundamental Education Division, UNESCO Headquarters, on Problems of Craft Training in Thailand, February 19, 1958.

Director General Education, Ministry of Education, to Chief of Mission on Transfer of UNESCO Experts to Ministry of Education, June 26, 1958.

Chief of Mission to Fundamental Education Division, UNESCO Headquarters, on Need for Development of a Pottery Industry, June 17, 1958.

Deputy Head TUFEC on the Influx of Theories and Theoreticians at TUFEC, to Chief of Mission, UNESCO Regional Office, Bangkok, June 20, 1958.

Chief of Mission to Fundamental Education Division, UNESCO Headquarters, on Disintegration of FEO Teams, June 1958.

Deputy Director TUFEC to Chief of Mission, on Relations with Thai Personnel at TUFEC, July 2, 1958.

Chief of Mission to Fundamental Education Division, UNESCO Headquarters, on Need for Different Type of Program as Replacement for Fundamental Education, August 14, 1958.

"Questionnaire on Effective Use of FEOs" (Bangkok, 1958).

Chief of Mission to Director of Education, UNESCO Headquarters, on Need for Longer Tenure, Field Experts, August 4, 1958.

Myrtle Imhoff to Director of Education, UNESCO Headquarters, on Her Terms of Reference as Researcher, Pilot Project, November 4, 1959.

Chief of Mission to Director of Education, UNESCO Headquarters, on Absence of Data, Pilot Project, November 5, 1959.

Director of Education, UNESCO Headquarters Paris, to Teaching Adviser, TURTEP, Declining his Request for Funds for Educational Materials, December 23, 1959.

Internal Memorandum on "Underlying Principles for Evaluating TURTEP Villages," undated.

Head South East Asia Section to Chief of Mission on Compiling of Historical and Other Records, June 19, 1960.

Wahland, Sten, *Technique of Evaluation: Paper No. 13: Evaluation of Fundamental Education Projects,* Paris, UNESCO/SS/Eval/13, March 30, 1956.

Wilson, R. W., *Cha Cheong Sao Project Recommendations to UNESCO Committee and Under-Secretary of Education,* Bangkok, January 2, 1951.

———, *Survey on the Cha Cheong Sao Vocational Training Plan,* Cha Cheong Sao, March 8, 1952.

———, *Outline Curriculum for "General Workshop" for Boys,* Cha Cheong Sao, March 31, 1953.

UNITED NATIONS TECHNICAL ASSISTANCE BOARD

Faris, Donald K., *Community Development Training in Thailand,* New York, TAO/THA/IO, August 11, 1959.

Fox, Morris G., *Thailand: Community Development Programs, Part I: A Report By the Social Welfare Adviser to TAA*, Bangkok, June 26, 1957.

GOVERNMENT DOCUMENTS: THAILAND

Central Statistics Office, *Bulletin of Statistics*, Vol. XI, No. 3, Bangkok, 1963.

Central Statistics Office, *Thailand Population Census: Whole Kingdom, Changwads Cha Cheong Sao and Ubol*, Bangkok, 1962.

Ministry of Agriculture, Royal Irrigation Department, *The Greater Chao Phya Project*, Bangkok, Thai Watana Panich, 1957.

Ministry of Defense, Mobile Information Team I, *Report on First Trip to Remote Areas in Amphur That Phanom and Amphur Khemma-Rat January 22–February 4, 1962*.

———, Mobile Information Team I, *Report on a Second Trip March 15 to April 4; Area Visited: Villages in Amphur Saeka and Bungkhan, Changwad Hong kai*.

———, Mobile Information Team II, *Report and Analysis of the Assignment to Visit Remote Villages in Amphur Chiengkan, March 15 to April 3, 1962*.

Ministry of Education, Abhai Chandivimol and others, *Statement on Cha Cheong Sao Pilot Project Policy and Means*, Bangkok, 1954.

———, Bunthin Attaeara, *Report on a Visit to UNESCO By Thailand's National Commission for UNESCO*, Paris, November 21, 1950.

———, *Education in Thailand*, Bangkok, External Relations Division, Ministry of Education, June 1960.

———, *Information on the Education Plan at Cha Cheong Sao*, Bangkok, 1957 (in Thai).

———, Letter from Under-Secretary to Chief of Mission, transferring FEO's from Ministry of Education to Ministry of Interior, undated.

———, *Report of the Evaluation Committee: Cha Cheong Sao Pilot Project*, Cha Cheong Sao, August 16, 1957 (from the files, Ministry of Education, Bangkok) (trans. Smorn Guntilaka).

———, *Report on the Results of an Enquiry into the Morale and the Working Conditions of 27 FEO Teams in Thailand*, Bangkok, January 1959 (trans. M. R. Sermsri Kasemsri).

———, *Report on an Investigation into Educational Conditions in Five Provinces in North East Thailand, 1955* (in Thai).

———, *Report of the Primary School Division on the Cha Cheong Sao Pilot Project*, Bangkok, March 1, 1957.

———, *Report on Teacher Training at Cha Cheong Sao by The Teacher Training Department*, Bangkok, January 12, 1956.

———, Under Secretary of Education, *Report on TURTEP: Annex I,* Bangkok, September 1960.

———, *Terms of Reference and Appointment of a Directing Committee for the Pilot Project,* Bangkok, February 27, 1958.

Ministry of Health, *Health Services of Thailand,* Bangkok, Siva Phron Printers, 1961.

Ministry of Interior, *Annual Reports on Community Development for 1960, 1961 and 1962,* Bangkok, 1962 (in Thai).

———, *Community Development Budget for 1961 and 1963,* Bangkok, 1963.

———, *An Explanation of the Methods for Implementing the Five Year Community Development Plan,* Bangkok, 1962 (in Thai).

———, *The Community Development Bulletin,* Vol. 1, Nos. 2 through 9 and Vol. 2, No. 1, Bangkok, May 1962–January 1963 (in Thai).

———, Letter from Under Secretary for Community Development to Chief of Mission UNESCO Regional Office, on TUFEC's Role in Proposed National Development Program, May 1959.

———, *Report on and Papers Presented at the Seminar on Community Development in Thailand,* Bangkok, 1960.

———, Pakorn Augususingha & Others, *Report from the Thailand Delegation to the Six-Country Seminar on Planning and Administration in Community Development under the Sponsorship of the United Nations and the Thai Government,* Bangkok, March 1959.

———, *The Plan for National Community Development,* Bangkok, 1963 (in Thai).

National Community Development Department, *National Community Development Plan,* 1959 (in Thai).

———, *Guidelines to Thai Officials Relative to Peace Corps Volunteers,* 1962 (in Thai).

———, *Operational Plan for Thai-SEATO Regional Community Development,* Technical Assistance Center, 1962 (in Thai).

Office of the Prime Minister, "Act Transferring Affairs of the Re-organized Ministry of Interior," September 29, 1962, *Royal Thai Government Gazette,* 2 (October 7, 1962), 39–42.

———, "Act for the Revision of the National Education Plan," June 19, 1949, *Royal Thai Government Gazette, 1* (March 1, 1949), 293–96.

Public Relations Dept., *Vistas of Thailand,* Bangkok, 1963.

UNITED STATES OPERATIONS MISSION

Haynal, Andrew P., *Thailand's Rural Health Program and the Role of U.S. Assistance in Its Recent Development. Report for the Period May 10, 1956–February 17, 1959,* Bangkok, March 1959.

Polson, Robert A., *USOM Advisers Report on the National Community Development Program of Thailand*, Bangkok, 1961.

Shepherd, Frank W., *Recommended Changes in Selection and Pre-Service Training of Village Workers for the Community Development Department of the Ministry of Interior, Thailand*, Bangkok, December 1, 1962.

Turner, Sheldon J., *Further Comments on Community Development in Thailand*, Bangkok, August 18, 1959.

———, *The Thai-USOM Community Development Program*, Bangkok, undated.

MISCELLANEOUS

Development Assistance Committee Co-ordinating Group, *Compendium of Technical Assistance to Thailand, 1963*, Bangkok, Thai-American Audio-Visual Services, May 1963.

South East Asia Treaty Organization, *Report on the SEATO Conference on Community Development*, Baguio, Philippines, CDC/60/Rep, December 1960.

PART II—SECONDARY SOURCES

Apostolic Delegation to Thailand, *The Catholic Directory*, Bangkok, Thai Publications, 1963.

Chaiyong Chuchart, *Costs and Returns on Korat Farm Enterprises, 1957*, Bangkok, Kasetsart University, December 1959.

———, *Farm Success and Project Administration: Cooperative Land Settlement Project: Part I*, Bangkok, Kasetsart University, 1962.

Chang, C. N., *The Present State of Agricultural Extension Development in Asia and the Far East*, Rome, FAO, 1961.

Claude, Inis L., *Swords Into Plowshares: The Problems and Progress of International Organization*, New York, Random House, 1959.

Cleveland, Harland, and Gerard J. Mangone, *The Art of Overseamanship*, Syracuse, Syracuse University Press, 1957.

Cochrane, Robert, "Approaches to the Solution of Engineering Problems in Rice Production," unpublished paper read before Kasetsart University Rice Seminar, Bangkok, November 1962.

———, "Some Thoughts on Bringing Agricultural Science to the Small Cultivator," unpublished paper, undated.

Collison, Robert, "The Continuing Barrier: Translation as a Means of East-West Communication," *UNESCO Bulletin for Libraries, 16* (December 1962), 296.

Coughlin, Richard J., *Double Identity*, Oxford, Oxford University Press, 1960.

Doob, Leonard W., *Becoming More Civilized: A Psychological Exploration*, New Haven, Yale University Press, 1960.

——, *Communication in Africa: A Search for Boundaries*, New Haven, Yale University Press, 1961.

Embree, John F., "Thailand—A Loosely Structured Social System," *American Anthropologist*, 52 (1950), 181–93.

FAO, *FAO in Asia*, Bangkok, Vichitrasilpa Press, 1962.

——, *Thailand and FAO*, Bangkok, Regional Office, undated.

Fradier, Georges, *East-West: Towards Mutual Understanding?*, Paris, UNESCO, 1959.

Hambidge, Gove, "The Food and Agricultural Organization at Work," *International Conciliation*, No. 432, New York, Carnegie Endowment for International Peace, June 1947.

Human Relations Area Files, *Thailand*, Country Survey Series, ed. Thomas Fitzsimmons, New Haven, HRAF Press, 1957.

Huxley, Julian, *UNESCO: Its Purpose and Its Philosophy*, Washington, D.C., Public Affairs Press, 1948.

Imhoff, Myrtle M., "The Cha Cheong Sao Pilot Project of Thailand, 1949–1959," an evaluation study prepared for UNESCO, unpublished, undated.

Ingram, James C., *Economic Change in Thailand since 1850*, Stanford, Stanford University Press, 1955.

Juvigny, Pierre, *The Fight Against Discrimination: Towards Equality in Education*, Belgium, UNESCO, 1962.

Keeny, S. M., "If I Were a Minister of Health in Asia," *The Lancet* (July 2, 1955), pp. 30–31.

Kikkert, Robert, "A Pilot Village Study in North Eastern Thailand," South East Asia Survey Research Report No. 3, prepared for USIS, Bangkok, October 1960.

Klausner, William, "The Ministry of Interior and Community Development," *The Community Development Bulletin*, 2 (February 1962), 38–46 (in Thai).

Kukrit, Pramoj, *The Red Bamboo*, Bangkok, Bangkok Press, 1956 (in Thai).

Laves, Walter C., and Charles A. Thomson, *UNESCO: Purpose, Progress, Prospects*, Bloomington, Indiana University Press, 1957.

Lerner, Daniel, *The Passing of Traditional Society: Modernizing in the Middle East*, Glencoe, Ill., Free Press, 1958.

McClelland, David, *The Achieving Society*, New York, D. Van Nostrand Company, 1961.

McFarland, George Bradley, *Historical Sketch of Protestant Missions in Siam, 1828–1928,* Bangkok, Bangkok Times Press, 1928.

Manich, Jumsai, M. L., *Compulsory Education in Thailand,* Paris, UNESCO, 1951.

Millikan, Max F., and W. W. Rostow, *A Proposal: Key to an Effective Foreign Policy,* New York, Harper Bros., 1957.

Millikan, Max F., and Donald L. M. Blackmer, *The Emerging Nations,* Boston, Little, Brown, 1961.

Ministry of Education, *A School History of Thailand,* 2, Bangkok, Ministry of Education, 1952 (in Thai).

Moerman, Michael H., "A Memorandum on a Northern Thai Village," unpublished South East Asia Survey Research Report, prepared for USIS, Bangkok, May 1961.

Montgomery, John D., *The Politics of Foreign Aid: American Experience in Southeast Asia,* New York, Frederick A. Praeger, 1962.

Morris, James, *The Road to Huddersfield,* New York, Pantheon Books, 1963.

Mosel, James N., "Thai Administrative Behavior," *Toward the Comparative Study of Public Administration,* ed. William J. Siffin, Bloomington, Indiana University Press, 1957.

Polak, S., "UNICEF in Thailand," Text of an Address to the Provincial Health Officers Conference, Cholburi, Thailand, July 5, 1962.

Prajuab, Tirabutana, *A Simple One: The Story of a Siamese Girlhood,* Ithaca, New York, Cornell University Data Paper No. 30, 1958.

Pye, Lucien W., *Politics, Personality, and Nation Building: Burma's Search for Identity,* New Haven, Yale University Press, 1962.

Quaritch, Wales, H.G., *Ancient South East Asian Warfare,* London, Bernard Quaritch, 1952.

Radcliffe, Lord, *The Problem of Power,* The Rieth Memorial Lectures 1951, London, Secker & Warburg, 1952.

Sai Hutacharaoen, "Our New Community Development Program," *The Community Development Bulletin, 1* (December 1962), 3–6 (in Thai).

Santa Cruz, Hernan, *FAO's Role in Rural Welfare,* Rome, FAO, 1959.

Sermsri Kasemsri, M. R., "The Fundamental Education Center and the United Plan for Adult Education Development," prepared privately for the Minister of Education, June 30, 1962 (in Thai).

Sharp, Walter R., *Field Administration in the United Nations System,* New York, Frederick A. Praeger, 1961.

Sitton, Gordon R. et al., "The Growing Importance of Upland Crops in the Foreign Trade of Thailand," *Kasetsart Economic Report No. 16,* Bangkok, Kasetsart University, November 1962 (in Thai).

Snow, C. P., *Science and Government,* New York, Mentor Books, 1962.

Snyder, Harold, *When Peoples Speak to Peoples,* Washington, D.C., George Banta Publishing Co., 1953.

Stokes, William S., "The Drag of the Pensadores," *Foreign Aid Re-Examined: A Critical Appraisal,* ed. James W. Wiggins and Helmut Schoeck, Washington, D.C., Public Affairs Press, 1958.

Tasniya Isarasena, "The Development of Elementary Education in Thailand," unpublished Ph.D. dissertation, University of Wisconsin, 1953.

Textor, Robert B., *From Peasant to Pedicab Driver,* Ithaca, N.Y., Cornell Monograph No. 9, 1961.

Thompson, Sinclair, "Integration of a Mission School System in Thailand," unpublished M.A. dissertation, Cornell University, 1950.

Turner, Sheldon, "The Capacity for Self Growth Through Community Development," *The Community Development Bulletin, 1* (November 1962) (in Thai).

―――, "The Fifth Freedom: A Proposal for Inducing Social Change and Stabilizing Technical Assistance Gains," prepared for USOM, Bangkok, unpublished, undated.

Ubol Havananda and Charoon Vongsayanha, *Statistical Data of a Decade of Educational Development in Thailand,* Bangkok, Chatri Press, 1955 (in Thai).

UNESCO, *Men Against Ignorance,* Paris, UNESCO Press, 1953.

―――, "What Is UNESCO?" *UNESCO Information Manual,* Paris, UNESCO, 1956.

―――, "Technical Assistance: The Role of UNESCO," *UNESCO Information Manual No. 2,* Paris, UNESCO, 1959.

―――, "International Aid for Progress: The Role of UNESCO" *UNESCO Information Manual, No. 4,* Paris, UNESCO, 1962.

―――, *Education in a Technological Society: A Preliminary International Survey of the Nature and Efficiency of Technical Education,* Paris, 1952.

―――, *Cultural Patterns and Technical Change,* ed. Margaret Mead, Paris, 1953.

Wilson, Howard E., "The Development of UNESCO," *International Conciliation,* No. 431, New York, Carnegie Endowment for International Peace, 1947.

INDEX

Italicized page numbers refer to tables.

Agency for International Development, 3
Agriculture, 2, 3; Cha Cheong Sao crops, 20–21; marketing, 26–27; enterprise in, 28–29; land-power-climate ratio, 27–28; and TUFEC, 73–75
Aliens, integration of, 158–64
Army, Royal Thai, 62, 105
Assumption College, 146
Automobile industry, training in, 135–39
Automotive trades, 64

Ban Muohy village, 61
Bangkok, 3, 20; shipping center, 23; administrative center, 24, 30; trading agencies, 27; schools, 146
Bangpakong Commune, 53–56
Baptist Church, missionary activity, 143
Bodet, Dr. Jaime Torres, 12
Bridge building, 58, 61–62
Bureaucracy, 77, 115–22; Thai relation to U.N., 110–15; informal roles, 123–25

Cambodia, 105; Cambodian minority, 21
Canals, 20, 60
Cash economy, 26, 29
Catholic missions, 144 ff.
Cattle raising, 23
Cha Cheong Sao (town), 20–22, 24; crops, 20–21
Cha Cheong Sao Education Pilot Project, 2, 21–22, 30, 34; concepts of, 37–38; fellowships, 39, 133; operations,

43–47; activities, 52–57; vocational training, 64–68; rote teaching, 72; recreation, 72–73; language problem, 79–81; bureaucracy, 110–15; achievements, 126–30; comparison to missions, 151
China, Republic of, 34
Chinese (minority group), 21; and metalworking, 64–65; immigration of, 99
Chulalongkorn, King, 98, 99, 111
Church of Christ, missionary activity, 143
Claude, Inis, cited, 16
Coconuts, as crop, 20
Colonialism, 1; and U.N. aid, 187–92
Communications: mass media, 24–25; language problems, 79–81, 83–84; interbureau, 118–22; in German Institute, 141; in the field, 155–58; integration of aliens, 158–64; core problems, 164–73; breakdown of, 176–86, *178–79*
Community Development Plan, 52
Consolidated Land Act of *1908*, 99
Constitutional Revolution of *1932*, 95
Corn, as crop, 20, 23, 26, 28
Corvée labor, 98, 99
Cotton, as crop, 28
Crafts, village, 3
Curriculum, school, 14

Dam building, 57–58
Dansai village, 61
Defense, Ministry of, 111
Dhammayat School, 23
Diseases, 68–70, 155

Ecumenican Mission, 143

Education, 2, 11; Fundamental Education Centers, 4, 35–36, organizers, 38, 49, 59; illiteracy, 11, 14, 71; adult, 14; and UNESCO, 17, 71; in Cha Cheong Sao, 21; in Wad schools, 21, 23, 34; survey of Thai, 31; in Thailand, 32, 33, 47; GED Project, 46, 47; book boxes, 71–72; economic motivation, 73–74. *See also* Thailand UNESCO Fundamental Education Center

Education, Ministry of, 31, 34; and UNESCO projects, 39; relations to projects, 110; and missions, 144, 147

English language, widespread use, 79–81, 83

Enterprise, peasant, 28

Ethnocentricity, 1

FAO. *See* Food and Agricultural Organization

"Felt needs," 57–60

FEOS. *See* Fundamental Education Organizers

"Filth diseases," 69

Food and Agricultural Organization, 2, 36, 53

Fundamental Education Center, concept of, 4, 35–36. *See also* Thailand UNESCO Fundamental Education Center

Fundamental Education Organizers, 38, 49; training of, 59

Fundamental Education Project, 4

Furniture making, 67

Gambling shops, 99

General Educational Development Project (GED), 46, 47

German Junior Technical Institute, 139–43

Ground nuts, as crop, 28

Headmen, as links between project personnel and villagers, 31

Health, 3; programs for, 68–71; and missionaries, 144

Huxley, Julian S., cited, 10, 11, 12

Illiteracy, 11, 14, 71

ILO. *See* International Labor Organization

Interior, Ministry of, 49, 53, 62; and TUFEC, 111–15

International Centers for Applied Mathematics, 11

International Institutes for Home and Community Planning, 11

International Labor Organization, 2, 36

International Reconstruction Camp, 11

Jute, as crop, 23, 26, 27, 28

Khon Kaen Institute of Technology, 140

Korat Plateau, 22

Kroms (departments) of Thailand, 111

Land-power-climate ratio, 27–28

Language: of U.N. experts, 79–81, 83–84; in automotive industry, 137; in the German Institute, 141

Laos, 22; de facto Communist seizure, 105

Loeie, bridge building near, 61, 105

Madge, Sir Charles, quoted, 36

Madge Report, 42

Malaya, 23, 105, 106, 107

Marketing, 3; and the peasant, 26, 74

Mass media, impact of, 24–25

Mater Dei Girls School, 146

Matoon, Dr. Stephen, U.S. Consul (*1851*), 145

Mekong River, 22, 62, 105

Metalworking, 64–65

Military conscription, 26

Missionaries, 143–52; Protestant, 143, 144, 146; and health, 144; Catholic, 145–46; and Buddhism, 147; time in Thailand, 148; compared to U.N., 149; policies, 150–52

Missions, 143, *144*, 145–52; and Ministry of Education, 144, 147; comparison to TUFEC, 150
Mobile Development Units, 105
Moh ram (traditional rhyming duets), 73
Mongkut, King, 98
Montgomery, John, cited, 4
Moslems, 21, 106, 107
Movies, popularity as means of communication, 25

National Community Development, Department of, 52
National Community Development Plan, 101, 105
National Theater Institute, 11
Northeast Region, 22, 23, 57, 61

Overseas Missionary Fellowship, 143

Packaging, changes in, 26
Pakistan, jute production, 26
Peasants, 2; eating habits, 20–21; in Cha Cheong Sao, 21–22; use of drugs, 25; marketing knowledge, 26–27; enterprise, 28–29; "felt needs," 57–60; furniture, 67–68; health programs, 69–71; reading among, 71–72; recreation, 72–73
Personnel, 82–84, 173–75; undefined roles, 76–79; adjustment to milieu, 83–87; friction between UNESCO and Thai, 88–91; empathy, 91–92; integration of, 159–61; difficulties in obtaining, 164–66; orientation, 167–69; social mobility, 169–71; adaptation, 171–72; personal relations, 172–73
Pilot Project. *See* Cha Cheong Sao Education Pilot Project
Pineapples, as crop, 20, 26
Platu (sea food), 20
Population density, 43
Power limitations, effect on agriculture, 28

Presbyterian Church, missionary activity, 143
Primary Education Act of *October 1, 1921*, 32, 47

Radio, importance as communication medium, 25
Ramwong (festival dance), 73
Recreation, peasant, 72–73
Resources: of UNESCO, 15; indigenous, 60–64
Rice, 20, 23; as major export, 26, 42–43; culture of, 28; in Bangpakong, 54; and malaria, 69
Rinderpest epidemics, 85–86
Road building, 58–60
Roles of U.N. experts, 76–79, 123–25
Royal Irrigation Department, 60

Sanuk, definition and significance, 73, 92
Sargent-Orato Report, 31, 32
Schools, 14, 146. *See also* Education
Seventh Day Adventists, missionary activity, 143
Shell Oil Company, aid efforts, 3, 64
Slavery, 98, 99
Social institutions, 111–15, 156, 157, 158
Songkram, Field Marshal Luang Pibun, 95

TAA. *See* Technical Assistance Administration
TAB. *See* Technical Assistance Board
Taxation, 27
Teachers, 14, 31, 33–34; tenure, 81–82, 138, 157–58. *See also* Education
Teachers' Assistance Fund, 147
Teachers' Training College, 21
Technical Assistance Administration, 2, 36
Technical Assistance Board, 2
Technical Assistance Operations, Bureau of, 2
Television, significance in communications, 24, 25

Temple (Wad) schools, 21, 23, 34
Tenure, teacher, 81–82, 138, 157–58
Thailand, 2, 17, 19; physical characteristics, 20–21; minority groups, 21, 22; government, 27, 47, 95–97; economic expansion, 43; the elite, 101–04, 108; development boom, 104–05; relations with neighbors, 105–07; bureaucracy, 110–25; institutions, 111–15; missions, 143–52
Thailand UNESCO Fundamental Education Center, 2, 22, 30, 37; concepts of, 38; fellowships, 39, 133; operations, 48–52; administration, 50; activities, 55; well system, 57–58; and indigenous resources, 63; vocational training, 64–68; recreation, 72–73; economics, 73–75; language problems, 79–81; Thai objectives, 107–09; bureaucracy, 110–15, 116–18; achievements of, 127, 130–33; comparison with missions, 150
Thailand UNESCO Rural Teachers' Education Project, 71
Thanarat, Field Marshal Sarit, 47, 95
Therevada Buddhists, 21, 147
Training Village Center, 50
Training, vocational, 64–68
TUFEC. See Thailand UNESCO Fundamental Education Center
TURTEP. See Thailand UNESCO Rural Teachers' Education Project
TVC. See Training Village Center

Ubol, 22, 23, 24, 38
Underdeveloped countries, 1, 2, 13
UNESCO. See United Nations Educational, Scientific and Cultural Organization

UNICEF. See United Nations Children's Fund
United Nations, 1; field operations, 2–3; and UNESCO, 9–19; lack of adequate knowledge, 29; overall plans, 39–41; roles of experts, 76–79, 123–25; and Thai objectives, 107–09; aid and national plans, 176–79; aid and colonialism, 187–92
United Nations Children's Fund, 2, 68
United Nations Educational, Scientific and Cultural Organization, 2, 36; philosophy, 9–11, 14, 16–19; practical operations, 12–16; resources, 15; and education, 17, 71; and Ministry of Education, 39; "grand view" of, 179–83
United Nations Relief and Rehabilitation Agency, 12
United States Information Service, 62
United States Operations Mission, 2, 46, 64
UNRRA. See United Nations Relief and Rehabilitation Agency
USOM. See United States Operations Mission

Village organization, 3

Wad Saotorn, 21
Water, 21, 53–54; conservation, 58
Welfare, village, 3
WHO. See World Health Organization
World Health Organization, 2, 36, 68, 155
World War II, 1, 32

Yaws, 69, 155

YALE STUDIES IN POLITICAL SCIENCE

1. Robert E. Lane, THE REGULATION OF BUSINESSMEN. Out of print
2. Charles Blitzer, AN IMMORTAL COMMONWEALTH: THE POLITICAL THOUGHT OF JAMES HARRINGTON
3. Aaron Wildavsky, DIXON-YATES: A STUDY IN POWER POLITICS
4. Robert A. Dahl, WHO GOVERNS? DEMOCRACY AND POWER IN AN AMERICAN CITY
5. Herbert Jacob, GERMAN ADMINISTRATION SINCE BISMARCK: CENTRAL AUTHORITY VERSUS LOCAL AUTONOMY
6. Robert C. Fried, THE ITALIAN PREFECTS: A STUDY IN ADMINISTRATIVE POLITICS
7. Nelson W. Polsby, COMMUNITY POWER AND POLITICAL THEORY
8. Joseph Hamburger, JAMES MILL AND THE ART OF REVOLUTION
9. Takehiko Yoshihashi, CONSPIRACY AT MUKDEN: THE RISE OF THE JAPANESE MILITARY
10. Douglas A. Chalmers, THE SOCIAL DEMOCRATIC PARTY OF GERMANY: FROM WORKING-CLASS MOVEMENT TO MODERN POLITICAL PARTY
11. James D. Barber, THE LAWMAKERS: RECRUITMENT AND ADAPTATION TO LEGISLATIVE LIFE
12. William J. Foltz, FROM FRENCH WEST AFRICA TO THE MALI FEDERATION
13. Fred I. Greenstein, CHILDREN AND POLITICS
14. Joseph Hamburger, INTELLECTUALS IN POLITICS: JOHN STUART MILL AND THE PHILOSOPHIC RADICALS
15. Hayward R. Alker, Jr., and Bruce M. Russett, WORLD POLITICS IN THE GENERAL ASSEMBLY
16. Richard L. Merritt, SYMBOLS OF AMERICAN COMMUNITY, 1735–1775
17. Arend Lijphart, THE TRAUMA OF DECOLONIZATION: THE DUTCH AND WEST NEW GUINEA
18. David P. Calleo, COLERIDGE AND THE IDEA OF THE MODERN STATE
19. Ronald C. Nairn, INTERNATIONAL AID TO THAILAND: THE NEW COLONIALISM?